Sitting Ducks

BY
BETSY HITZ-HOLMAN

SEVEN SEAS PRESS INC. NEWPORT, RHODE ISLAND

For Jim, who offered his life for mine

PUBLISHED BY SEVEN SEAS PRESS, NEWPORT, RHODE ISLAND, 02840
EDITED BY JAMES R. GILBERT

LIBRARY OF CONGRESS CATALOGING IN PUBLICATION DATA
Hitz-Holman, Betsy, 1951–
  Sitting Ducks.
  1. Hitz Holman, Betsy, 1951–   . 2. Cheers
(Yacht : U.S.)   3. Voyages and travels—1951–
I. Title.
G475.H53   1984   910.4'5   84-1442
ISBN 0-915160-60-9

DESIGNED BY IRVING PERKINS ASSOCIATES
PRINTED IN THE UNITED STATES OF AMERICA BY R. R. DONNELLEY & SONS

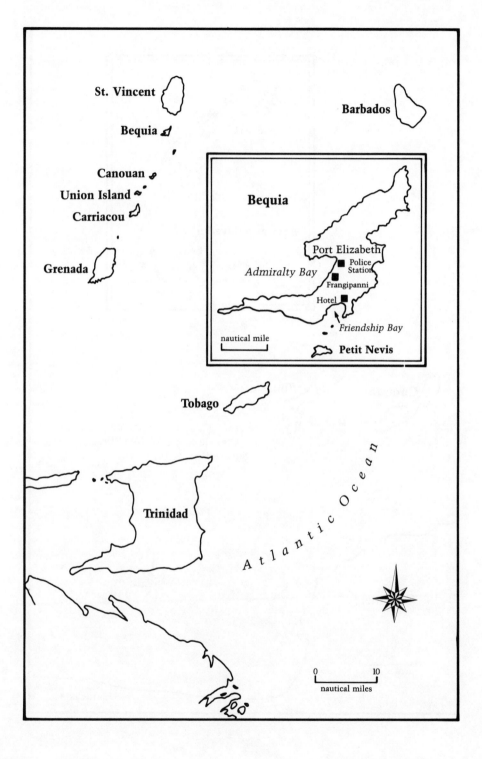

St. Vincent

Barbados

Bequia

Canouan

Union Island

Carriacou

Grenada

Bequia

Port Elizabeth

Admiralty Bay

Police
Station

Frangipanni

Hotel

Friendship Bay

nautical mile

Petit Nevis

Tobago

A t l a n t i c   O c e a n

Trinidad

0   10
nautical miles

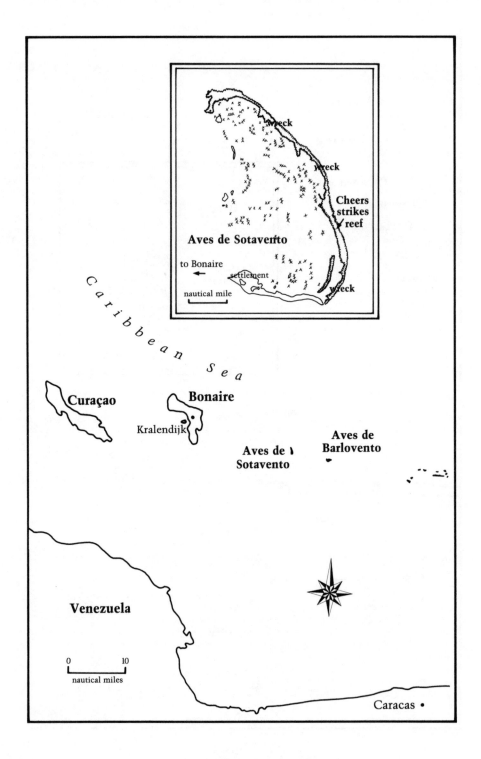

Wreck

Wreck

Cheers
strikes
reef

Aves de Sotavento

to Bonaire

settlement

Wreck

nautical mile

C a r i b b e a n   S e a

Curaçao

Bonaire

Kralendijk

Aves de
Sotavento

Aves de
Barlovento

Venezuela

0   10

nautical miles

Caracas •

"*Love is not looking into each others' eyes, but looking together in the same direction.*"

—ST. EXUPERY

Part One

PROLOGUE

———————————————— This story begins not on the sea, but at its very edge, in Spanish Water on the Dutch Island of Curaçao in the Netherlands Antilles.

Cheers lies cradled just a whisper away from the blue Caribbean, her battered hull supported by a makeshift cradle in an empty gravel lot. Her gleaming white hull is scarred with deep lacera-

1

tions. Her once-pristine varnish is flaked like yellow fish scales. A mixture of diesel fuel and saltwater still drips from deep fissures in her disfigured keel. On a sawhorse lays her mast, and on the ground, her rusted diesel engine.

When cruising friends stop by these days, they find Jim and me wearing bandanas, paper face masks and heavy coveralls taped at the neck and cuffs to keep out the irritating fiberglass particles as we work to rebuild our boat, and our lives. Our daylight hours are filled with the whine of a heavy industrial grinder as we fair the hull and lay in new fiberglass. But in the evening, when the electric cord is pulled and we climb the ladder and light the kerosene cabin lamp after a day's work, we still can hear the beckoning call of wavelets lapping the shores just beneath us.

And even now, as *Cheers* lies in her cradle, her bowsprit points west—toward Panama, the Galapagos, Tahiti.

*   *   *

The low afternoon sun was casting long shadows on the gravel lot when I noticed movement above the nearby mangroves. Standing in the cockpit, 15 feet above the water, I could just barely see the twin spars of a ketch picking her way among the meandering tributaries of Spanish Water. Slowly, carefully, she motored up the channel turn after tight turn. Though her hull was shrouded by the mangrove-covered headland, I recognized the familiar rake of those wood masts.

"It's *Walu!*" I called down the ladder to Jim.

He pushed his goggles to the top of his head, put down his resin pot and scurried up the ladder. The blue Australian ketch anchored just off the yacht club where *Cheers* was cradled.

"I'll be damned," said Jim with quiet pleasure. "Diapers drying in the rigging. It's *Walu* all right."

I watched from across the harbor as Richard climbed aboard *Walu's* dinghy and held it alongside for his wife, Robyn, and baby daughter, Joelle.

"Jim, do you think they heard what happened to us?"

"We'll soon find out."

We pulled off our coveralls, climbed into our swimsuits, descended the ladder and hosed one another off. Then we raced for the dinghy dock and greeted them with the warm embraces reserved for lost friends.

Suddenly the smile vanished from Richard's face. He held Jim by both shoulders at arm's length. "Jim, what's happened to you? My God, mate, you look like a skeleton!"

Robyn planted a well-aimed elbow in Richard's ribs. She placed her long arm around Jim's waist.

"And he wonders how Australians get their reputation," she said, casting her own surreptitious glance at Jim's deeply-scarred chest.

In the awkward silence that followed, I scooped the baby up in my arms. Together, we all headed up the dock toward *Cheers*.

"Joelle's grown so since we left you in the Grenadines," I said, adding, "A lot has happened in those two months."

Together, we all began walking up the dock toward *Cheers*. At first sight of our boat, Richard and Robyn stopped dead in their tracks, a mixture of dread and horror showing on their faces. Robyn's eyes filled with tears.

Richard walked all around the boat, shaking his head in disbelief. "My God! What's happened to you—to your beautiful boat?"

"We should have known something was wrong," said Robyn. "We waited for you in Grenada. It just wasn't like you not to show up. Something horrible has happened."

I tussled Joelle's downy hair. "Thank goodness we separated. But come up," I invited. "I'll mix a rum punch and tell you about it."

Jim cleared the tools from the cockpit while I filled four glasses and passed them around.

"When we parted you were going back to Bequia," recalled Robyn, "to pick up your charts for the passage west out of hurricane country."

"Ah, the charts," I sighed. "I'll start at the beginning, the afternoon we returned to Bequia, to Friendship Bay . . .

CHAPTER ONE

———————————— With calloused hands I clung to the headstay, swaying as the bowsprit beneath my bare feet leapt and plunged through the closely-spaced seas. I could feel my salt-caked skin crackle as I squinted against the low tropical sun.

"Strong current," I called to Jim at the helm.

He glanced over his shoulder to check our set against Petit Nevis, a tiny crumb of land we were leaving in our wake.

"It's okay," he shouted, "I allowed for that."

Cheers cut a clean path northward, throwing up spray as she plunged into each trough. As *Cheers* climbed each wave crest, the palms lining the distant beach rose on the horizon, only to be quickly swallowed by the next blue wave.

Returning to Bequia felt like going home.

"I can just make out the entrance to Friendship Bay," I shouted aft.

Jim glanced at the chart folded in his lap. "Just keep an eye out for the reef that makes out from the southeast shore."

In half an hour we would be anchored in Friendship Bay. Though we'd spent three weeks settling into island life while anchored in Admiralty Bay on Bequia's western shore, we never had explored Bequia's south shore. I tried hard to picture the harbor in minute detail. It was a game I liked to play—to see how close my mental image would come to the real port.

Pastel-painted houses came into view on the tall hill marking the entrance to the shoe-shaped cove—a larger settlement than I'd expected. A white sand beach fringed with palms and deadly manchineel trees ringed the harbor.

"Can you see the reef, off the point to starboard?" I called to Jim.

"Yes. It's just breaking."

"Right. And the long shoal to port? See that—between the tall cay and the shore?"

"Yes," he mumbled past the pencil clenched between his teeth.

Jim started the engine and could no longer hear me over its noisy idle. I walked aft to the cockpit and swung out the depthsounder and adjusted the red blip. Five fathoms. I switched the dial from fathoms to feet for a closer look at the bottom contour.

"Good water."

"Here, you steer while I drop the sails," said Jim. "Let's round up between this cargo schooner and that hotel with the pier. Keep an eye on your depth."

We ducked into the lee of the hilly eastern shore and dropped anchor in 15 feet.

"Notice anything strange about this place?" I asked as we furled the mainsail.

He looked around and shrugged.

"No pesky boat vendors! Show me one," I challenged.

"It's half past four. Maybe they've gone on home. Let's go below and lay low for another hour, just in case."

The cabin was still buttoned up against the sea. Jim made a few notes in the log while I opened all the portholes and hatches to get a fresh breeze moving through the stuffy saloon. Then Jim mixed us both an iced drink while I sponged the salt off my body.

"You're fried," he said, pressing the iced glass to my red shoulder. I squirmed just out of reach.

"Hey, don't mess with the cook. Why don't we take the dinghy into the beach and have a look around. It's nearly low tide and there might be some good shells."

"Oh no. I'm not eating any more snails. Not this boy."

"Those were West Indian tops," I corrected him.

"All right, I'm not eating any more tops. Or sea slugs. Or squid or even kelp bread. Remember me? I'm the guy from New York— the guy who doesn't even like fish. Sneaking around with flashlights, prying our supper off the underside of a rock is not my idea of *haute cuisine.* Look where it got Euell Gibbons: bleeding ulcers and an early grave."

I picked up a cleaver and began cutting coarse chunks of onion into a skillet. "I merely wanted to look around. Will you row in with me in the morning to explore?"

"Sure. Sunday morning. Then we can sail around to Elizabeth Harbour tomorrow afternoon, then check the mail for those charts first thing Monday morning."

He leaned over my shoulder sniffing. "What's that you're making?"

"Oh, octopus stew," I teased. "Manhattan style."

He grinned.

"How about Indian curried chicken?"

"With mango chutney?"

"Homemade."

"And coconut?"

I tossed him a nut from the hammock overhead. "Do you mind grating it?"

*   *   *

We returned to the cockpit with heaped dinner plates and ate silently, contentedly by the glow of an oil lamp. Outside the protected horseshoe cove the wind-driven current flooded west with the speed of a river. But inside all was peace. A lone frigate bird, silhouetted against the rose-colored sky, spread bat-like black wings to soar high over the shallow water covering the western reef. A light breeze from the east tugged at the inflatable dinghy bobbing off our stern. Only the mournful wail of a bleating goat broke the still air.

Not a soul stirred on the beach, nor on distant porches, nor even on the two multihulls with which we shared the anchorage. Far away on the pier a man and a young boy sat fishing.

"Peaceful isn't it?" I yawned.

"Mmmm. I think I'm getting to like the tropics."

We both knew, however, that hurricane season was approaching. It was time to return to Bequia to pick up our long-awaited charts and move to a safer part of paradise.

*   *   *

I washed up the last of the dinner dishes and left Jim on deck to check the anchor rode. I visited the head, stripped off my bikini and slipped into bed in the forward cabin. It was too warm for a clingy nightgown. The cotton top sheet felt cool against my sunburned skin. A square ceiling of stars shone through the open hatch overhead and a warm breeze stirred through the cabin.

I reached up, opened to the bookmark in Tristan Jones' *The Incredible Voyage* and began reading. Jim wound the ship's clock, gave the barometer his customary three taps, then slipped out of his shorts and beneath the sheet with Herman Wouk's *Don't Stop The Carnival*, which shortly had him chortling and guffawing like a lunatic. Soon he had me laughing, too.

Jim was on another wave length. I read on.

Although sometimes I had to strain the limits of reason to believe certain episodes of Jones' novel quest to sail the highest and lowest bodies of water in the world, it was impossible to avoid comparing our cruising experiences with his. Cruising this past year, I thought to myself, had been so safe, so . . . predictable. Where was the adventure? Every port that once seemed so exotic, so remote, once visited becomes benignly familiar. But still, I'd never known the kind of freedom, the thrill of discovery, the inner contentment I'd found while cruising. At that moment, however, I yearned for high adventure.

Had we become too cautious? Too sterile in our approach. Where were the hair-raising landfalls and close encounters? We might return from this trip without one good story to tell. Nothing but suntans, empty pockets and a few lousy slides.

I plowed vicariously back into Jones' adventure and in a moment was charging headlong down the Red Sea fleeing a pirate attack.

A boat at anchor is seldom silent. No matter how well she is put to bed. A boat, like a baby, has a repertoire of countless sounds that tell the attentive parent the precise complaint. Invariably the sound begins only after one has collapsed in bed after a tiring day. If one ignores the fussing child the noise sometimes will stop. But a complaining boat always requires a visit topside.

It was such a noise, a gentle sound halfway between a whisper and a football, that interrupted my reading. It was a sound I could not place. I read on.

Again, the subtlest patter, right over my head. A strumming halyard?

"Did you hear that?" I asked Jim.

In seven years of togetherness he'd perfected the art of tuning me out and we both read on.

Three bells: 9:30. Again the subtle sound.

"Jim, did you check the anchor rode?"

"Yes."

"Then I bet it's a halyard. I'll check it out."

"Nope, here I go," Jim said, putting down his book.

He stood on the bunk, elbows on deck and peered around through the open hatch. Finding nothing slatting in the rigging, he ducked down the hatch, then walked aft through the cabin and climbed the companionway ladder.

"What are you—do . . ." Jim shouted.

I spun around in the bunk just as Jim tumbled backwards down the ladder. He scrambled to his feet. A dark silhouette jumped down after him swinging a long instrument. Jim leapt back and the figure lunged at him with a machete.

In seconds Jim's maneuvering room was gone. He was pinned against the forward bunk where I crouched. Naked, unarmed, cornered, Jim grabbed the only object within reach—his bed pillow—and held it in front of himself as a buffer.

The man, wide-eyed and wild, jabbed the rusty blade into Jim's abdomen. He withdrew and with tissue-tearing force, plunged the blade into Jim's chest. The blood-soaked pillow dropped to the floor. Jim fell backwards onto the bunk with me, choking on his own blood.

"Get out of here!" I screamed. A glass half full of water was the only thing within reach. I hurled it at the man.

"Get out of here! Get off this boat!"

He held the machete in front of him and just stood there in the light without speaking. No fear, no look of remorse, no sense of urgency. He was cool, in control. His wide eyes flashed with hatred. The brown skin of his muscular biceps and thighs shone beneath the overhead light. He was totally naked.

Our assailant then began to toy with us at knifepoint, reveling in our helplessness and in his total domination over us.

I put an arm around Jim; who was still conscious.

"Can't you see what you've done? Go and leave us alone," I implored.

The man shifted his weight from one foot to the next, the machete still raised, swaying like a tennis player covering the net. He stared at us with glistening, cold black eyes, daring us to move a muscle. The rusty blade was sharpened to a cruel point, poised and ready.

Suddenly he swung.

Splinters of glass flew through the air as the machete struck the shade of our kerosene hurricane lamp.

"What do you want?" Jim demanded, his voice rasping with pain.

The man looked around but did not answer. He was in complete control.

"What do you want?" I repeated angrily.

Our tormentor looked around casually.

"Money! Gimme money!"

We didn't move.

"Money," he ordered. "Money!"

"There's money behind you," I said. "In my wallet."

"Bring it. You bring to me."

"It's right there, right behind you. In my purse there's a wallet with money."

"You get it," he ordered again.

"Shall I?" I whispered to Jim.

He nodded.

I tensed, fearing what reaction my next move would bring. My purse sat atop the hanging locker just behind the man's left shoulder.

I clung to the top sheet and dragged it with me as far as it would reach. I tugged. The sheet dropped on the bunk.

I snatched my purse and returned to the sheet, drawing it up to my neck.

I fumbled inside the purse and withdrew my wallet. In plain view of the man, I opened the wallet like a book, reached inside and withdrew all the paper currency it contained, about

$200 Eastern Caribbean dollars ($80 U.S.). He snatched the money with his right hand, looked at it in his fist, but did not count it.

"Now won't you go?" I urged. "Go and leave us alone."

"More money!" he demanded.

"That's all we have," I insisted. "See for yourself."

I extended the wallet. He grabbed it, then rummaged through my purse, examining its contents one piece at a time. A lipstick, a key ring, a scarf. Finding nothing of value, he dropped the purse.

"More money!" he ranted.

"Look in the other cabin," said Jim.

"Take whatever you want," I added, "radios, booze—take it all. Then get off this boat."

If we could just get him to go aft, just through the doorway three feet away, we could slam the stateroom door shut and block-ade it. A fire extinguisher was mounted on our side, just behind the door. If we could just get to it . . .

"Gimme money!" he repeated. "More money!"

"There is no more money," I pleaded. "You have all our cash."

"More money," he chanted, "more money, more money, more money," until I could no longer think.

"Hey, where y'all from?" he asked in a sudden, curious change of tone.

"From Rhode Island," Jim answered bleakly.

The man stared at us vacantly.

"It's in America," I added. "Now why don't you leave? Can't you see you've got all the cash we have?"

"I from Union Islan'," he said matter-of-factly.

"We've been to your island," I replied. "A wonderful island." And in a softer voice I added, "Now go and we won't tell anyone you came."

But it was no use. We'd reached a dreadful stalemate. Tonight, perhaps for the first time in his life, our frightening visitor was in command. He was master and we were his subjects. He was revel-ing in his blood bath and meant to have some more fun, beginning with me.

"You," he motioned with the machete to Jim. "Up on de deck." His intention was plain. I knew then the dreaded act was inevitable and wondered only whether he would rape me before or after he killed me.

When Jim didn't move, he became enraged.

"Go!" he ordered.

The ship's clock struck four bells: 10 o'clock. The man cocked his head listening.

Jim leaned toward me on the bunk. "On deck and over the side," he whispered.

I stared straight ahead letting his words sink in, trying not to see the man's nakedness. The thought of this man straddling me was terrifying, repugnant. In seconds I could be in the water, swimming for shore. But Jim would pay with his life.

"I am pregnant with child," I blurted out, searching desperately for a soft spot. "This is the father of my unborn child." I lied, giving Jim a motherly embrace. "He needs a doctor. Go now and we will tell no one."

But the monster only laughed.

"Oh, I kill you both. I cut you into little pieces," he declared, twisting the machete.

"First I want you." He motioned at me lasciviously.

"My husband is a man of God. Baptist minister. He will ask God's forgiveness for what you have done. Go now. We won't tell anyone. I will get him a doctor but no police. Go now and God will forgive you."

Jim saw the futility of my ploy. Slowly he leaned close to me, putting himself directly in our attacker's path.

"On deck, over the side," he ordered in a harsh whisper.

In one motion I sprung through the hatch over my head. I landed with both feet on deck and stepped to the rail. Then I froze. I couldn't leave Jim.

A second passed but the man didn't follow me through the hatch. Two seconds. Leap or be killed. Three seconds. Footsteps. I looked aft. The silhouette emerged from the cockpit and rushed at me on the foredeck.

I jumped back down the forward hatch, closed it and dogged it. As I fumbled frantically with the large thumbscrews, he tugged at the hatch with all his strength, but the first screw was set.

I turned. Jim was alive beside me. He took something from my purse.

"Get to the companionway," I shrieked. "Lock it. I'll get the skylight."

Jim staggered aft, clutching his chest. He reached the ladder. Too late. The black silhouette had one foot on the top step and was coming down. He raised the machete over Jim's head. The instrument of death, however, remained suspended. Jim raised his arm, as if to protect himself. Suddenly, the naked black executioner groaned loudly. In an instant, it was over.

I stared, incredulous, as our devil turned suddenly and jumped over the side.

Jim hung motionless in the companionway, watching as the man first swam frantically toward the open sea, then turned for shore and disappeared into the black night.

"He's gone?" I asked in disbelief. "But how? What did you do?"

Jim dropped his arm and a leather key ring fell to the cabin sole —the key ring containing a small vial of mace, which for years lay forgotten in the bottom of my seldom-used pocketbook.

My only thought was to get medical help for Jim, who seemed to be losing consciousness. I grabbed some paper towels to press against his wounds. I helped him down the companionway ladder, then I tried to lie him down on the port side. But he resisted. I bent over and put my ear to his lips.

"Can't lie down. Lung . . . losing air. Help me sit . . . up."

I propped him up then ran forward, forgetting the splinters of broken glass from the shattered lamp, which stabbed and cut my bare feet. I pulled a dress over my head and slipped a pair of shorts on Jim.

"Get the gun," he whispered.

"We've got to get help," I insisted. "We've got to find a doctor."

"Get the gun," he repeated.

"Right, the gun. Gun, where's the gun?" I mumbled to myself. "Locker. Key! Get the gun."

I rummaged through the chart table and found the key. Then I raised the starboard settee cushion, unlocked the compartment and lifted the hinged lid. The greased Smith & Wesson .38 revolver was near the top. I ripped off the oily plastic bags which covered it and handed the gun to Jim.

"Bullets," he rasped.

"Bullets! Right, bullets," I stammered. I plowed back through the same locker spewing out jars of molasses, cookie boxes, vegetable tins, a boarding ladder, shotgun shells—everything but bullets. By now my hands had begun to shake uncontrollably. I could not find the bullets.

I hurried on deck and made one loud cry for help. The harbor was black. Not a light shone on the distant shore nor on any boat. The only noise was the sound of crickets on the far shore.

I looked aft and was startled to see an orange inflatable dinghy bobbing next to our own gray inflatable. I went below and told Jim.

"He'll be back. Maybe with friends. Arm yourself," he whispered.

I took the largest knife from the galley and returned to the stern pulpit. In one motion I severed the orange dinghy's painter and sent it drifting away toward shore.

I hurried below, turned on the VHF radio and switched to Channel 16. Surely some yachtsman would be monitoring the distress frequency.

"Mayday, mayday. This is the yacht *Cheers*, yacht *Cheers*, anchored in Friendship Bay, south shore of Bequia. Our boat was boarded. The captain's been stabbed. Request help immediately. Any vessel in the area please reply. Repeat, this is the yacht *Cheers*. . . ."

I broadcast the message every five minutes over the next half hour and wondered if the tall hill hemming in Friendship Bay was blocking transmission to Admiralty Bay, where perhaps 30 yachts were berthed. Between broadcasts I tried to find the bullets, load the flare gun and tend to Jim's wounds. In so doing, I accomplished nothing at all. I produced shotgun shells for the pistol and loaded the flare gun improperly. None of the three flares I fired ignited. One by one they fell out of the barrel and into the water.

I returned below. Jim was soaked in blood and had turned ashen white. His eyes were closed but he remained conscious, his thinking clear and decisive.

"Get the bullets," he ordered. "Forget everything but bullets."

In the final recess of the locker I found the box of .38 shells and placed them next to Jim. I assisted as he slipped five bullets into the chamber.

"Help me . . . on deck," he groaned.

With great exertion he scaled the companionway ladder while I steadied him and pushed from behind. He sat on the coach roof, badly winded and in obvious pain.

"I want you to start the engine. Cut the anchor rode. Get underway for Admiralty Bay. Can you find the harbor by yourself?"

"Yes, but that will take two hours, maybe more. You may not . . . make it."

"Forget about me. Can you do it alone?"

"Yes, but. . . . someone's coming!" I pointed toward the noise of an outboard motor approaching from shore. "Oh God, there're more of them this time."

"If I black out, take the gun," said Jim. "You must use it. Five bullets. If it's him, shoot to kill, then the others."

I grabbed a flashlight from the chart table and held it away from my body, playing the beam on the three figures in the wood skiff that idled down and approached our port side. Jim sat in darkness, the gun in his lap.

"Who are you?" I called. "You from Union Island?"

"From dis' islan'," replied the man in the bow. "Someone stole our rubber boat. We call police but no one come. Then we heard someone scream."

I searched their faces. All teen-agers. Our assailant was not among them, but I feared they could be his friends.

"The man who stole your boat came here. He robbed us and he stabbed the captain. Get help, *please*. Is there a doctor on the island?"

"Yes, but he's home now."

"Find him. Go to his home or call him on the phone. Bring him here. Hurry!"

The boys sped toward shore and disappeared into the night. Jim and I remained on deck, watching. I propped Jim up and reassured him of that which I doubted myself, that he would be all right. We waited.

When the boys returned the doctor was not with them.

"De doctor say he don't make house calls," they shouted. "He say you come to de clinic."

"How far's the clinic?" I asked.

"Over in Port Elizabeth. We call for a taxi."

"How long will it take for the taxi to get here?"

"Not long. We'll see the car lights," he said, pointing to shore.

The three looked innocent enough; the one who spoke sounded genuinely concerned. Still I suspected a trick. How could a doctor refuse to come? Again I searched their faces as they clung to our port rail. They hadn't seen the gun in Jim's lap. We had five bullets —five bullets for three men at close range. There was little choice but to accept their help and hope.

I leaned Jim against the boom gallows and slipped below. I found the mace on the cabin sole and dropped it and the box of bullets into my purse. Then I grabbed a white shirt for Jim and shoes for us both. The cabin was a grizzly collage of blood-stained upholstery, broken glass, canned goods and shotgun shells. The microphone dangled from the VHF, which crackled with static. I flipped all circuit breakers to OFF and climbed the ladder. I dropped three boards in the companionway and locked the hatch.

"Taxi's here," one boy announced, pointing to headlights at the head of the cove.

I took the gun from Jim and concealed it in the folds of my dress. I steadied Jim from behind as he inched weakly toward the rail. Two of of the youths helped him into the skiff.

As we pushed off toward shore I shone the flashlight back to the blood-spattered deck. The portholes were open to the weather. A flare gun, half a dozen unused cartridges and a valise lay on deck. Our own Avon tender and the intruder's severed dinghy painter trailed astern.

We sped full throttle for the bright headlights on shore. The boys ran the skiff right up on the beach with little concern for their motor. All together, they lifted Jim over the gunwale and supported him as we crossed the beach and walked through a manchineel forest and coconut grove to the road. Grazing goats bleated invisibly in the darkness and my bare feet found their still-warm droppings. One of the sandals I was carrying dropped to the ground, but I didn't stop to retrieve it.

The driver opened the front passenger door and helped Jim into a shredded bucket seat. I jumped into the back where bare rusted coil springs were all that remained of the seat. The driver floored the accelerator pedal and we began bouncing along the deeply-rutted dirt road at a good clip. The floor beneath my feet was entirely rusted out and each puddle we hit sprayed me from feet to face. Worst of all, the passenger seat was not bolted down, so that at every deep rut or turn in the road, Jim was thrown into the windshield or catapulted backward into my lap.

"How far to the clinic?" I asked.

"Oh, 'bout two, three miles," said the driver.

"Slow down," moaned Jim.

A crowd was gathered outside the primitive clinic's doors when we arrived. A mob of Bequians filled the hallway and examining room, their faces filled with sympathy, curiosity and awe. We had a long wait, but finally an East Indian doctor sauntered in, still in his pajamas.

"That's Dr. Kavala," whispered the nurse.

I tried in vain to shoo away the onlookers who even squeezed behind the small examining screen. But I was far outnumbered. I grimaced when the nurse placed Jim on a blood-soiled examining cot, but when the doctor began suturing Jim's wounds without cleansing them first or offering anesthesia, I reached for the phone. Jim sat upright and never flinched.

In a rare burst of efficiency, the overseas operator came on the line. I hoped his father, an orthopedic surgeon in New Jersey, could arrange for a specialist, a flight to the States, or whatever it would take to save Jim.

Despite the fast but typically poor connection, my words finally broke through. I interrupted a surprise birthday party for Jim's younger brother, Bill.

"There's a fast powerboat waiting here at the dock to take us to the hospital in St. Vincent. No, don't come to Bequia. There's no hospital and no airport. We're going to the hospital in St. Vincent. It's a larger island just five miles north of here. The doctor told the nurse his right lung is collapsed. I don't know any more than that. Better make plane reservations for St. Vincent just in case. I'll call you from the hospital when I know more."

Their voices were comforting. Doc had been at Jim's side in more than one hospital over the years and it was a tremendous relief to know he could be on hand.

A tall black man of about 25 wearing blue jeans and a wrinkled, open-neck shirt squeezed through the pack of onlookers and tapped me on the shoulder.

"Please," I urged, "just leave us alone while the doctor . . ."

"Police," he said. "Can you tell me what happened?"

I took a seat next to the policeman in front of a small table in the examining room and spared no detail in relating to him the incident and describing our assailant.

"Black male, 20 to 25 years old. Height about five feet, 10 inches. Totally naked, carrying a machete . . ."

"Naked?" his eyes widened.

"Naked," I continued, "carrying a machete about 15 inches long. But the tip was sharpened to a point." I drew him a picture.

"Well built," I continued. "Not fat, not lean. Muscular yet wiry —about your build."

He drew himself up in his chair and threw his shoulders back.

"Weight about a hundred and fifty pounds. Quite fine facial features. Very round brown eyes. Close-cropped hair. Are you getting all this?"

"Yea," he insisted.

"Don't you want to write some of it down?"

"It's okay," he assured me, tapping his temple. "It's all up here. Go on."

"Angular, smallish nose. Perfect teeth. No scars, no acne, no stubble. Complexion about like yours, maybe a little lighter. Oh yes, a small goatee."

"Gold teef?" he asked.

"No, a goatee—a small chin beard. Whiskers only on the chin," I motioned, "like this."

He nodded.

"The boat waitin' for you at the dock," called the nurse. "The doctor's finished."

"What's your husband's name?" asked the officer.

"Jim Holman. And we're not married."

"Please," I said to the officer, "go to Friendship Bay tonight. Talk to the boys who brought us ashore. The driver said their name is Mitchell. Search the beach and the woods. You might find his clothes on shore. Maybe the machete. He was still carrying the machete, the cash and maybe my wallet when he jumped. I'll call you in the morning."

Dr. Kavala handed me a sealed envelope to present to the doctor in St. Vincent, but declined to speculate at all on Jim's condition.

"An ambulance will meet you at the dock," I thought he said in a thick East Indian accent.

A cab brought us the short distance from the clinic to the end of the town dock. There we were greeted by a kindly rotund black man who helped Jim aboard a large powerboat.

"Chester Peters," he said, extending his hand. "I run the *Sunny Caribee*. Sure am sorry 'bout your husband there. Such a mean thing," he said, shaking his head.

"You're very kind to help us," I said.

Then a man stepped out of the crowd and passed me Jim's shoes. I looked at his face—strong and kind with the mixed blood of a Bequian. I'd seen him before, but where? He helped me aboard the cruiser and had one foot on deck, about to follow, when he was pushed aside in the shuffle of bodies. The lines were cast off and the man disappeared into the crowd as the cruiser maneuvered away from the pier.

Jim was settled into a living room-type sofa below in the cabin as Chester headed west out of Admiralty Bay. Once out, we sped north for St. Vincent.

There was little I could do for Jim except to keep him from falling over by bracing him with my arm around his shoulder.

I kissed his forehead and spoke to him softly.

"We were dead, you know."

He nodded.

"You turned the tables. You saved my life. You saved *our* lives. God, you took a chance."

With the hem of my dress I rubbed the dried blood from his arms and legs and draped the white shirt over his shoulders. I made him as comfortable as possible as the cruiser negotiated the lumpy seas.

"I'll find the guy who did this, Jim. I promise you that."

CHAPTER TWO

SATURDAY EVENING, JULY 11

The nine-mile trip to Kingstown seemed an eternity. I was gravely concerned about Jim, who didn't speak and who could draw only quick, shallow breaths. It scarcely seemed possible we were still alive, so inescapable was our predicament little more than an hour before. I could not shake the feeling that I was living outside my body, living on borrowed time after my own death.

Out of the fuzzy octagons of light magnified by the spray-drenched windshield of the cabin cruiser emerged the Kingstown waterfront. How ironic, I thought as we approached the brightly-lit cement pier, to be coming to St. Vincent for help.

Making our way south in *Cheers* some weeks before, we'd purposely given the entire island a wide berth, opting instead for sleepy Bequia as our base in the Grenadines. Now here we were in Kingstown, the lawless town on one of the roughest islands in the West Indies, seeking help.

We homed in on an oscillating red light atop a pair of headlights on the pier. As soon as our dock lines were secured, a pair of white-jacketed orderlies climbed over the rail and lifted Jim onto a canvas stretcher. I followed him into the back of the ambulance. Jim tried to sit up, but they forced him to lie down.

"Tell them," whispered Jim.

"His lung is punctured and he's bleeding internally," I explained, propping him up. "He must sit up."

They pushed him down again.

It was shortly after midnight when the ambulance pulled in front of the hospital. The ambulance doors swung open and the two orderlies carried Jim's stretcher toward the emergency room door. A light rain had begun to fall. The rear guard lost his grip and dropped the foot of the stretcher. The forward orderly broke into rales of laughter, but fortunately Jim stayed glued to the stretcher. We proceeded down a dimly-lit corridor to a dingy treatment room. Jim was placed on another blood-soiled examining bed and again we waited for a doctor.

The doctor, a young blonde man, arrived wearing a T-shirt, faded jeans and sandals.

"Mister Selwood," he announced with an aristocratic British air.

I extended my hand. "I'm Betsy Hitz, Dr. Selwood."

"It's *Mister* Selwood," he corrected me and walked past me to Jim.

The two of us were quite a sight, and I wondered what he was thinking. It wasn't long before we found out.

He removed the two bandages and peered closely at the sutured wounds, but seemed more intrigued with some previous scars, the result of a boating accident years ago, which transversed Jim's chest like a road map.

"Got in a little knife fight, huh fellow?" he remarked as a veterinarian might to an alley tomcat. "Well, Saturday nights we see a lot of these. What happened this time?"

Jim struggled for words, but could not speak above a rasping whisper.

"Speak up!" the doctor ordered, standing a bed length away.

"Our boat was boarded . . ." Jim managed to say.

"I can't hear you! Can't you talk?"

"Doctor, may I explain?" I asked. Without waiting for comment I began. "He was stabbed twice with a rusty machete, here and here. Dr. Kavala in Bequia sutured the wounds. He sent you this note." I passed him the envelope. "He hasn't been given tetanus or an antibiotic."

"Let him tell me himself. Wait outside, will you?"

Marcus Welby, he wasn't. Why, he's no older than I am, I thought. But if he's good, that's all that matters.

I took a seat at the empty nurse's station and looked around. But if he's good, I wondered, what's he doing in a place like this? I watched the minutes on the clock drag by.

A very large cockroach paused briefly on the bound ledger that lay open on the desk beside me. Without thinking, I removed my one sandal and smacked it into a pulpy mess in the gutter of the ledger. The head nurse caught this and glared at me disapprovingly. Embarrassed for my breach of hospital etiquette, I flicked the carcass on the floor, bowed my head and folded my hands in my lap.

"Mister" Selwood emerged from the examining room drying his hands with a paper towel. "The knife punctured his right lung all right—hemopneumothorax," he said matter-of-factly. "The cavity is filled with blood and air. The abdominal wound doesn't appear to have caused injury to internal organs, but we'll have to keep an eye on it. For now, we've got to drain that pleural cavity and give the lung a chance to expand."

"Will that require surgery?" I asked.

He smiled with a hint of despair and thought long before he spoke.

"I'm an orthopedist. If we were home—in the U.K.—I'd have a thoracic man go in and have a look. But this," he said with a theatrical sweep of his hand, "quite obviously is not the U.K. The chief surgeon is on leave and I'm doing all the surgery now. We simply do not have the facilities, the staff to do. . . . This is not America, you know."

"I realize that. Could he, should he be flown to the States for treatment?"

"Not in his condition. I'm taking him to the operating theatre now to insert a tube in the pleural cavity to try to drain off the fluid that has collected there. Then with luck, the lung will expand. Problem is, I don't have the proper tube. They're looking for one now, but we may have to make do with another type, a urinary catheter. Sterile, of course."

He handed me Jim's shoes and clothes. "You'll find him later in male surgical."

The double doors to the examining room swung open and Jim whisked by on the hand-borne stretcher to surgery. I touched his hand and forced a smile. His eyes met mine and then he was gone.

Resuming my seat, I nervously kneaded Jim's soiled clothes, thoroughly consumed with worry for this man from whom I'd not been apart in the year since we left on our cruise.

Alone with my thoughts, I recalled the six months of planning and anticipation while we kept our ownership of *Cheers* a secret from our employers. They were exciting days of poring over pilot charts and world maps, sticking pins in the exotic ports of call we hoped to visit. For nearly a year we lived in the future, accumulating food stores, canning one last bumper harvest from our garden and adding to our library, paring belongings down to the essentials, gathering spare parts, collecting charts.

By the time we'd announced our plans, we'd sold our house and owned *Cheers* outright. We didn't want to be burdened with mortgage payments, insurance premiums and teetering checkbook balances. We watched our pennies, tightened our belts and saved enough for four years of cruising—if we were careful. In four years, we could reach the faraway ports of our dreams, or circle the globe if we wished.

Back in those days I wondered how we would fare day in, day out, sharing the confines of a boat smaller than most living rooms, with only each other for company. Finally last fall, the day of truth arrived. In the dark hours of October 4, we slipped our lines and sailed south from Newport, Rhode Island. And from that moment on, we lived each day in the present and never looked back with a moment of regret.

Life under sail was richer, more rewarding than any time we'd ever known. Clock time mattered little as each day unfolded without schedule. Living on deck as much as below, we needed no alarm clock to awaken us. We slept when we were tired, ate when we were hungry and planned our itinerary by the seasons.

The simplest things in life took on new significance. Dinner was the highlight of each day. Whenever possible it included new foods we'd picked from trees, foraged from shore or bartered in colorful open-air markets. Meals were savored slowly in the cockpit by the glow of a kerosene lamp. A black rubber bag slung from the rigging gave a luxuriously warm freshwater shower. A nozzle and a long hose converted the sun awning to a rain catcher to top off tanks in a downpour. A mail drop bringing word from friends and family was a big occasion, which we'd prolong by taking turns reading our letters aloud over morning coffee. Evenings we learned to find the planets and trace the constellations.

Then it dawned on me: This is all a nightmare. There's been no intruder—no stabbing. Wake up! The nightmare's over and Jim is beside you sleeping. I shook my head violently, then pinched my arms.

But it wasn't a dream. Two o'clock came and went. Unconsciously I kneaded Jim's clothes, folded in my lap, as though the fabric remained my last link to his life.

I'd never tired of this man who'd been my best friend and lover, psychiatrist and watch mate. He was as uncomplicated and direct as any man can be, yet complex enough that after seven years I was still learning new things about him.

I thought back to that autumn day when his best friend succumbed to lung cancer. Jim threw his pack of cigarettes into the sea and kicked his two-pack-a-day habit for good. He christened our self-steering vane "Harper" in honor of his blue-eyed, martini-drinking friend. And now and then when Harper wouldn't perform, Jim would disappear below, make a dry martini—no olive—and pour it over the vane. "Cheers, Harper," he'd say. "Why yes, now that you mention it, I think I should have one, too."

How I adored this man who long ago had chosen a seaman's life over a college education. Yet Jim devoured books and delighted in reading aloud to me. Propped up in bed, in our lamp-lit forward cabin, he read me every one of Sherlock Holmes' mysteries while I bit my nails in suspense. He read me Treasure Island and Kenneth Norris' wonderful accounts of porpoise-watching. From his lips I heard the tale of Robinson Crusoe's long, isolated sojourn, and the swashbuckling stories of Pitcairn Island.

I remembered the closeness we shared during midnight battles with rebellious sails off Cape Hatteras, the terror I felt when I awoke for watch and found no one at the helm . . . and the flood of relief when Jim crawled aft from the bowsprit.

I thought of that day in the Abacos when Jim leapt to the boom, leaned back into the full, billowing sail and rode the mainsail as *Cheers* rolled and tried to dip the end of her boom in the swells.

I recalled how eagerly he donned face mask and fins to explore beneath the surface of each new anchorage, setting the anchor by hand. And how I'd hold the tip of his flipper, draw a breath and hitch a ride through underwater coral gardens.

I remembered the thrill of discovery the day we rowed inside an underwater cave in the British Virgins and shot with the surge from one dank wall to the next, the feeble beam of our flashlight illuminating stalactites that had never seen a ray of sunlight. Those were carefree days of ultimate freedom and self-discipline slowly learned when workaday rules no longer applied.

From a close friend grew my love for this man of quiet humility who never spoke of conquests past, whether storms at sea or women.

I discovered in Jim a man of subtle contrasts who professed to detest fish, but who raved about the delicate taste of the few I caught, a man who couldn't sew on a button, but given a needle and palm could repair a sail and tuck perfect herringbone stitches in elk hide.

Being with Jim was undemanding fun. We never clung to one another in body or spirit. But now, how I wished for something to cling to.

*   *   *

"Phone for you," said the nurse. "Your husband the one up to the theatre? Phone's down the hall, turn left."

It was Jim's mother, Jean.

"He's still in surgery," I explained. Then I recounted to her what Selwood had told me.

"We're flying down first thing in the morning, by way of Barbados," she said. "We'll get a cab to the hospital and will meet you there tomorrow afternoon."

"Good, I'll find you a place to stay."

"Fine. Here's Bob." Jim's father came on the line. "I'd like to speak with Jim's doctor when he's out of surgery," said Jim's father, who everybody simply called Doc.

Just then Selwood appeared in the doorway.

"Doctor, Jim's father is on the phone from New Jersey. He's a doctor, too, and would like to speak with you."

Selwood glanced at his watch.

"It's three o'clock in the morning," he snapped. "I'm going to get some sleep."

He left.

*　　*　　*

I threaded my way through wood-floored corridors with grimy, graffiti-covered walls and felt my way up the dark stairway to the sign that read "Male Surgical." There I found three interconnected wards with between six and a dozen beds in each.

Jim's stark white face was easy to find. I found him asleep in a center bed, one of six in the ward. A nurse in a starched white uniform and prim cap entered and pulled a string overhead, which lighted a bare bulb that dangled from the center of the high ceiling. Armies of cockroaches scurried in pandemonium up the walls, across patients' beds and into wide cracks in the wood floor. The nurse bit the edge of a white rag and tore off a strip. Then she balanced atop a vandalized kitchen chair and, with the rag, slung an intravenous bottle over Jim's bed.

A worn and cracked red rubber hose led from a new orifice in the right side of Jim's chest to a two-gallon jar, half-filled with water, which sat on the floor beside his bed.

"You stayin' the night?" asked the nurse as she adjusted the flow of intravenous fluid.

"Yes, if it's all right."

"It's all right," she said, offering me the backless chair.

Jim opened his eyes, looked at me, then fell back into a deep sleep. I watched each shallow breath he drew throughout the night and kept the roaches at bay with my sandal.

CHAPTER THREE

———————————————— The first rooster crowed at 5 a.m. Just before dawn the ritual began. A lone, haunting whistle started at the far end of the first ward. The man in the next bed picked it up and the mournful tune carried from pursed lip to lip throughout the three wards. By sunup, all the men were awake and beginning their morning routine. They chatted lazily.

"How you be this morning, Vibert?"

"Can't complain. I'm still alive."

"You feel that rain?"

"Feel that rain? Damn wind like to blow me outta my bed!"

"John, how are you?"

"Oh, been better, been better. That woman doctor going to take my stitches out today."

"Vincent, you had a bad night there. How's the leg?"

"All right, I guess. It's Sunday. My family comin' to see me."

Bashfully at first, then with brazen curiosity, the other inmates dropped by to see the new arrival and "his woman." And little wonder they did. Not only were we the only white people in the 250-bed hospital, but word was out about the circumstances of the "accident," as I'd begun to call it.

I felt very much out of place and wished to give the other patients their morning privacy. Jim was asleep, so I picked up my

26

pocketbook and took a stroll. The pocketbook was heavy with the weight of the revolver and 50 rounds of ammunition. I knew little about guns and felt uneasy carrying a loaded weapon. I found a ladies' room and ducked inside, ill-prepared to find a full-length mirror.

In my haste to leave the boat I'd thrown my loose-fitting smock dress on backwards. The front was spattered with blood and mud and the back soiled with rust and rips. My one sandal was caked with cockroach remains and my bare feet were encrusted with caked sand and goat dung to the ankle. I splashed water on my face and tried to comb my snarled hair with my fingers. Then I took stock of the contents of my seldom-used pocketbook. I had no comb, no wallet and no identification. I had not one Eastern Caribbean cent, no place to stay and I knew no one on the island. Things could only improve.

I went inside a stall, carefully removed the loaded gun and dumped the contents of the purse on the toilet seat. My old Timex was still running. It was 8 a.m. The ferry *Grenadine Star* would be arriving soon from Bequia. If my hunch was correct, Jim's attacker would try to catch the first ferry off tiny Bequia and flee to St. Vincent, where he could get lost in the crowd. But I would be there waiting. Whether driven by the desire to bring him to justice or plain and simple revenge, I'm not sure, but I was determined that Jim's attacker would not go free.

I examined the pistol and tried to remove the bullets, but the revolving chamber wouldn't spin. I fumbled and fussed, but could not release the catch. I was reluctant to force any moving parts for fear of accidentally firing the pistol and inelegantly meeting my Maker in the toilet stall of a roach-infested hospital. I decided to wait and ask someone to help me. Carefully, I put the gun back in my purse.

Then I found among the litter in my purse, a name Jim's father, Doc, had given us nearly a year before: Bill Little, Bequia Slip.

"Bill's wife has been a patient of mine for years in New Jersey," Doc had said. "Bill owns a waterfront restaurant and slipway down in Bequia. Be sure and look him up if you stop there on *Cheers.*"

We hadn't.

I sat on the seat and with a safety pin, removed glass slivers from my foot. Then I washed both feet in the sink.

I looked in on Jim and, finding him asleep, I asked to use the phone at the nurse's station. I rang Bequia police, identified my-self, and asked to speak with the ranking police officer.

"Sergeant Allen here."

"Did you find the man?" I asked.

"Find the man!" he exclaimed. "How we gonna find the man with you in St. Vincent? If you want us to find the man, you better get yourself on the next ferry to Bequia."

"But I talked to one of your officers at the clinic last night. I gave him a thorough description of the man—every detail."

"You had no business leaving the island," he interrupted. "There's nothing we can do till you come back here and cooper-ate."

"But, please understand. I had to look after . . ." My voice broke and I couldn't finish my sentence. "I'll call you later," I choked and hung up.

I walked outside to the breezeway and tried to fight back the tears. I was ashamed and angry with myself for losing my grip. More importantly, I didn't want to get off on the wrong foot with Bequia police and jeopardize the investigation.

Struggling to pull myself together, I stood at the second story wood railing and stared below at a pair of scrawny hens strutting and pecking at the refuse from an overturned garbage can in the cement courtyard below. Suddenly a painfully-thin boy of eight or nine dashed in from the street, past two hospital watchmen in their stand-up guardhouse, and knelt at the refuse pile, scattering the clucking hens.

One guard gave chase. In his hand was a coiled bullwhip. The boy snatched from the ground the heel end of a discarded loaf of bread and stuffed as much into his mouth as he could before the guard reached him. Now inside the courtyard, the guard dropped the tail of the whip to the ground and approached the boy threat-eningly. The street urchin backed up, still tearing off hunks of bread with his teeth. He wore only a pair of soiled, cut-off khaki shorts large enough to accommodate four boys his size. He held the shorts up with one hand and continued stuffing bread into his mouth with the other as he scrambled to keep beyond the whip's reach.

I could scarcely believe what followed. The guard cracked the whip on the pavement inches short of the boy. The two of them shuffled round and round like sparring boxers, the boy keeping just beyond reach of the cracking whip. The guard obviously was toying with the boy and, curiously enough, the boy seemed to rise to the challenge of grabbing free food without receiving a beating. Finally, the guard chased the boy back into the street with fervor. I couldn't help but think it a cat-and-mouse game they frequently played.

Beside the bizarre spectacle, my worries seemed mundane indeed. I pulled myself together and returned to the ward, where I penned a quick note to Jim: "Gone to the dock to meet the ferry. Be right back. Love you, B."

Then I wrote a letter to a man on Bequia I'd never met:

Dear Bill Little,

Jim Holman and I have been cruising the Grenadines aboard our cutter *Cheers*. I believe you know his father, Dr. Robert Holman, who has often treated your wife in New Jersey.

While anchored in Friendship Bay last night, our boat was boarded by a man who stabbed Jim and robbed us. I am with Jim at the hospital in St. Vincent, but have no identification or money.

Could you possibly lend me $100 E.C. for a few days? If so, please send it to me with the ferry Captain. I'll repay you when I return to *Cheers* in Bequia, and look forward to meeting you then.

Many thanks,
Betsy Hitz
Kingstown, St. Vincent
Sunday, July 12

I sealed the letter, slipped my feet into Jim's shoes and struck out for the dock, although I had only the vaguest idea where I'd find it.

I walked downhill until I reached the water, then turned left past some waterfront warehouses until I found the cement pier.

Scores of boisterous school-age boys splashed and swam from the dock trying to impress a handful of tough-looking Rastafarian youths with their bravado. I was fair game for their catcalls and their leers.

The *Grenadine Star* was late. I waited. I no longer pushed from my thoughts the terror wrought by last night's naked intruder. Rather I let his very being flood my mind until I could see his outline, focus on his face, hear his demands. So vivid was his image, the air seemed charged with the same violence I had experienced less than 12 hours ago.

But what if he disguised himself? Shaved the goatee? How would I recognize him?

I'd still know him.

Suppose he hid beneath sunglasses and a hat?

It wouldn't matter. It wasn't only his face. There was an unmistakable aura about him. He could crop his hair, shave his goatee, or hide beneath clothing. It made no difference. I was dead certain I could pick the man I sought out of any crowd.

But then what?

I heard the *Grenadine Star* before I saw her approach. A mixture of canned reggae and gospel blared from a pair of loudspeakers mounted atop the bridge, while thunderclaps of spirited hands kept the beat. Carnival in St. Vincent, the gala event of the year, had ended just two weeks before. But the frenzy, however, was still in full swing this Sunday morning for hundreds of gaily-dressed young people returning from a religious retreat in the Grenadines.

They thronged the decks and bridge of *Grenadine Star,* a gray-hulled replica of a World War II landing craft, their undulating bodies a sea of suggestive movement. Clapping, stomping, dipping and twirling, they sang:

> *Don't stop it now, mon, Carnival,*
> *Do it, do it now, mon, Carnival!*

Girls with girls, boys with girls, singly, in circles and in line formations, everyone boogied and wailed:

> *Everybody here say, Carnival,*
> *Here to stay, mon, Carnival!*

It would have been easy to get caught up in the moment as the *Star* nosed her bluff bow right up to the shore. The pier began to swell with friends and family who'd come to greet the passengers. I spotted two uniformed and armed policemen and stood near them on the shore end of the pier.

Finally, the *Star's* broad bow ramp swung down onto the beach and passengers began to disembark. Clasping the canister of mace, I scanned the crowd, searching every male face for the one I sought, holding tight to the vision of him in my mind. When I saw him there would be no mistake.

I found a man of his build—no, too dark. An angular face with a sparse goatee—no, too tall. A pair of round eyes with that same cold stare—no, bad teeth.

The ferry was now empty but for the captain and crew.

I stepped aboard and searched the passageways for stragglers. Suddenly a man emerged from the head, his back to me. The height was right. I waited for him to turn around. Wrong face. Then I asked the mate if I might speak with Captain Hazel. He led me up winding steps to the wheelhouse.

"I knew your brother Jayford in the States," I told him. "He was in Newport, Rhode Island, last winter caulking the decks of the *Rose* and *Black Pearl,* and a good job he did. We had him home to supper and he told us a lot about Bequia and about the 'two-bow' boats he used to build here."

Then I told the captain about our trouble and he promised to hand-deliver my letter to Bill Little when the *Star* returned to Bequia. I thanked him and left.

It was after 9 a.m. when I returned to the hospital and found Jim awake. American voices filled the next ward, sending roving patients scrambling back to their beds. I strained to hear their conversation as they approached.

"Not another Saturday night stabber," said a woman. "Why me?"

A team of blue jean-clad young people worked their way through the wards, looking more like picnickers than medical personnel. A petite white woman of about 25, unmistakably an American, stopped at the foot of Jim's bed. A stethoscope dangled from her neck. In her hand was a clipboard. She clenched a pencil between her teeth. Her large brown eyes looked at us in bewilderment from beneath a fringe of black bangs.

"Morning. I'm Rima Matevosian," she said. "What happened?"

As I told her briefly about our mishap, her face filled with compassion. I judged her to be an intern or an extern, not yet hardened by experience. She took Jim's vital signs, glanced at his chart and increased the rate of his intravenous droplets.

"Has Mister Selwood been in to see him since surgery?"

"No," I replied.

"Well, we're pretty shorthanded now. You look like you could use some sleep," she said to me. "How about a shower and breakfast at my place? Do you have a change of clothes? No? Well, I'll lend you something."

Before I could answer, she placed a hand on Jim's shoulder. "Can you spare her for a couple of hours? I'll have her back by noon."

"Go with her, Betsy," Jim whispered.

Rima finished her Sunday morning rounds, collected me and we piled in her rented compact sedan. She stomped on the gas and we whined out of town, snaking southward along narrow, twisting lanes.

Rima chattered non-stop, foot to the floor, one hand on the wheel, the other hand embellishing the story as we tore southward. We spoke of our similar suburban childhoods, the carnival just past and snowfalls in New England; college professors and the fuel crunch; the near assassination of President Reagan and the green flash—all things of the past, ignoring the present for the moment.

My ears popped as we crested verdant hills planted in plantain and sugar cane. My stomach leapt to my throat as we plunged through valleys dotted with drowsy villages. The stench of the island hospital vanished on Rima's adrenaline ride through the clean countryside, still dripping from its morning shower.

Rima looked at my white-knuckle grip on the dashboard. "Sorry, I'll slow down," she apologized, pressing on the brake.

"Funny," I laughed, "I guess I've come to think of six knots as really moving. We never get above sea level. It's been a while since I've ridden in a car. This is a thrilling ride. Please, carry on."

Rima nailed it, sending a flock of chickens scurrying for cover. We talked, almost as old friends, while green scenery raced by in a blur.

I tried to answer in a nutshell her question of what compelled us to leave behind the security of home, good jobs and close friends for what now seemed an ill-fated voyage.

"We left not to run away from life, but to keep it from escaping us, I suppose. And we weren't searching for paradise, Eden or even a better place to settle. Just a way of living free from all the trappings—shopping malls and disco fever, blow driers and tax-eroded take-home salaries."

"Junk mail and traffic jams," she laughed.

"You know, then, Rima."

"I think so."

And then it was my turn to ask the questions.

"You could have chosen to be a nurse, Rima. You'd have your cap by now, maybe be married to a doctor."

"Wouldn't that be easy? And I'd be hustling bed pans in Hoboken," she laughed, "working the night shift while my husband crammed days for his neurology boards. No, like you, I guess I wanted something more. My older sister's a doctor, you know. We're very close. I've always admired her. I suppose that's why I'm going to be a doctor."

She turned left into a long driveway and with a screech pulled up to a sprawling white stucco compound.

"Villa Lodge," she announced, jerking back the hand brake. "It's a long way from the hospital, but there aren't many places on St. Vincent I'd feel safe living."

Rima led me past a chlorinated swimming pool where a lone couple fresh from the north was sipping frozen piña coladas from stemmed glasses, oblivious to the panoramic view of the blue Caribbean far below and their own blistering skin.

Rima waved to the white-jacketed poolside bartender who was busy at the blender and led me up a short flight of winding stairs to her apartment. She fumbled through her overstuffed bag, turned the key and ushered me inside a tidy efficiency, tastefully decorated and Arctic cold. A slender, kerchiefed maid was just finishing up last night's dinner dishes. She dried her hands on her apron, gave a polite nod and left.

After living aboard a boat with as much floor space as an abbreviated bowling lane, even the simplest dwelling seems an opulent place to travel-weary eyes. Hurtled in just a few short minutes from rough-and-tumble Kingstown to condominium-style island affluence—complete with hot water, pile carpeting, scented soap and gleaming porcelain—left me momentarily in culture shock.

Rima poked her head in the steamy bathroom. "Cheese omelet all right?"

I dried off with an oversize Turkish towel, combed my wet hair and felt human again.

Noting that I was a full head taller than herself and put together rather more ruggedly, Rima had thoughtfully selected a forgiving mid-calf-length frock that would yield to my more muscular, less curvacious frame. I pulled the gossamer dress over my head, adjusted the thin spaghetti straps and tugged at the clingy bodice. I blushed at the image of Lolita in lavender staring back at me from the full-length mirror. But I felt clean, covered and deeply grateful.

Over a fresh pot of coffee and a box full of her roommate's imported cigarettes, we talked like mad as only women can—candidly, openly, frankly. In the space of a couple of hours we solved some immediate logistical problems and got down to the ultimate concern, Jim's recovery.

Villa Lodge had a good restaurant, she said, and also rented rooms on a short-term basis. So we reserved for the Holmans an efficiency apartment on a day-to-day basis. They could commute to the hospital with Rima or by taxi. She offered to meet them at the hospital that evening and bring them to the lodge, while I stayed the night with Jim.

"Have you thought about moving Jim to a hospital in the U.S.?" she asked delicately.

"Sure. I want his father to examine him first. Right now he's hooked up to so many tubes. Dr. Selwood seems to think . . . I mean Mister Selwood. Which is it?

"It's Mister—English system."

"Mister Selwood wants to see some improvement. Then, just as soon as Jim is stable enough to travel, I want to move him to the States for further treatment."

"Improvement. That's the important first step," said Rima. "The lung is a curious organ. Its recuperative ability is amazing. The tissue can knit together in a day or two. Selwood probably explained to you the urgency of draining the pleural cavity and expanding the lung, right? The big risk with such an injury is infection, especially in the tropics. You've seen the hospital. Patient care is not what it is in the States. The level of sanitation is, well, deplorable. Jim should be getting the expertise of a thoracic specialist and attentive, round-the-clock nursing. That's impossible here."

"I'm not a doctor," she said. "Please understand that."

"You're an intern?"

"I'm not even an intern. I'm twenty-three years old. The other Americans you saw me with this morning were classmates of mine in medical school in St. Georges, Grenada. Technically, we're still in med school and are assigned to the general hospital on St. Vincent as externs. When we go to St. Joseph's Hospital in New Jersey in September, we will be interns."

"That's where Jim's father practices: St. Joseph's in Paterson. He's the director of orthopedics there."

"Really? Well, right now we're in training where we're needed most, treating patients in an environment that's, well, you saw it, not what you'd find at home.

"Betsy I don't want to alarm you, but I don't want you to expect miracles from a hospital that's understaffed, underequipped and underfinanced. One physician now is treating two hundred and fifty-odd patients. He's an orthopedist but is doing all the general surgery—mastectomies, ouphratemies, pneumonectomies, hysterectomies—you name it. And he's got the outpatient day clinic on top of that."

Rima shrugged and went on.

"The rest of us, we're only a handful of students, but we're doing our best to keep those poor people alive. We're green, we're over our heads, but there's no alternative. The hospital is poor and the patients still poorer. The per capita income on St. Vincent is less than five hundred dollars a year. Of the Caribbean Islands only Haiti is poorer. Patients here have died for lack of a ten-dollar antibiotic. Even if it were available here, the dispensary couldn't requisition funds for it.

"Oh, it's excellent training. We're treating diseases we'd never see in a lifetime of stateside practice—yellow fever, elephantitus, leprosy, gangrene and a variety of tropical and parasitic diseases. On this island there's no such thing as preventive medicine. Most people live with an injury or illness until they can no longer function. Then they come here. Often it's too late for us to help.

"Did you meet Mr. Chase, the elderly man with the bandaged

hand in the bed to Jim's left? He was crossing the road in front of his house on the north end of the island when a motorcycle came around the corner and hit him, injuring his left hand. He wrapped it in banana leaves for a few days and waited until he couldn't stand the pain any longer before coming to us. He was admitted four weeks ago with a broken metacarpal and a low-grade infection. Now the hand is gangrenous and may have to be amputated. There are too many cases like his, cases of gangrene setting in *in the hospital.*"

Another key turned in the lock and I was introduced to Rima's roommate, Molly, a pretty Chinese woman a bit older than Rima. She poured herself a cup of coffee, kicked off her shoes and put up her feet. Molly, also a medical student, had been assigned to the male surgical ward the previous month. Though she was now working in internal medicine, she was full of questions for Rima about the condition of her former patients. They thumbed through their notes and flipped through the pages of a pharmaceutical text, searching for alternative treatments in available drugs.

Rima explained to me that St. Vincent leads the Caribbean in birth rate—and mortality rate.

"These people have large families and they learn at an early age to live with death. They're afraid to come to the hospital, but once admitted, they're the most submissive patients in the world. They demand nothing, ask few questions and are grateful for anything that's done for them. Their stay costs them less than a dollar a day, on the average, and if they can't afford that, their friends and extended families help out.

"Today's Sunday, the big visiting day. Watch Mr. Reynolds, in the bed across from Jim. He gets the most Sunday visitors. You'll see them all stuffing red dollar bills in his hand or under his pillow."

"He's still making money?" exclaimed Molly. "That poor, sweet man. He must be worth a small fortune by now."

"He was admitted six weeks ago with a urinary tract infection," explained Rima. "With the right antibiotic and judicious hygiene, he'd be home now. But the nurses are funny about such things and again we didn't have the desired antibiotic. His penis became gangrenous and was amputated two weeks ago."

"Do you know he gave me a sack of mangoes after that?" said Molly. "The big grafted ones. He had his wife bring them in along with a couple of hands of bananas, he was so grateful."

"Grateful!" Rima shook her head. "Grateful for what? House pets in the States get better medical care than those people get here."

"Easy, Rima."

"I'm sorry. I don't mean to be morbid."

"You've got to toughen up."

"How do you learn not to feel?"

Molly rummaged through her purse. "Here's the rest of your Ampicillin," she said, changing the subject.

"Creative medicine," said Rima. "So many drugs we need are unavailable on the island. So we carry our own kits. My sister sends me whatever free samples she can, and I pay for some prescriptions myself. But it's a losing game. There's no way to cure the ills of the world on my small allowance."

"You aren't paid for your work at the hospital?" I asked.

"Paid? No. But I'm fortunate that my family is putting me through medical school, so I don't have to stop and work like so many others. It's a long enough road with just the schooling. You've probably noticed, I'm younger than the rest."

"Like me, kiddo?" intoned Molly. "It's true. This is my second career."

"And your first?" I asked.

"I was a piano player," said Molly.

"A concert pianist," corrected Rima, "and a fine one."

"Well that was long ago, back in China."

"You grew up in China?" I asked. "But you speak English like an American."

"Thank you. I spoke only Chinese until I was twenty-two. Learning English then was difficult for me. I'm forty and foolish enough to think I'm not too old to study medicine."

"Do you plan to specialize?" I asked.

She laughed. "I want to practice medicine someday not spend my life studying it. I have to complete a year of internship and a two-year residency before I become a general practitioner. And I must work along the way. I have a husband and two children waiting for me in the States."

"You must miss them," I said.

"I miss them very much," Molly sighed. "But what do you do when there's a voice inside you that gives you no peace until you either reach your goal or your spirit is broken trying? Is there a word for that in English?"

I thought. "Maybe it's what sailors used to call a siren song. Usually the siren's voice led them to disaster, but always her song was too sweet, too enticing to ignore. It's a song I've heard."

Rima emerged from her bedroom carrying a pair of high-heeled sandals. "It's almost noon and I made Jim a promise. Let's get you back to the hospital. Here, Betsy," she handed me the shoes. "Try these on."

I coaxed my size eights into her six-and-a-halfs. "They'll be just fine." I said.

"Your heels are hanging over the edge a full inch," laughed Rima, "but I guess they'll have to do."

I wobbled unsteadily out of the door ahead of Rima, having long ago lost the knack of walking in heeled shoes.

"Like riding a bike," coached Rima, "you never really forget how."

Rima's blue sedan pulled up to the front gate of the hospital and she pressed 80 Eastern Caribbean dollars into my palm. "You'll need this," she said casually.

"But . . ."

"I know you're good for it," she insisted. "And I can lend you more if you need it. When the shops open in the morning you can buy Jim some things the hospital doesn't provide.

"If you're going to stay with him, Betsy, better be prepared to nurse him yourself. Just stay out of the nurse's way, especially those on the night shift. Here's my phone number. Call me if anything comes up. I'll look in on Jim this evening when I pick up the Holmans."

"How can I thank you, Rima?"

"You can look after that man of yours."

I turned and wobbled up the steps to Jim.

CHAPTER FOUR

——————————————————— A sallow-faced teen-ager sat at the foot of Jim's bed wearing carpet slippers and a plaid cotton bathrobe. The two patients merely looked at each other. Jim was in too much pain to talk and his young friend too shy.

"Meet Damian," whispered Jim.

The boy's right arm was withered, so I offered my left.

"Happy to know you, Damian. I'm Betsy."

We shook and he explained in a timid voice that he was being treated for epilepsy. He was very homesick but he'd been here many times before. His grandmother, who was his guardian, was due on the afternoon bus. That's why Sundays were his favorite, he said.

I looked at the withered right hand and then at his strong left hand. Suddenly it came to me: Our attacker was left handed, like Damian! Think now. He held the fist full of cash in his right hand, the machete in his left. On deck he was only a silhouette, but while he was below, standing beneath the overhead lights, he held the machete with his left. When he swung and broke the lamp, he held the machete in his left hand. But when he stabbed Jim? I couldn't be sure which hand he's used, for Jim's back partially obstructed my view. I saw only his crazed face, heard only the sound of the blade as it penetrated.

I had to call Sergeant Allen.

A young nurse in a gray pinstripe dress stopped at Jim's bed and with two claps of her hands sent Damian shuffling back to his bed in the next ward. She reached in the pocket of her white apron

39

and handed me a note: "Call Bill Little, Bequia Slip. 83272," it read.

"Thank you, nurse. His IV seems to have stopped again. Could you check it please?"

She regarded me sourly, adjusted the flow and left without speaking.

Bill Little picked up the phone on the first ring. There was a touch of wild west in his voice. He spoke fast and non-stop.

"Captain Hazel personally delivered your note," he said. "Christ, it took me almost an hour to find you in that town. I assumed you'd go to the Botanic Hospital, you know, Cyrus's clinic. What in blazes you doin' in the general hospital? Only good thing to come out of that place is Doc Cyrus and they threw him out 'cause he was the only one in the bunch knew how to practice medicine."

"Dr. Holman is flying in tonight," I explained. "As soon as Jim is stable enough to be moved, we're going to move him to a hospital in the States."

"Christ, didn't you people have a gun on that boat? Either of you know how to use it? Then why the hell didn't you blow that son of a . . . Well it's too late now. Jeez, I wish you'd a come to see me 'fore goin' 'round to Friendship Bay. Everyone here knows it's a smuggler's haven.

"Your boat still there? Listen, I got a boat of my own, a pretty little Perry design sittin' right out front of my place. How 'bout if I go 'round to Friendship an' bring that boat of yours back here. 'Fore they strip her. I got a mooring an' she can sit right in front of Bequia Slip till this thing blows over, till Jim's better. One of my boys can keep an eye on her for you. He'll check her every day. It's July, you know, hurricane season.

"Barbara—she's my partner—Barbara here's written you a letter an' we're sending you some cash on the late ferry. The *Seimstrand* gets into Kingstown 'bout six o'clock tonight. You only asked for a hundred E.C. That's only forty U.S. dollars, you know. That won't get you far. I'm sending you three hundred E.C. in cash, just so you know. It'll be in an envelope on the evening ferry.

"An' for Christsake don't go down to that ferry dock yourself— not after dark. That town's nothin' but a ghetto. I got a cab driver named Lester I use whenever I'm in St. Vincent on business. He's white Vincentian. Lester's good people. You wait there at the hospital and Lester'll bring you the envelope. An' don't pay him. I'll take care of him later.

"Now, anything else I can do for you? Oh, they got a lead on this guy. That ought to cheer you up. Maybe by now they've brought someone in. He's got a gold tooth, right? Isn't that what you told the cop? A big black buck with a gold front tooth? No? You sure? It's all over the island: The guy had a machete and a gold tooth. Well, don't quote me. Better call Allen yourself.

"Hey, so Doc's comin' down. That's fine. An' Jim's mother, too? You folks ought to think 'bout that Cyrus Clinic. If Jim's as bad as it sounds. Jeez, so that sucker really carved him up, huh? Look, call me if you need anything."

I thanked Bill Little for his kindness, gave him instructions on starting *Cheers'* engine, and told him where to find spare keys to the ignition and companionway locks.

"The boat looks like a battlefield," I explained. "Would you please hide the shotgun, flare pistol and all the ammunition in a locker? But before you go aboard, let me first call Sergeant Allen and see if he'll examine the boat. Maybe there's some evidence we overlooked. He might even be able to get some fingerprints. I explained to the policeman who came to Bequia Clinic last night that the man had a goatee—a chin beard—not a gold tooth. I thought he understood that, but I better clarify it again with Sergeant Allen. When Jim's better we'll find a way to thank you in person for all your help, Bill."

I hurried back to Jim to share the good news that the police might have a suspect, but he was asleep. His IV passed only three drops a minute. I mentioned the IV to the nurse at the station. Then I telephoned Sergeant Allen in Bequia.

I apologized for losing control during our morning conversation and assured him that I wanted to help with his investigation in every way possible. "Do you have a suspect?" I asked.

"Look, I told you, there's nothing we can do till you come back to Bequia and talk to us."

Summoning all the self-control I could muster, I explained that I could not leave Jim in this condition. "Please, take down this number at the hospital. I'm here day and night and you can call me any time. It's not a toll call. I can check in with you several times a day, as often as you wish, but I can't come to Bequia yet, not until Jim's a little better. Do you have my description of the assailant? The one I gave to your officer at the clinic last night?"

"All I know's the man got a gold tooth. You know how many men on this island's got a gold tooth?"

"The man who boarded our boat had a *goatee*—a small beard only on his chin. Not gold teeth. Our assailant had perfect, white teeth. The police officer must have thought I said gold tooth when I said goatee, meaning a chin beard. Do you understand?"

"He said you said gold tooth. You changing your story now?"

"No. I said goatee. Please, can we start from scratch on the description? I can give you every detail now, over the phone. Then you'll have something to go on."

I repeated to him the description I'd given his officer. "Did you get all that?"

"I'll send a CID man 'round to get your statement."

"A CID man?" I asked.

"Criminal Investigative Division. In plain clothes. He'll be there tomorrow, or maybe Tuesday."

"The assailant could be on another island by then," I said.

"An' you can thank yourself for that, Ma'am."

"Listen, my boat is still at Friendship Bay. Bill Little can take you out to it. He'll have a key to the cabin. There's bound to be some evidence there. The assailant had to have grabbed the stanchion when he came aboard from the stern. It's stainless steel. Maybe you can get some fingerprints. The forward hatch, he grasped the chrome-plated handle on the forward hatch. And the main hatch, it's varnished wood. He touched that, too. Can you take fingerprints?"

"Only in St. Vincent. Not here."

"Can you bring fingerprint equipment from St. Vincent to my boat in Bequia?"

"It's a waste of time."

"It's a waste of time to do nothing. Have you talked to the Mitchell boys?"

"Who?"

"Three teen-agers who brought us ashore in Friendship Bay. At least two of them are named Mitchell. They live there, overlooking the bay. It was their orange rubber dinghy that the assailant stole from shore to come out to our boat last night. After the man jumped overboard, I cut the dinghy painter so he wouldn't return for the dinghy. The severed dinghy painter is still tied to my stan-chion, starboard side. You're bound to learn something if you go there and talk to them. Look at my boat. Her name is *Cheers*—the white cutter, a double-ender with a bowsprit.

"When the man jumped overboard he was still carrying the ma-chete and a fist full of cash, about two hundred E.C. in small bills. He also may have been carrying my wallet, a maroon billfold, a dark red leather billfold with credit cards and identification in my name, Elizabeth R. Hitz. He might have dropped something. Maybe you'll find his clothes on shore."

"Look, you're wasting my time," the sergeant interrupted. "You can tell it to a CID man or you can come back here and cooper-ate."

"Sergeant, you find me a suspect and I'll be on the next ferry to Bequia. Find me anyone to look at who fits the description. Can I talk to your CID man today?"

"Today's Sunday."

"Tomorrow morning, then?"

"Sometime tomorrow."

"I'll be waiting in the male surgical ward."

Exasperated, I hung up the phone. How could he be so thick-headed? But what if Bill Little's information is correct? What if the police do have a suspect but don't want to pick him up for ques-tioning until I'm back on the island? A suspect can only be held for a few hours before he must either be charged or released?

Maybe Allen was a West Indian Columbo—dumb on the out-side, crafty and cunning on the inside. But if Allen had a suspect, why wouldn't he tell me when I'd agreed to be on the next ferry?

I wished for patience. A criminal mind. An old dog to kick.

*   *   *

By early afternoon, the wards were filling with visitors dressed in their Sunday finest. Many brought gifts of green drinking coconuts and fresh fruit from the plantations.

Jim was still asleep, soaked with perspiration. A small transistor radio sat at the foot of his bed aimed at his face, playing gospel music. The middle-aged man in the next bed beamed.

"I think he likes it," he whispered. "See how deep he is sleeping? Like a baby!"

"That's very thoughtful. The sleep will do him good. My name's Betsy."

"Vincent John, Miss Betsy. When he wakes up, you give him some of this, hear?" He produced a big green bottle of green liquid. "Acolado. It's good for everything."

"Do you drink it?"

"No," he laughed. "You rub it on his skin." He offered me his brown, wrinkled wrist. "See how good it smells? It cools a body."

"He's very hot. I'm sure this will help."

The ward was now bursting at the seams with visitors. Jim awoke with a start. He always liked to sleep with his feet sticking outside the covers, and his white toes lured a curious little girl with big pink bows in her braided pigtails. With her small pink tongue curled over her upper lip, she stood at the foot of Jim's bed pinching his toes. Jim forced a grin and soon was surrounded by other children who gathered around his bed, wide-eyed and silent, kneading his toes. They were joined by parents, cousins and aunts who stopped by to satisfy their curiosity and, it seemed, to pay their respects. Few spoke, but all cast glances of deep sympathy for this stranger, who was remarkable only in that he was white and they were not.

Shoulder to shoulder, they thronged around his bed while others filed past. The air was thick with body heat. Jim looked as silly as a corpse watching his own wake. He grinned. I chuckled. He laughed and grasped his chest in pain. Then they all laughed and we joined in.

Jim, it seemed, was getting better.

*   *   *

The parade continued until four o'clock, when everyone left as quickly as they'd appeared and the roaches returned to their usual haunts. On communal bedside night stands, the patients laid in their larder of drinking nuts, bananas and mangoes to last the coming days. Many would have no visitors until the following Sunday.

The ward no longer seemed so alien. I'd met all five of Jim's roommates and many of their families. Mr. Reynolds even gave Jim one of the drinking nuts from his burlap sack. He whacked off the top of the coconut with an abbreviated machete and I poured Jim a small glass. With a smile, Jim feigned enjoyment of the sweet, slightly carbonated liquid. For days after, Mr. Reynolds kept him supplied with drinking nuts.

Vincent John lost his gospel station at five o'clock and wasted no time in tuning in another for Jim while I splashed the aromatic green liquid on his feverish head and shoulders.

"Whew," he whispered, "I smell like a French whore."

"Can you believe they bottle it right on Curacao?"

"Oh, wait till my mother gets a load of this place," he groaned.

"Do you think she's ever seen a cockroach?"

"They're mahogany beetles. Remember that."

*   *   *

"You look like the lady I'm looking for," said the tallish man holding a white envelope. "Betsy Hitz?"

"Yes. You're Lester?"

"That's right. Then this is for you. Bill Little sent it."

"Thank you," I said opening the envelope. "It came on the *Seimstrand?*"

"Right again."

"How long ago did she arrive?"

"Not more than five minutes ago. Bill Little said it was important, so I came right here."

"Do you have a few minutes?"

"Sure. What for?"

"Would you take me to the dock? I'm looking for someone who might have come on the ferry."

"Sure can. Hey, I heard what happened. How's your husband doing there? He don't look so good."

I told Jim I'd be back soon. "Try to get some sleep. Darn, your IV stopped again. Try to tell a nurse or I'll fix it when I get back. Sorry I have to run."

We hurried to Lester's compact station wagon and sped to the dock.

Most of the passengers had already left the ferry when we arrived. But many still milled around the dock area. It was just getting dark, so Lester drove onto the concrete pier and trained his headlights on the bright orange ferry.

"I think you've given me a pretty good idea of what the guy looks like," he said, helping me out of the cab. "You stay here behind the headlights while I check the ferry."

Lester searched the *Seimstrand* while I scanned the dock. He returned a few minutes later.

"Nothing," he shrugged.

"Did you check the men's head?"

"I looked in the men's toilet and in the engine compartment."

"When's the next ferry from Bequia?"

"*Grenadine Star* is due again in about 20 minutes."

"Can you wait with me?" I asked.

"Sure. We should see lights coming from over there," he pointed, "anytime now. Let's wait in the car."

I hope Bill Little's right about this guy, I thought. He seems trustworthy.

"Do you know anything about guns?" I asked awkwardly.

"A little. Why?"

"Have you ever used a revolver?"

"Look, lady, I'm not going to shoot anyone. Not here, not to-night."

"I didn't mean that. Could you release the catch on a revolver and unload it?" I pulled the gun out of my bag.

"Good kind Jesus!" he exclaimed.

"Would you try to get the bullets out for me?" I asked inno-cently.

He looked around, then switched on the overhead light, clicked the release catch and spun out the revolving cylinder. Five bullets dropped into his hand.

I sighed with relief. "Now, can you show me how to load and unload it?"

"Just a minute. You seem like a pretty gutsy lady. You're sure no dumbo. If you had this, what's your husband doing in that hospital bed while the guy who stuck him's out free?"

"We weren't prepared. The gun wasn't loaded."

"Think you could use it next time?"

"Yes," I said without hesitation, "show me how."

By the time the *Grenadine Star*'s lines were secured, I'd prac-ticed loading and unloading the revolver a few times and no longer felt uncomfortable with it in my purse, where I zipped it, un-loaded, into a side compartment.

Lester turned on his headlights and we repeated the same drill, searching the ferry and dock. Again we turned up nothing. We returned to the hospital. Lester insisted on walking me to Jim's ward.

"At least you know he's still on Bequia," he consoled me.

"Unless he got a ride on a private boat."

"Right. Or stole one."

"Or stole one."

The ward was dark and silent when I returned from the ferry. Jim was in considerable pain and together we counted down the minutes until his eight o'clock injection. Again his IV fluid had stopped.

Jim's parents reached the hospital at 9 p.m. Sunday after an unscheduled five-hour layover in Barbados. They embraced me, then Doc examined Jim while his mother and I spoke outside.

Jean didn't gasp when she discovered cockroaches covering the hospital walls and her son's bed sheet. Her quiet concern and Doc's professional knowledge were just what was needed.

"He's in no condition to be moved just yet," concluded Doc after examining Jim.

"Nurse, I'd like to speak with his doctor. Could you get Dr. Selwood on the phone for me, please?"

"The doctor's not at home."

"Then who's filling in for him?"

"No one fillin' in," she said defensively. "Mister Selwood be in in the morning." She left the ward.

Doc shook his head. I want to get Mike Rumundo on the phone. He's a fine thoracic surgeon and a good friend. Please call us, Betsy, if there's any change in Jim."

Rima Matevosian looked in on Jim, then drove the Holmans to Villa Lodge.

Again that night I stayed at the hospital with Jim. I became adept at dozing in the backless chair. There were no call buttons to summon nurses, and patients were expected to fend for themselves as much as possible. So I was happy to stay by him nights if only to fetch him a glass of water, massage the stiffness from his back, or shoo the bugs away—anything to enable him to sleep.

By a shaft of moonlight that streamed in the window behind his bed, I tried again and again throughout the night to sketch the face I remembered. I wadded up dozens of squares of bathroom tissue trying to commit to paper the vision that had become my obsession. The images I drew were laughable, but served to keep the face fresh in my mind.

CHAPTER FIVE

Monday, July 13

———————————————— At seven o'clock sharp the next morning, an armed guard in military uniform marched past and took his post by the first bed in the next ward, relieving from duty the other armed guard. I craned my neck to see the object of their surveillance.

A dusky youth of perhaps 20 lay in the bed nearest the guard. I'd seen him whenever I used the telephone at the nurse's station, but he was always asleep. Never had he moved a muscle. But now he struggled to sit up. Every patient watched; no one helped. He wore his hair in matted Rastafarian dreadlocks. His chest was bandaged in a white mummy wrap and an intravenous tube led from a bottle overhead down to his left forearm.

"Lord, he's going to get up!" exclaimed Vincent John.

"Why do you think he's kept under guard, Mr. John?" I asked.

"He's a wicked man. He robbed a bank. The police was on strike. Wasn't nobody to stop him. So next he robs a store, he shoots a man dead. No police will come. Finally somebody calls the retired police chief at his home and he comes to the store and shoots the man. Shot him good from the looks of it. The man supposed to die. Doctor say he wouldn't ever wake up."

Lying on his back, the man pulled the tape off his left forearm and removed his own intravenous needle. He put his weight on his elbows and struggled to sit up, then rolled out of bed, landing on his feet. He steadied himself on the edge of the bed, then picked up his waste bag and swaggered down the hall past us, clad only in his chest bandage.

The armed guard followed him through all three wards.

"Now I seen it all," exclaimed Vincent John. "D'you suppose some people just too mean to die when they's supposed to?"

"I don't know, Mr. John."

*　　*　　*

The patients passed Monday morning caring for themselves and one another. Though white-capped matrons walked through from time to time, nursing care was non-existent.

In this hospital, patients bathed themselves or stayed dirty. One single cold water tap over a fetid sink served the laundry, drinking and washing needs of three wards. A sign over the sink read "This sink not for patients' use."

Patients with beds were jabbed with steel coil springs that protruded through torn mattress covers. In Jim's ward, two of the patients, who now numbered eight, had no bed at all. One slept on a canvas army cot; the other on a bed roll on the floor. These makeshift beds were removed during the day, so the two men wandered the corridors without a home base until night, when their beds were brought out of storage. Sheets were soiled, torn and seldom changed. Patients provided their own pajamas, razors and drinking vessels or did without. They emptied their own waste bags. Ambulatory patients frequently emptied bed pans for their bed-ridden neighbors.

It was tantalizing to think what the money so generously lent to me by Rima and Bill Little could do. The stores would open at 8:30, so I looked around and took stock of what Jim and the other stubble-chinned men might need.

There was only one morning ferry from Bequia on Mondays, so I first stopped at the pier to scan the arriving passengers, but again turned up nothing. I was beginning to lose hope that I would ever find Jim's assailant on St. Vincent.

Then I began spreading that wonderfully filthy money from shop to shop until my arms bulged with bags and the money was gone. I bought pajamas and boxer shorts; roach bomb and rubbing alcohol; soda straws and a case of cold fruit juices, tooth brushes, toothpaste and Kleenex; deodorant, razors, shaving cream and soap; face cloths, plastic pitchers and drinking cups; playing cards, checkers, cigarettes and mints. It took two trips to carry all the bulging bags back to the hospital since I'd not thought to save enough for bus fare.

When I returned with the second load, two teen-age girls—one pretty, one plain—stood at the foot of Jim's bed. In their hands were brown paper shopping bags. They'd stopped by to see how Jim was doing, they said.

The pretty one spoke. "My name is Janet. We came on the morning ferry from Bequia. It was my boyfriend, Roderick Mitchell, who took you two off your boat Saturday night."

I took a pad of paper from my parcels and led them outside to a wood bench on the second floor breezeway. For the next half hour Janet related all she knew of the incident, while I asked questions and made notes.

She remembered correctly that there were three other sailboats anchored in Friendship Bay Saturday night. One was a catamaran owned by an American. He might have been asleep below at the time of the incident. The second boat was also a multihull, whose owner was off the island. In his absence, Janet's boyfriend had been entrusted to care for his tender, an orange inflatable dinghy that was kept tied to shore. The third boat was *Wave Dancer*, a typical island-built cargo schooner of about 45 feet, owned by her boyfriend's father. *Wave Dancer* was still under construction and bobbed light on her lines at anchor, awaiting her rig.

That Saturday night, Janet related, Roderick Mitchell and his brother, Orbin, watched from the porch of their house overlooking Friendship Bay as a figure crept along the beach. They saw the figure get into their orange inflatable dinghy and row it out into the bay. At 9:45 p.m. they telephoned Bequia police and reported the dinghy theft. Then they waited. The police did not arrive. They heard a scream from a boat in the harbor and again they phoned the police. When the police still did not respond, they summoned another friend, launched the Mitchell's blue outboard skiff, came out to our boat and finally took us ashore.

The cab driver who took us to the clinic was their friend, Noel Oliver. The Mitchell boys followed our taxi in another car. After

Jim was treated and he and I had boarded the power cruiser for
St. Vincent, the Mitchell boys returned to Friendship Bay. They
saw a figure crouched under the pier by the Friendship Bay Hotel.
This they immediately reported to Bequia police. They watched
the man hiding there throughout much of the night. The police
never came. In the morning the man was gone.

"If you find the man," Janet concluded, "look at his feet. There's
lots of sea urchins under that pier. Big urchins with long black
spines that break off when you step on them. Very painful."

I wanted to question her about the man and young boy we'd
seen fishing from the pier on our arrival at Friendship Bay. But
she and her companion wanted to make the midday ferry back to
Bequia.

As they left, two men who had been waiting to speak to me
approached.

"We're from the CID," said one in heavy island dialect.

"Sergeant Allen told me to expect you," I said. "I'm glad you
came."

The agents wished to take separate statements from Jim and
me, so one plainclothesman took a seat beside Jim's bed while
I followed the other to a secluded porch away from the other
patients.

In longhand he recorded verbatim my account of the incident.
It filled five pages. I read it and signed it.

"Do you think you can find the assailant based on this description?" I asked.

"I can't say. Our job is to take your statements and send them
to police in Bequia to aid their investigation."

"And your department—the CID in St. Vincent—doesn't it get
involved?"

"Only if Bequia police call us in on the case."

"In other words, they call in the CID if they're unable to find
the assailant?"

"Yes."

"Do you—does the CID—have fingerprint equipment?"

"No Ma'am."

"So it's not possible to lift fingerprints from my boat to help
track down the assailant?"

"We can't do it."

"Do you have mug shots—books containing photographs of persons with criminal records?"

"We used to. But we had to stop that. The bookkeeping was too complicated to keep track of everyone, I guess."

"How long ago did you stop keeping photographs?"

"I dunno. A long time ago."

"Can I ask your opinion about something? Suppose for a minute you were the assailant. The heat's on in Bequia. What would you do?"

"I'd try to get away."

"You wouldn't go into hiding?"

He thought for a moment. "No, Bequia's too small. Everybody knows everybody, and most of 'em are related. I'd get off the island somehow. Then hide."

"Where?"

He paused. "Here, probably. Kingstown."

"I think so, too. Could your department stake out the pier in Kingstown? Check out passengers arriving from Bequia to see if you can find someone matching the description I gave you?"

"How do you know he didn't already do just that?"

"I've checked every ferry arriving from Bequia since Sunday morning. But I can't keep it up indefinitely."

"I'm sorry. We can't act until police in Bequia call us in on the case."

Before he left I got from him the names of the key police officials in St. Vincent: Police Superintendent Jackson; his superior (and his cousin) Police Commissioner Jackson; and, overseeing the entire police department, Hudson Tannis, minister of tourism, foreign affairs and home affairs. I added these names to a growing log I now kept and then returned to Jim.

His parents waited outside the ward while the CID man strained to get Jim's statement. Jim was in extreme pain and the statement filled only half a page.

When the investigators left, Doc found Mister Selwood and finally got his consultation.

Jim's mother and I unwrapped my parcels and schemed how to share the loot from my morning shopping trip without embarrassing the men or antagonizing the nurses.

It was obvious to all that we weren't natives but Americans, we reasoned. And as all the world presumes, all Americans are sinfully rich. We hoped Jim's fellow patients would feel no shame in accepting gifts from people with more money than good sense. Anyway, Jim was in the same boat they were. They had shared their luxuries with him and he was doing likewise. We somehow even rationalized giving cigarettes to postsurgical patients.

Though our logic may have been groundless, the gesture was greeted with appreciation by the other patients without a hint of wounded pride or resentment.

So what if none of the men knew how to play checkers? They soon made up their own rules, and fortunes in cigarettes were made and lost. So what if the Brand X roach bomb seemed to attract more roaches than it killed? Mr. Chase didn't know what one is supposed to do with a box of tissues, but he marveled at their ability to change colors as the next popped up in place of the last. Mr. Reynolds preferred his warm drinking nuts to a can of cold orange juice, but he was a shrewd horse trader who swapped the juice for chocolate mints, which could thaw even the frozen face of the head nurse. The men delighted in shaving their stubbly beards, and we were lifted with their bolstered spirits.

It was three o'clock when Broom Hilda, the hospital's starstruck maid, swept in. I first heard the din from her hip pocket, and then I saw her. Twining with her homemade broom, she danced up a storm of dust as she thundered through the ward. I leapt out of her path just as her broom handle snared Jim's IV and brought him up short in a tangle of tubes. He growled savagely and I grabbed for the tube. But she heard only the seductive voice of Bob Marley whining from her transistor. Without even knowing what she'd done, Broom Hilda mamboed off in a cloud of dust.

Vincent John sat on the edge of his bed shaking his head. "That girl's gonna hurt somebody with that broom someday," he sighed. He turned in some Rock of Ages gospel music and placed his radio at the foot of Jim's bed. "Now just sleep, Son."

"Why don't you come back to the lodge with us tonight and get some rest," Jim's mother urged after Doc had finished his consultation with Selwood. "You can't keep going without some sleep."

"Jimmy seems stable," Doc added. "Selwood got the tube he's been waiting for and he's taking him to OR tomorrow to switch tubes. I think he'll need you more tomorrow night."

"Rosie Brisbane, owner of Villa Lodge, says it's lobster for dinner tonight. We'll get Arthur the bartender to build you a nice big drink."

"I'll look after our boy," offered Vincent John.

There was no convenient restaurant near the hospital, and I realized without ever feeling hungry that I hadn't eaten a real meal for two days.

We caught a cab to the lodge, showered off the day's grime and made a beeline for the bar, where at owner Rosie's orders, Arthur filled his blender with fresh fruit and plied us with one frozen concoction after another.

We were sitting at a round table in the lodge's fancy third-story lounge overlooking the canopy of palms stretching to the blue Caribbean far beyond when a short, round-faced East Indian man approached and cleared his throat, waiting to be introduced. Jean grimmaced and Doc excused himself to make a call to Mike Rumundo, the thoracic surgeon in New Jersey with whom he was consulting over Jim's case.

"Betsy, meet Harry Maharaj, from Trinidad," said Jean.

I shook a pudgy hand encrusted with gold rings.

"Mr. Maharaj is a guest at the lodge," Jean said awkwardly. "We met him here just last night."

"My good friends call me Harry," said the barrel-shaped man, pulling up a chair beside me.

"Ah, care to join us?" I said belatedly.

"Bartender, Scotch and water," he ordered.

"I am not a violent man. You must understand that. But these people," he searched, "these people, the um . . ."

"Holmans," intoned Jean.

"The Holmans. Thank you dear. The Holmans are my very good friends. I feel like they are my own family." He sucked on his drink, leaned back and began cracking the knuckles of his left hand.

Jean's eyes roamed the room, looking for an exit.

"I am a gentle man. A kind and gentle man." *Crack!* "But when someone hurts one of my family," *Crack!* "I know how to take care of him." *Crack, crack!* He leaned forward and whispered. "I know how to rub him out."

Harry switched to the right knuckles and continued. "The one who stabbed their son is not a man." *Crack!* "He is an animal." *Crack!* "No better than a savage in the wilds." *Crack, crack!* Then the left hand again.

Jean flinched with each crack and I didn't dare look her in the face. So I stared at his hands and listened, mesmerized by the seven gold rings. Three were heavy gold with some engraving. One held a ruby of about three carats, one a chunk of polished jade, one a star of 10-point diamonds, and one an emerald-cut black stone I didn't recognize. They all looked genuine.

"How do you propose to do this?" I looked around. "To rub him out?" I whispered, wondering, half amused, where the conversation might lead.

"First we must find where he is hiding," he said. "Now that would be easy in Trinidad . . ."

Harry Maharaj ordered another Scotch and water and went off on a tangent about his homeland; the pocket pistol his wife carries in her apron and the revolver he keeps over the refrigerator; his brother the new prime minister of Trinidad and Tobago; the pervert he dropped with a .38 through the head when he tried to tamper with his seven-year-old daughter; his architecture practice and his deeper love for justice.

Rosie must have sensed we needed relief, for she called us early to dinner.

We rose from the table and Harry withdrew his wallet. He extracted a red one dollar bill, turned it over and showed me the engraving of the Central Bank of Trinidad and Tobago with an oil rig in the corner. On it he wrote, "Happy days ahead. Best of health. Long life. From Harry Maharaj."

"Isn't *he* a piece of work?" I said dryly when we joined Doc at the dinner table. "Do you think he's really a hit man?" I asked.

"No, he's really an architect," said Doc. "He showed us the blueprints for a hotel he designed."

"I think he'd make a better hit man," laughed Jean. "You don't really think his brother is the prime minister of Trinidad and Tobago, do you, Bob?"

"I don't know," said Doc. "Could be, they just had an election."

"Serious or not, he gives me the creeps," said Jean.

After dinner I stopped in for a cup of coffee at Rima's apartment. She and Molly were working on their cases and, as usual,

Molly was consulting her pharmaceutical tome. Something very disturbing evidently had happened that day at the hospital involving one of Molly's patients.

"The nurses are hopeless," said Molly. "There are a few good sisters and one or two good one-stripers, but the rest are . . ."

"Well, how about this," interrupted Rima. "Every patient in male surgical has a normal temperature. Young, old, fat, thin, terminal or recovering from surgery. They all have the same strong pulse and blood pressure of one-twenty over seventy. Impossible? We read their charts and that's what the nurses tell us: all perfectly healthy specimens.

"Betsy, you remarked about Jim's IV fluid not flowing, even after you'd mentioned it to the nurses several times. I checked his chart this evening. He's been on the same bottle of fluid for two days and it's still nearly full."

"You mean they turn it off?" I asked.

"It happens too often in these wards to be a mistake," said Molly. "If the bottle doesn't drip, it doesn't get empty. If it doesn't get empty, you don't need to change bottles."

"Jim's not received any antibiotic since the morning after he arrived," said Rima, "yet he was written up for an injection each day. I spoke to the head nurse and will check his chart again in the morning. It's a crucial time in his recovery and infection now could mean trouble.

"Watch them, Betsy. The next time a nurse takes Jim's blood pressure, look at the cuff she uses. Two of the three cuffs in those wards are torn. They cannot build up pressure, so an accurate reading is impossible. I've told the sisters to throw them out, but they keep turning up. Watch a nurse take a patient's temperature sometime. She'll leave the thermometer in his mouth for 30 seconds, jot down a normal reading and go back to her girlfriends.

"It's a good thing Jim's father is here. He handles Selwood well. It's a delicate situation and any strong intervention now will do Jim more harm than good. Another couple of days and I think Jim might be out of the woods."

"You think we could fly him home that soon?" I asked.

"That's not for me to say. The risk of infection is still great, but tomorrow is his third day. That will tell us a lot."

CHAPTER SIX

TUESDAY, JULY 14

———————————————— What do you say about a place like the general hospital? Looking back, I feel I spent a large part of my life there. But it was only four short days—four days of tragic comedy without intermission.

When the spectre of death was too overwhelming in Male Surgical, I would retreat to the new modern maternity wing where life was beginning for a new generation of Vincentians.

This was Jim's third day at the hospital, and it was now becoming evident that he was in serious trouble. There was nothing more this hospital could do for him, short of sending him to the morgue.

Early Tuesday morning the Holmans and I hurried to the hospital to see Jim before he was taken to the operating room to switch tubes. But we found only an empty bed.

"They took our boy to the theatre," said Vincent John.

"How was his night?" asked Doc.

"Bad. Pain was awful. The nurse knows he gets a pain shot at midnight. She made him wait till three o'clock. He didn't sleep a wink. He was out of his head. Couldn't none of us sleep for worrying."

When Jim returned from surgery, his pain was severe. Later in the day it spread throughout his chest and abdomen. His breathing

was short and labored. Jim's father observed him closely throughout the day with growing concern, watching, hoping the new tube
would drain the pleural cavity. It didn't. That afternoon the intravenous feeding was discontinued in favor of solid food. But when
the dinner trays arrived, there wasn't one for Jim.

"Must of forgot," shrugged the nurse.

"He's showing some early signs of infection," said Doc as they
left for the lodge late that evening. "I want to get Mike Rumundo
on the phone. Call us if anything changes, Betsy."

*   *   *

By 7 p.m., involuntary muscle spasms brought on by pain
gripped Jim's chest and constricted his breathing. He was running
a temperature and was soaked with perspiration. Jim wouldn't let
me summon Nurse Roberts, with whom he'd had the trouble the
previous night, for fear of angering her and missing his 8 o'clock
pain injection.

By 8 o'clock his chest jumped and seized in spasms of pain. I
summoned Nurse Roberts and reminded her of the injection.

She fingered his chart. "Not ordered," she said icily.

"Right here," I pointed. "Fifty milligrams Pethadrin every four
hours. His last one was at four p.m. It's after eight now."

She shrugged and walked away. We waited. She did not return.

The pain grew more intense and his cries echoed through the
corridors. I sat him up as he struggled to get his breath and laid
him back down when the pain became unbearable. Up and down,
up and down as he directed. The spasms by now were continuous,
jerking his torso like a puppet. He gasped to draw each shallow
breath.

"Head nurse," rasped Jim. "Run!"

I ran through the corridors and finally found Sister Bosworth,
the head nurse in another wing of the hospital. She was on the
phone, reliving carnival, when I broke in.

"Jim Holman—Male Surgical. He's having spasms that are cutting off his breathing. He's been written up for . . ."

She held up her hand, then cupped the phone. "I'll be along."

She went back to her conversation.

"Don't you understand? He cannot breathe!"

She turned her back and chatted on.

I ran back to Jim. His hair was soaked in perspiration and his upper body continued to be seized by spasms. His roommates sat on the edges of their beds, staring in morbid fear.

I ran to Nurse Roberts' station. "Get Mister Selwood on the phone. Now. *Please.*"

"He's out to dinner."

"He must have told you where to reach him."

"I'll see." She began counting pills into little cups for her rounds.

I grabbed the phone and dialed Rima. It was 9:30. No answer. Then I dialed Jim's father.

"We'll be right there," said Doc.

I dialed Rima again and caught her as she was walking in the door of her apartment.

"Put Nurse Roberts on the phone," she said.

The nurse listened expressionlessly, then handed the receiver back to me.

"I've ordered an additional fifty milligrams of Pethadrin to be given immediately," said Rima. "If we can relieve some of the pain, it should ease Jim's breathing. I'll be there as soon as I can."

I hurried to Jim's side. I was aware that I'd broken hospital protocol and hoped the nurse wouldn't take it out on Jim. She did.

At 10 p.m., when the Holmans arrived, Nurse Roberts gave the injection, two hours late, and half the prescribed dose.

At 11 o'clock Rima arrived with another medical student and Dr. Columbo, a young visiting pediatrician from Ohio, in tow. "I've been trying to get Selwood on the phone," she said, "but no one knows where he is."

Rima took Jim's vital signs, then handed her stethoscope and pressure cuff to Jim's father so he could examine Jim.

Finally she reached Selwood at home by phone, and after they spoke, she took me outside.

"These nurses are tough," she said. "If they give you any more problems, call me. I want you to take Jim's temperature and pulse every hour. Count the number of breaths per minute. I've got a flashlight in my glove compartment and I'll get you a thermometer from the nurse's station. Do not let the nurse see it. This aspirin will help keep his temperature down. If it goes above a hundred and two, call me. You can rub him down with alcohol and a cool face cloth. Try to get him to drink some water. Forget the nurses, forget the chart. Do you have some paper? Keep your own chart. Write down his vital signs every hour and anything you observe that's out of the ordinary.

"I've doubled the dosage of Pethadrin. He should get another injection at midnight, but this one was late, so I'll write it up for two a.m., then another at six. If it's late, ask once, then ask the nurse to call me."

Then Rima and her entourage left. The Holmans and I waited for Selwood to arrive.

The head nurse, Sister Bosworth, finally finished her phone call and stood at the foot of Jim's bed. "Ain't nothing wrong with that boy the good Lord won't fix if He sees fit. Now you folks just get outta here. Treating him like he's something sooo special. Just go on home and leave him alone."

Doc listened to his son's chest, took his vital signs and ignored the nurse.

About midnight Selwood arrived and examined Jim. He ordered an injection of Valium, which was given immediately to relieve the spasms.

Outside he confided to Doc, "This is what I feared—that infection's set in. It's the new tube. Well, nothing to be done tonight. See you tomorrow."

Without Selwood's order, indeed nothing more could be done. He did order an antibiotic, but it was never given. Doc stayed by his son's side late into the night.

WEDNESDAY MORNING, JULY 15

Lines of strain and concern were etched on the Holmans' faces as I bade them goodnight at 3 a.m. and settled into my chair.

This night marked the turning point in Jim's fight to recover. We might have chanced flying him to a hospital in the States a day or two after the stabbing. Instead we waited and watched for signs of improvement before moving him. He stabilized, but improvement never came.

Now, four days after the accident, he was emaciated, weak and full of infection. His pain was unbearable and his breathing shallow and labored. Neither tube had drained the pleural cavity and the lung had not reinflated. Normal body functions were deteriorating.

Doc had consulted daily by phone with thoracic surgeon Mike Rumundo, who offered to fly to St. Vincent. But of course he, like Doc, had no license to practice in the country. Selwood, we felt was too proud to consult Doc's chosen specialist even had Dr. Rumundo flown in. We feared such intervention would do Jim more harm than good.

Early Wednesday, after a couple of hours' sleep, the Holmans looked in on Jim, then struck out on foot to investigate the Cyrus Clinic, a private, 12-bed hospital not far from the general hospital. From the beginning, we were reluctant to move Jim twice, but now an interim hospital was imperative if Jim was to improve enough to be flown to the States.

The Holmans returned to the general hospital later that morning to speak with Selwood about transferring Jim.

"I see no reason to move him to the Cyrus Clinic," said Selwood angrily. "Aren't you out of your territory, Doctor?" snapped the young physician.

"Until now I've not interfered with anything you've done for my son. I've tried to be a father and leave the practice of medicine to you. You probably saved my son's life, and for that I'm most grateful, so please understand that my removing him is no reflection on you."

His voice was calm yet firm.

"But I do see the limitations of the facilities here. The nursing care is deplorable. Last night I watched the nurse take Jim's vital signs. Then I took them. She recorded his pulse as seventy-two when it really was a hundred and twenty-four and his respiration as twenty when it was thirty-five. His temperature was over a hundred and one, not ninety-eight eight, as she noted. With this kind of chart, you are not getting the proper information. And furthermore, your orders are not being carried out."

"You're an orthopedist, Mister Selwood, and so am I. Let's be honest. Thoracic medicine is not our field. Infection has complicated his condition, and unless something is done, and done soon, he's going to be in serious trouble."

"I resent your interference in my case."

"Mister Selwood, maybe when you've been practicing medicine for forty years and have children of your own, you'll understand better why I'm taking him away today."

The young doctor turned on his heels and left.

"We're taking you to another hospital, Jim," was all his mother said.

His father clamped off the hose leading from Jim's chest cavity, and with the aplomb of midnight body snatchers, we whisked Jim into a waiting taxi-wagon and up the hill to the Cyrus Clinic.

✻   ✻   ✻

The taxi whined up the hill and stopped in front of a sparkling clean building set within what seemed to be a lush botanical garden.

A genteel Canadian nurse showed Jim to a cheery yellow private room with a private bath and a small, first-floor terrace overlooking the expansive, tree-shaded grounds. We followed.

She pulled back a crisp white cotton top sheet and eased him into a regulation hospital bed. A white-uniformed cook entered with a covered tray, placed it on the rolling table in front of Jim and left the room. A sprig of magenta bougainvillea in a tiny vase spilled its bright papery petals in a corner of the tray.

"You're just in time for tea, Mr. Holman," said the nurse. She cranked Jim up in bed and draped an oversize white linen napkin across his lap. "Dr. Cyrus will be along in a few minutes, Dr. Holman," she said, then closed the door behind her.

The four of us stared at the tray.

"Tea time?" I exclaimed. "What? No pumpkin gruel?"

It was worth your life to get so much as a pan of porridge in the general hospital, where patients' meals, if they came at all, were the same fare as that served to inmates at the city prison. Bread, when there was any, was baked by female prisoners at Fort Charlotte.

With a flourish, Jean rolled back the linen cloth, exposing a delicate, flaky croissant, a dollop of creamery butter and a spot of fresh mango preserves. The tray also contained a steeping hot pot of aromatic English tea, complete with prewarmed china, coarse brown sugar and dairy cream.

"Jim," I smiled, "I think you've come to the right place."

And for the first time in four days he ate.

Jim's father stepped outside for a consultation with Dr. Cyrus, a serious, soft-spoken Vincentian with graying temples, a gentle manner and articulate speech.

When they left the room, Jim's mother checked the hallway then quietly closed the door. Quickly, we crammed all of Jim's belongings into a plastic bag, emptied half a can of roach bomb inside, cinched up the neck and hid the bag in an empty bottom bureau drawer. The rest of the can we sprayed inside our own pocketbooks and inside Jim's shoes.

Jim began to improve immediately under Dr. Cyrus's care. His medication was changed to a broad-spectrum antibiotic, which soon cleared up the infection. The red rubber hose was removed and the pleural cavity was drained in steps by syringe. Pain medication was administered as needed, enabling Jim to breathe with greater ease, and thus helping to expand the lung, which eventually reinflated over the course of his week's stay.

Nursing care was excellent and nothing was spared to make Jim comfortable. Five trays of savory home-cooked meals were brought to him each day, and he had only to ask and the kerchiefed cook would dash outside to the garden with a long stick and return with fresh breadfruit, papaya, mango, limes or bananas for his tray.

For the first time since the attack I felt confident he would recover. The same afternoon Jim was transferred to the Cyrus Clinic I checked the ferry schedule, then phoned Sergeant Allen in Bequia and made an appointment to meet with him the next afternoon. I was more determined than ever now to find Jim's attacker.

Part Two

Spanish Water is dark. A light rain has begun falling in *Cheers'* cockpit and the punch pitcher is dry. The kerosene lamp atop the cabin flickers and winks out. Baby Joelle, cradled in her father's arms, naps as I relate my story. Jim's eyelids are heavy with sleep. But Australian friends Richard and Robyn continue their rapt attention.

"Then what happened?" asked Richard. "Did the police find the cussed bloke?"

Robyn glanced at her nurse's watch. "It's almost midnight. We really should be going. Betsy, Jim, come tomorrow night for tea," she invited. "Then tell us the rest."

*   *   *

The following night Jim and I rowed out to *Walu.*

"I thought about you two all night long," said Richard. "You know, we stopped in Friendship Bay just a few days before your attack. Your story has been haunting me. I . . . I look at Robyn, I look at Joelle and I think, it could have been us. All night long I just lay there wondering, what would I have done in your shoes? How would I have defended my family? By all counts, Jim, you should be dead and gone to Fiddler's Green. A hundred times last night I asked myself, what would I have done?"

"You would have done the same, Richard," said Jim. "It wasn't bravery just survival."

Robyn held her baby to her breast and the infant nursed greedily.

Tell us, Betsy, what happened then? Did the police find the attacker?"

"Where was I? I remember. I had just phoned Sgt. Allen in Bequia . . .

65

CHAPTER SEVEN

——————————————— "I'll be on the *Friendship Rose*, which gets into Port Elizabeth at three," I told Sergeant Allen. Then I phoned Bill Little and learned that he had powered *Cheers* around to Admiralty Bay as promised and that she lay on one of his moorings, right off Bequia Slip.

"But don't stay on that boat, for Christsake. Not alone, not with that guy still loose. You can bunk with Barbara here in the house. C'mon by after you talk with Allen."

There was no ferry returning to St. Vincent until the following day, so I gratefully accepted Bill's offer to stay overnight.

The bald-headed schooner *Friendship Rose* plied nearly the same course Jim and I had taken to first reach Bequia some three weeks before in *Cheers*. I couldn't help but remember with a tinge of sentiment the excitement I'd felt back then when we'd made our landfall before the incident.

In no other West Indies island had I felt quite so at home as on Bequia. There, in Admiralty Bay, we set two anchors against the easterly trade winds and settled into the quiet, langorous pace of island life, anchored little more than an oar's length from a score of congenial waterfront watering holes.

Friendship Rose rounded the point of Devil's Table and sails were sheeted home for the hard-on-the-wind motorsail up Admiralty Bay to Port Elizabeth. It felt strange to be traveling as a nonparticipating passenger on a sailing vessel and I yearned to return to *Cheers*, bobbing alone at the far north end of the harbor.

Lines were heaved ashore and secured to the dock. I stepped over the tall bulwarks and crossed the street to the tiny government complex at the head of the harbor that housed the post office, customs and immigration and police.

I asked at the front desk for Sergeant Allen and was directed around the back of the building to an office at the head of an outside flight of steps. I entered a plain, institutional-looking room where an expressionless man with a very round, brown face sat behind a schoolteacher-style wood desk. A row of white shirt buttons strained to conceal an amazingly large belly.

"Sergeant Allen?"

"Yes?"

"I'm Betsy Hitz," I said, offering my hand.

He remained seated and gave me a limp-fish handshake.

"Well, now we can begin," he said. He reached in his top desk drawer and began thumbing through the pages of handwritten text on lined paper.

He read a little, then looked up at me. "I don't mind telling you that you've fouled up this investigation," he admonished me. "You had no business leaving Bequia."

"I've heard the lecture before," I reminded him.

"Just so you know," he scowled.

"I'm here now," I said, "and I've already given you plenty to go on. I talked to your policeman at the clinic Saturday night. I gave you the same description over the phone. Isn't that my statement in front of you there?"

"This, yes."

"I've told you everything I know. I've phoned you every time I've thought of something new. Have you talked with the Mitchell boys?"

"What for?" he asked.

"Because they *saw* the man, that's what for. Has it occurred to you that the man might be a Bequian? And maybe that's why he's not fled, at least not to St. Vincent? That if he is a Bequian, the Mitchell boys might just know who he is?"

"All I know's that the man's got a gold tooth. That's what you told my officer and that's what the Mitchell boys say."

"The man does *not* have a gold tooth. I've told you that. Did the Mitchell boys actually tell you they saw a man with a gold tooth?"

"No."

"Have you talked to them?"

"Not yet."

"Have you searched the area around Friendship Bay?"

"It's too late for that."

"What about Saturday night? I'm told the Mitchell brothers saw the man crouched under the pier in front of the hotel after the incident. Why didn't your police search that night? The Mitchell boys called the police Saturday night."

"They did not."

"Then why was there a police officer at the clinic? How did he know what had happened?"

"By then we knew what happened."

"Then why didn't you search the area Saturday night? Or Sunday? Or Monday or Tuesday or Wednesday? What's wrong with right now?"

"Don't tell me how to run my investigation."

"What investigation!"

I stopped myself. "I'm sorry. Please forgive me, I didn't mean to lose my temper. I only want to find this man. Can we start over?"

The sergeant fingered the statement and after a long silence he spoke. "Let me ask you a few questions. How much money did this man take from you?"

"About two hundred E.C., mostly in small bills. It says so in my statement."

"I see. And can you tell me how he was dressed that night?"

"He was naked. Stark naked! I think that's a rather important detail. Haven't you read my statement?"

"It only arrived here yesterday. I was just about to read it when you came."

"Well how about this: Why don't you read my statement and send me in a car with one of your officers around to Friendship Bay. We could search the area and then drive around until dark looking for the man."

"I warned you, don't tell me how to run my investigation."

"Has your investigation turned up any leads?"

"We're working on it."

"Any suspects?"

"Now that you say the man didn't have a gold tooth, I guess we'll have to start over."

This man must have the I.Q. of a hard-boiled egg, I thought. Maybe he can't think in the abstract.

Four young Bequian policemen, all in their 20s, were milling about the hallway and back stairs of the barracks. I asked Sergeant Allen to call them into his office.

"He's built like this," I gestured to a muscular man in sweatpants and a T-shirt. "But his neck isn't as thick and muscular as this man's."

The young officer grinned self-consciously.

"His hair is short and well-groomed like this man's," I pointed to another, "and his hairline is very similar, squarish and not receding at all."

His buddy poked him playfully in the shoulder.

"His complexion is about yours," I said to another officer. "Yes, just about the same skin color as yours."

Sergeant Allen heard me out, then said impatiently, "What are you trying to prove? That one of my men did this?"

A look of fear and distrust displaced the grins of the officers.

"No," I reassured them. "I was merely making a comparison."

They looked at me apprehensively.

"No, none of you did it. I'm not accusing any of you, honestly."

I tried a new tack. I reached in my handbag, produced the vial of mace and laid it on the desk.

"This key ring contains a small cannister of mace," I said popping open the snap on the leather sheath and exposing the aerosol pushbutton on top of the vial. "This is the mace Jim used to get the assailant off the boat. See, it's caked with dried blood—Jim's blood. Maybe you've heard of CS gas. That's another name for mace, CS gas."

They looked at me with blank stares.

"No? Well, it's like tear gas in a way, but it shoots a stream of liquid, not a gas or vapor. It causes temporary blindness and severe irritation to the eyes and nose. This is what got the man off our boat. Jim squirted it in the man's face."

I placed some paper on the floor in the corner of the room and shot a stream of mace at it until it was wet. I picked up the paper.

Carefully I smelled the paper, which irritated my nose and made me sneeze. They were not impressed with the mace's effects.

"Are you finished?" asked the sergeant impatiently.

"Yes," I acquiesced, placing the key ring on his desk. "You can keep it as evidence."

"It's no good to us."

"It might be important later. The stuff causes temporary blindness. Maybe his eyesight is still impaired."

He pushed the key ring toward me, then called two privates over to his desk and dismissed the other two. Lapsing into island dialect, he whispered something to the remaining pair and they left the room.

"I've just ordered two of my best men to go to the pier and see if the assailant is there," he announced, pleased with himself.

"In Friendship Bay?" I asked.

"Here!"

"Here, in front of the police station? Do you really think he'd be hanging around . . ."

We were off again in a flurry of bickering. It just didn't seem possible for us to exchange more than a few syllables without butting heads.

As far as I knew, Allen was the ranking police officer on Bequia. He sat at the only desk in the only office on the second floor. The way to stimulate results, I figured, was not to demand to speak to his superior. Allen was all I had.

I rose and picked up my key ring. "I have some things to do on my boat. Will you come out and have a look at the scene?"

"I'm too busy."

"Then will you send one of your officers with me?"

"What good would it do now?"

"Forget it." I had to admit he was right, since the police had no way to analyze evidence. "Listen, the man—our assailant—told me he was from Union Island. It's in my statement. I don't know whether to believe it or not. Can you call the police in Union Island, tell them what happened and read them my description of the man? They might know of him."

"You really believe he'd tell you if he was from Union Island?" he mocked.

"I don't know. But what's the harm in checking it out? One phone call."

"Leave this investigation to me."

"Will you call Union Island?"

"The man's not from Union Island, I can assure you of that."

"You say he's not from Union Island and he's not from Bequia. Where's he from then?"

"Look, I'm getting a little tired of your superior ways. I don't need some woman telling me how to do my job."

"I'm returning to St. Vincent tomorrow on the midday ferry. I'm staying tonight at Bequia Slip." I wrote the phone number on a piece of paper. "Call me there if anything comes up. If I'm not there, I'll be on my boat, and you can leave a message with Bill Little. I'll do whatever I can in person to help your investigation between now and noon tomorrow. But if you don't turn up anything by then I'm returning to St. Vincent and we'll have to communicate by phone."

"If you see the man, come tell me. I'll bring him in," he assured me.

"Thank you," I heard myself say.

Discouraged that Jim's attacker would ever be found, I turned north and walked around the harbor road to Bequia Slip, where a long man sat facing me at a stool in the open-air second-floor bar. He looked like he was waiting for someone.

"Bill Little?"

"You're Betsy?"

I shook hands with a tall man with rugged good looks and longish blonde hair changing subtly to gray. He introduced me to his partner, Barbara Frauenpreis, a tall, sturdily-built woman somewhat younger than Bill, formerly a textile designer from New Jersey. We had a round of drinks, I thanked them heartily for their kindness and repaid Bill his loan with money I'd borrowed from Jim's parents.

Then I walked down to the dock where my inflatable dinghy was tied, got the oars and a key from the dock hand and rowed out to *Cheers*. I surveyed the harbor for any boats I might know, but all our cruising friends had fled the Grenadines in the wake of hurricane season.

I climbed aboard *Cheers*, turned the key and slid open the companionway hatch. No need to worry about disturbing evidence, I thought. Just clean up the mess and forget about it.

A sickening stench issued from the cabin. Newly-hatched flies covered the upholstery and overhead. The eight-day ship's clock still ticked. It seemed inconceivable it was Jim who had wound it just five days before. Two bells struck: five o'clock. My heart beat quickened. I sensed the presence of an intruder. I picked up the revolver and slowly, methodically, searched the boat. The cabin was empty, but the aura of our intruder still was there.

I lit off a can of Piff Paff bug bomb, then closed the hatch while I sat in the cockpit, fingering the revolver, waiting for the insecticide to work. A pool of dried, brown blood stained the cabin top where I'd propped Jim up against the boom gallows.

Maybe we should lay a trap for him, I thought. He might already know I'm back on the island. If he thinks I'm alone on the boat, he might come for me. I envisioned Sergeant Allen, crouching in the head over his ample belly, waiting in ambush.

I checked the mooring rode, added some chafing gear and returned below, where scores of flies buzzed. I loaded the revolver and placed it on the far corner of the chart table, handy but out of sight to an intruder.

It wasn't the same boat I remembered, wasn't the comfortable image I'd been clinging to. Our once-cozy cabin had the haunting feeling of a room in which someone has recently died.

I lifted the lid of the top-loading icebox and began to empty containers of rotted food into the sink and trash can. Then I stopped, put the food back where it was and reached for my camera. On deck and below, I shot a roll of black and white prints, just for the record. I felt bitter bile rise in my throat as I filmed the macabre scene. I swallowed hard.

I raised the floorboards and found the bilges dry. I switched to the number one bank of batteries, started the engine, increased the revs and charged the number two bank. I emptied out the rotted food, bundled up the maggot-ridden garbage bag and stripped the forward bunk and settee cushions of their bloodstained covers. I swept up the broken glass and dead flies, then put the canned food and shotgun shells back in their locker.

With a bucket and rag, I scrubbed all traces of blood from the deck, cockpit, bulkheads and cabin sole, then stuffed some fresh clothes for Jim and me in a canvas tote bag. My wallet was nowhere on the boat. He must have jumped overboard with it. I scribbled a note on the back of my hand to remind myself to cancel my credit cards.

Just at sunset I dropped bags of trash and laundry into the dinghy, placed the loaded gun in the top of my canvas bag, cut the engine and locked up.

Rowing back to the dock, I stared at the severed dinghy painter that trailed into the water from the starboard stanchion. It was the only bit of evidence that remained, and I left it because I wanted to think about it. He tied two half-hitches—a round turn and two half-hitches.

I phoned the Holmans at the Lodge that evening and learned that Jim was better. Yes, I'd met with Allen, but no, the investigation was not going well. I'd be back tomorrow, but could they keep a secret until then? Good. I'd found where he's hiding. No, not the stabber—Idi Amin. The world believes he's holed up in Ethiopia or some such place. But he's right here on Bequia masquerading as a pea-brained police sergeant.

After a dinner of barracuda steak in her restaurant overlooking Admiralty Bay, Barbara led me up a stone path carved in the cliffs to her office apartment. She made up a bed for me on the studio couch in her living room, and when she retired to her bedroom, I tucked the loaded revolver under my pillow. I slipped beneath the sheets and waited for sleep that would not come.

Two huge picture windows broke the free form expanse of masonry walls, but where window glass would have been set in a conventional house, there was only the great outdoors. It was a charming island-style bungalow. A dozen times during the night, at the subtlest noise, I reached beneath my pillow and sat bolt-upright, gun straight-armed toward the huge black orifice in the wall, watching, ears tuned, waiting. It was silly and I knew it, but I couldn't help it. Night was terrifying.

CHAPTER EIGHT

FRIDAY, JULY 17

——————————————— I was sitting on the back steps on Friday morning waiting for Sergeant Allen when he came to work. I followed as he waddled up the stairs to his office and took his seat at the empty desk.

"Anything new, Sergeant?"

He leaned forward on his elbows, obviously annoyed. "Look, I told you I'd call you if anything developed. I didn't call, did I?"

"No."

"Then why don't you go on about your business and stop interfering with my investigation?"

"I left Jim in a hospital bed against my better judgment and came here at your request to assist with your investigation. Then I find you've done nothing and you plan to do nothing. Now you tell me I'm interfering. I'm not going to be your scapegoat in this case." My fist hit the desk.

I rose to my feet and left the building, this time choosing the left branch of the harbor road, which paralleled the water and finally trailed off into an eroded footpath that snaked over tree roots, in and out of the wavelets to the Frangipani Hotel and Yacht Services.

The Frangipani had been our watering hole during our three-week stay in Bequia before the accident, a place to mingle with other cruisers, pick up mail, and pass the time. This time it was the owner, Son Mitchell, not a cold beer, I sought.

I remembered reading in Doyle's *Sailor's Guide To The Windward Islands* that Son Mitchell is well known for "pulling one of the smartest political maneuvers of all time, getting himself the job in 1972 as head of government and party leader."

With this in mind I asked for him at the desk of the Fringipani.

"I'm sorry, Son is in St. Vincent on business," said Pat, Son Mitchell's demure Canadian wife. "Can I help you?"

I told her our tale and my concern that Jim's attacker would not be found. "I'm afraid I've blown it with Sergeant Allen."

"So you're the one," she said, closing the guest register. "I'd seen you in here several times, weeks back, but when I heard what happened over in Friendship Bay, I just couldn't place the couple on *Cheers*. Thank goodness you're all right."

Pat was a rare woman one occasionally meets at the heart of a country inn. A charming hostess with a keen business mind, Pat has managed to rear two lovely adolescent daughters and keep family life intact while opening her home-style inn to visiting wayfarers.

We shared a pot of coffee and got acquainted quickly, wasting no time on small talk.

"Betsy, let me tell you something. Other visitors have had problems here in the past—nothing as serious as this, but problems all the same—burglaries, assault, robbery, attempted rape, that sort of thing. You did the right thing by going to the police, but now you know.

"Some who've gone to the police have been subjected to extortion, insulting ignorance and even sexual harrassment from the police officers. If a victim knows Son and comes here first, Son takes down his statement and files it with the police. Sometimes it's lost, but in any case, nothing ever happens."

"That's what I'm afraid of," I sighed.

"Betsy, I think those policemen border on mental retardation. I'm very serious. I wish Son were here to talk with you, but he won't be back until tomorrow afternoon. There's someone you should meet. If anyone can help you, it's Nolly Simmons."

"Any relation to the sailmaker?"

"His son. Nolly is sort of an amateur private investigator. He had a scholarship to study architecture in Canada. To pay back his education he worked a couple of years for the district attorney's office there. He's very good at detective work. Nolly solved the last twelve or thirteen crimes on Bequia. He finds the suspect and turns him over to the police. They get the credit and Nolly keeps his cover. Oh, he doesn't do it for pay—he won't take money. He does it because he enjoys it, I suppose, and because he cares deeply about Bequia."

Pat Mitchell telephoned Nolly's mother. "He doesn't have a phone at his house, but his mother lives nearby and she said she would send him down."

A few minutes later I was introduced to Nolly Simmons, a name that went with a face I'd seen before. He was very tall and somewhat lanky, about 35, I guessed. He wore only a faded T-shirt and cut-off corduroy shorts. His skin was as light as my own, but his features showed the mixed blood of a Bequian. He was barefooted.

"Start at the beginning," he said. "and hold back nothing."

It took nearly an hour to recount the events of last Saturday and to give him a detailed description of our assailant. Pat listened and made notes to later give to her husband. But Nolly wrote down nothing. He listened intently without interrupting or asking a single question.

As the morning progressed, hotel guests began to stir, so Pat excused herself to tend shop while Nolly and I moved to another table in a quiet corner of the terrace, shaded from public view by a row of potted ferns. Only then did Nolly begin to ask questions and make notes.

"What time did you say you anchored in Friendship Bay?"

"About four-thirty in the afternoon."

"And you didn't go ashore?"

"No, we stayed on the boat."

"Did you see anyone in Friendship Bay when you arrived?"

"Yes. There were two people on the dock in front of the Friendship Bay Hotel. A man and a boy. They were fishing. They didn't seem to pay any attention to us, but since then I've wondered about the man. He was the only adult we saw ashore. And though I saw him at a distance of perhaps five hundred feet, his color and build were close enough to that of the assailant that I don't think we should rule him out as a suspect."

"Did you see anyone in a boat?"

"No."

"Had you ever been to Friendship Bay before?"

"No never."

"Did anyone know you were going there?"

"No."

"You told no one, even down in the Grenadines?"

"No."

"You said your last stop was Petit Nevis?"

"Right. We anchored there Saturday morning, explored the whaling camp, climbed around the volcanic debris, then moved *Cheers* to Friendship Bay that same afternoon."

"Did you see anyone at Petit Nevis?"

"No, we were the only ones on the island."

"No other boats?"

"Just the two whaling boats in the shed. No, come to think of it, there was another boat, a two-bowed boat out in the cut between Petit Nevis and Bequia. It was loaded with kids and two boys were rowing. The boat had no sail or motor and seemed dangerously overloaded. They were coming from sea, from the west, rowing into the wind toward Friendship Bay. The swells were running pretty high and I remember watching them, a mile or so away, and feeling concerned the boat might capsize. There were seven, maybe eight kids aboard, and very little freeboard."

"Did they see you?"

"Possibly. We were anchored at Petit Nevis at the time. They seemed to pay no attention. I assumed they were returning from fishing. They appeared to be pretty young, no more than twelve or thirteen, I thought, because there was no way you could squeeze that many adults into a boat that size."

"Can we backtrack a little? Tell me about your trip through the Grenadines—everywhere you stopped after leaving Admiralty Bay."

"We left Admiralty Bay on Saturday, the Fourth of July. We'd been waiting for charts to sail west to Curaçao and eventually the Panama Canal. I phoned my sister in Virginia that morning and learned that the charts hadn't yet been sent. She promised to airmail them Monday morning, July 6. We were getting concerned about hurricane season and wanted to be on our way west before then. So, with a week to kill before the charts could possibly arrive, we decided to cruise the Grenadines, in company with Australian friends on *Walu*, then return alone to Bequia, pick up the charts, then sail directly to Curaçao, 450 miles west.

"Our first stop in the Grenadines was Corbay on Cannouan. There was one other yacht in the anchorage. We never went ashore.

"Sunday morning we anchored in the Tobago Keys, next to our friends on *Walu*. Our anchor was down not more than half an hour when two men in a local skiff put out from the beach on Baradel island. Do you know the Tobago Cays?"

"Yes."

"This might be important. There looked to be a fishing camp on shore, with one or two lean-to tents. It was about 11:30 Sunday morning when they came out to our boat. I remember thinking, Oh no, not more boat vendors. The closer they got, the worse the two characters looked, and it was obvious they were coming to our boat.

"I was in the cockpit and Jim was below. I was wearing a bikini and I asked him to pass me up a shirt for a cover-up. My camera was in the cockpit, so as they approached the port side, I closed the case and started to pass it below to Jim. When they saw the camera in my hand, the one in the bow called, 'You take my picture it cost you a dollar.' Don't flatter yourself, I remember thinking. To the men in the boat, I said, 'I don't want to take your picture. I'm just putting my camera away.'

"I stood on the side deck ready to fend them off when they approached. They were in their mid-to-late twenties. The one in the bow was tough-looking, but the one rowing was worse. His teeth were rotted down to jagged black stumps and he had a bad eye. I don't remember which eye, but it looked abscessed. They clunked alongside, then the one rowing stood up on the thwart. Before I knew it he had one foot on our rail and was starting over the lifelines.

" 'Hold it!' I said, pointing at him. 'No one comes aboard this boat without an invitation. Now what do you want?' "

" 'I got something to show you,' he said, hanging on the life-lines."

" 'You can show me right from your boat,' I told him."

"He opened a plastic container and placed it on our deck. 'Black coral,' he said, showing me the usual junk. His buddy in the bow held up a turtle shell that hadn't even been cleaned and tried to sell it to me."

"Where was Jim?" asked Nolly.

"He was still below. It's sort of a drill we've rehearsed when guys like this come out to the boat. I talk to them on deck while Jim stays below. I make sure to say something to Jim so they know a man is below. Then if there's trouble, he can go for a weapon. But we've never had to resort to that."

"And he didn't go for a gun this time?"

"No. It was the middle of the day. Our friends on *Walu* were on deck, anchored nearby, and there were three charter boats anchored close by, three Peterson 44s.

"I told them the usual story we always give boat vendors—that we're cruisers, are not working, and only have money for essential things, like food.

" 'Gimme a beer!' the guy with the rotten teeth demanded. I told him we didn't have any beer, but he pointed to an empty Heineken bottle in the cockpit. Then Jim appeared in the companionway and told them we had no beer for them and asked them to leave.

" 'Give us some pot,' they said.

" 'We don't smoke pot,' Jim told them. Then they wanted paint, rope, old sails, gasoline and Coca-Cola. Jim told them to shove off and they left, shouting obscenities at us."

"Do you think there might be a link, Nolly?"

He shook his head and said, "Let's not rule out anything just yet. Was that the last time you saw them?"

"No. They rowed directly over to one of the Peterson 44s. The three sisterships all hailed from ports in Louisiana. They were on charter from Stevens Yachts and each had aboard two couples, so there were six couples in all. They were cruising in company through the Grenadines, and they were aboard the kind of boats that are immediately recognized as charter boats, a soft touch for the vendors. We weren't surprised when they hung alongside one of the boats for fifteen or twenty minutes. When we saw the charterers give them two beers, we shook our heads and went below. Then we heard shouting, went on deck and saw the guy with the rotten teeth standing in his skiff throwing bananas at the charterers and swearing. We thought the charterers had been given the bananas, because a full stalk was tied to their port shrouds, but later we learned differently."

"You talked to the charterers?"

"Yes, later. The vendors were so grim we decided to leave Tobago Cays the next morning, Monday. We sailed in company with *Walu* to Palm Island. The three Peterson 44s arrived soon after us. We met the charterers ashore. They were all from Louisiana. One of them, a doctor, was actually the owner of his boat, which he leases to Stevens Yachts. Anyway, he was there to enjoy his two weeks' use of the boat, but they'd had nothing but trouble in the Grenadines."

"What kind of trouble?"

"I didn't ask. Boat vendors, I guess, same as we'd had in every port from St. Lucia south."

"He'd made the same cruise the previous year and in the Tobago Cays had been approached by the same guy at the same anchorage. He recognized the rotten teeth and the droopy eye. Last year the guy actually got aboard his boat and began harassing his party. The owner ordered him to leave, but the guy only got more abusive. Finally the doctor went below, loaded his flare gun, pointed it at the guy and ordered him to leave. He left, swearing and throwing things at the charterers. The doctor said he reported this to officials in Union Island and to Bill Stevens."

"Did anything happen?"

"No. Officials in Union Island told him they knew there was a nest of troublemakers who camped out on the Tobago Cays, but for some reason, they hadn't cleared them out. That's right. I just remembered—the officials said the troublemakers were *from* Union Island—that they would cross to the Tobago Cays when they say a yacht anchored there. The doctor was certain this was the same guy who had boarded his boat the previous year."

"Yet you said you saw him give the same guys a beer this year?"

"No, the beers came from another boat in his party. They probably didn't know better."

"Does this doctor plan to pursue it with police?"

"I doubt it. His last effort was a waste of time. He's taking his boat out of charter in the Grenadines and moving it to the Virgin Islands.

"Nolly, maybe our assailant told the truth when he said he was from Union Island. At the time I was convinced it was a lie intended to throw us off the track, but maybe it was true."

"If he intended leaving you both dead, it wouldn't matter what you knew, would it?"

"I asked Sergeant Allen to contact police in Union Island, but he refused."

"Forget Allen," Nolly laughed. "He's going to sit on this thing till you go away and it blows over."

"It's just possible that our assailant is down there, that if he was able to get off Bequia, he's hiding out in the Tobago Cays with that pair."

"Would you be willing to go back there?" Nolly asked.

"To look for him, you mean?"

"To lay a trap," Nolly said flatly.

"Sure, I guess so. But he'd recognize *Cheers* right off."

"But he wouldn't expect you to turn up on another boat."

"Would you come, too, Nolly?"

"You bet."

"When can we go?"

"It's only an idea. Let's not rule out the possibility that he's still on Bequia. Okay. You were on Palm Island, then where did you go?"

"We didn't like the exposed anchorage at Palm, so we moved over to Union Island Monday afternoon. It was blowing and other boats were dragging anchor, so we didn't go ashore. We stayed at Union Tuesday night and Wednesday. We went ashore once, looked around and left Thursday morning."

"Did you have any visitors at Union?"

"No, just our friends from *Walu*, who also were there. There was only one vendor boat working the anchorage, and for some reason he never came out to us. We were anchored far out, in the lee of Newland's Reef, and the wind was fresh, about twenty knots from the east. We had no contact with locals at Union Island and anyway, we made three more stops before going to Friendship Bay.

"Thursday we anchored at Salt Whistle Bay on Mayreau. Friday back to Corbay on Cannouan, and Saturday, July 11, Friendship Bay."

"You said you were standing on the bowsprit when you entered Friendship Bay that afternoon?"

"Yes."

"What were you wearing?"

"A swim suit—a bikini."

"Did you ever that day appear on deck wearing less than a bikini?"

"No. I know what you're getting at. I'm not stupid enough to go topless or nude in a harbor."

"I don't think you're stupid, but it's an important point if we're going to establish a motive.

"Betsy, your description is good. The facial features you describe almost sound more like a white man than a black man: 'fine angular nose, thin lips, small ears tucked close to the head, prominent cheek bones,'" he recited from memory. "Was it your impression he was from mixed parents?"

"No. He was definitely black, a Negro. If he had any white blood at all, it must have been many generations back."

"Let's talk about skin color. That's a hard thing for white folks to pinpoint with accuracy. Was he darker than, say, that man over at that table—the man reading the newspaper?"

I turned around. "He was about the same color, no lighter. Maybe even a bit darker. It's hard to be exact about the shade. I saw him only under artificial light."

"Incandescent or fluorescent?"

"Incandescent lights, in our cabin."

"So on a scale of one to ten, would you say he was about an eight?"

"I guess so."

"You say he was well groomed."

"Yes. No face stubble except for a neat, rather sparse goatee. No acne, no obvious scars, white teeth."

"Did you notice his navel?"

"I didn't notice anything *unusual* about his navel, if that's what you mean."

"A lot of people from these islands have a flawed navel—a fingertip remnant of umbilicus protruding from their navels."

"I've seen that, yes, in children swimming. No, his navel was normal—an inny, I think."

"You say you think he was left-handed?"

"I said he held the machete in his left hand the entire time he stood there in the cabin. I didn't notice in which hand he held it when he stabbed Jim."

"A machete is a slashing tool. You describe a stabbing—a jabbing—assault on Jim."

"Yes, he used the tip of the knife, not the edge of the blade. I almost forgot!" I exclaimed rummaging through my bag. "His father and I measured his wounds yesterday and came up with some dimensions for the weapon that was used. We made some sketches."

I showed him my two crude drawings, one of a man's torso, the other of a modified machete.

"There are two wounds: here and here. The abdominal wound is superficial. The pillow must have taken the blow. But when he stabbed again, he lunged at Jim with the machete as though to run it right through him. The knife pierced the right side of Jim's chest and made a vertical incision here," I pointed to the drawing, "between the second and third ribs. The wound is one-and-a-half inches tall and about two inches deep, which gives us the shape of the tip of the knife. Because he held the blade vertically, his father said, the two ribs prevented the blade from going deeper. Had he held it horizontally or had the ribs broken, it would have gone much deeper.

"Here's a drawing of the machete based on what I remember seeing and what we measured from Jim's wounds. It's about fifteen inches long, including the handle. The handle was wood, weathered wood, I think, and the blade was black, maybe rusted."

"A machete's a common tool here," said Nolly. "Every household has at least one, I'd guess. But few are true machetes. Most people take a store-bought machete and grind the blade like so," he drew, "putting a finer tip on it. I'd call the knife you've drawn a sabre. It's a versatile knife for cutting down fruit, cleaning big fish —or cutting a man. Too bad, it's pretty common, especially among fishermen.

"You say the man was muscular? Describe his body."

"He looked very strong, in excellent physical shape. He was a wiry sort of muscular as opposed to a Herculean sort of muscular. There wasn't a bit of flab on his body, or an ounce of fat. His arms were well developed, but not as much as his legs. His thighs were like a pair of hams, sinewy and strong."

"Like swimmers' legs?"

"Yes. Exactly. Like swimmers' legs."

"Did he have an erection?"

"No. No, he didn't."

"Did you notice if he was circumcised?"

"I don't honestly think I could tell the difference. I'm sorry. Let me ask Jim. He might know. Actually I tried not to look at—his nakedness. His organ was very terrifying to me, almost as terrifying as the machete. Do you know what I mean?"

"Because you feared rape?"

"Sure I feared rape. In the back of my mind I guess I knew it was inevitable. He was naked after all; he didn't come to pay us a social call. But when I had to get my purse to get him the money, and I didn't have anything to cover myself with, then I knew it was just a matter of time. *I can get through that*, I remember thinking. *I can survive that*. But immediately it was obvious that Jim could not. He would sooner die than allow that man to touch me."

"And he never actually touched you?"

"No, he didn't."

"When you jumped up through the open hatch onto the deck, why didn't the man follow? Why did he run aft and come up through the companionway, which took him longer to reach you?"

"I thought he *would* follow. But Jim deliberately blocked my exit. He put himself in the man's path, so he would have had to kill Jim to get to me."

"Sounds like some guy, this Jim."

"He is."

Nolly closed his note pad. "You'd better get a move on if you're going to make the afternoon ferry."

"Right. And I have to stop at Bequia Slip for my bag first. Will you walk around with me?"

"Sure."

We took the path down along the water. I walked barefoot through small wavelets, while Nolly walked on well-trodden dry sand on my right.

"I've told you everything I can think of, Nolly, and you helped me remember much more. Do you think you can find this man, that is if he's still on Bequia?"

"I'm going to try," he said.

"Just give me your opinion on something." I turned to face him, but he was not beside me. I found him a few paces back, kneeling in the damp sand at the water's edge, drawing something with a twig. I turned and walked back toward him.

"This the face?" he asked, squatting in front of the outline.

"That's it!" I exclaimed. "That's him!" I dropped to my knees in the sand beside him. "Nolly, that's the face I've been trying to draw myself."

It was only an outline, yet it was so precisely accurate that he could not have drawn it without knowing who the man was.

"The rectangular head, the angular cheekbones, the slender, square jawline. You know who it is!"

"I think I've seen him around."

"An off-islander?"

"A Bequian."

"Do you think you can find him?"

"I'm going to try."

"Could you tell who did it just from my description?"

"Not just from your description. Come on, let's keep walking. It's something I've been thinking about, since Saturday."

He turned and faced me. "You don't remember me, do you?"

"I've seen you before. I can't remember where."

"I was in Friendship Bay that afternoon. I have a house I'm building there. I saw you sail in."

"You were there when it happened?"

"No, I'd gone home, to Port Elizabeth. I live on the hill just behind the Frangipani. I came to the clinic when I heard. I followed you to the dock and helped you on the powerboat."

"And you passed me Jim's shoes!"

"I started to come with you to St. Vincent."

"Why didn't you?"

"There was too much excitement. Too many people talking, pushing. I had a hunch who did it and I wanted to see if my hunch was correct."

"Was it?"

"I thought so. Then I heard you said the man had a gold tooth."

"That rumor again," I sighed.

"That rumor may have helped more than you think."

"How's that?"

"Word's out on the island that your attacker has a gold tooth. Wouldn't surprise me if the police are still looking for Gold Tooth. The guy who stuck Jim is going to relax. He's going to figure he's home free and he's going to slip."

"The face you drew—is he the same guy you suspected all along?"

"No, the guy I first suspected is up to it—murder, robbery, rape —Osborn's capable of most anything. I watched him, I tailed him that night. Sunup Sunday morning, the day after the stabbing, he got on a boat in Friendship Bay and left for Tobago Cays. He hasn't been seen since."

"But you ruled him out?"

"He doesn't fit your description, not in any detail. But I'll bet he knows what happened—and who did it."

Nolly stopped beneath the sprawling flamboyant tree at the head of the harbor. "This is as far as I go. Don't tell anyone you talked to me. I'll call you."

He turned and disappeared.

I collected my bag at Bequia Slip, ran back around the harbor and jumped aboard the ferry *Seimstrand* just as she was pulling away from the dock. Then, almost out of habit, I walked the decks and checked the upper saloon for the man. I didn't find him, but I met three very interesting people.

First was Dr. Columbo, the young visiting pediatrician from Ohio whom Rima had called in during Jim's worst night at the general hospital. He and his wife were returning from a weekend on Bequia. He was heartened to hear that Jim was improving and congratulated us for moving him to the Botanic Hospital.

"I'm afraid Rima's going to pay for that night," he said.

"What do you mean?" I asked.

"Selwood hasn't spoken to her since she and I looked in on Jim that night. She's certain to get a bad recommendation from him for her work there."

"That's unfair. Rima was just being conscientious."

"I agree. If anyone was remiss, it was Selwood for going out for the night without leaving an emergency number. There was no back-up. Besides, Rima didn't call me in; I volunteered to come. My wife and I were staying at Villa Lodge, you know."

"Did you explain that to Selwood?"

"He won't discuss it. But he's taking it out on Rima. I don't mean to tell tales out of school. I mention it only because I know Rima won't. That report will go with her to St. Joseph's."

"Jim's father is director of orthopedics there," I said. "Maybe he can check her file when she arrives and smooth it over somehow if there's a problem."

The second person I met aboard the *Seimstrand* was Terry Miller, a pretty blonde Canadian flight attendant on medical leave from the airlines, who'd taken a bungalow on the beach at Bequia for a few months. She was scared and was leaving Bequia. She'd heard about our trouble and told me about four recent cases of robbery and sexual assault on Bequia involving herself and three other women. I wrote down her name and added those of Melinda, Betsy Frisbee and a couple named Dudly and Sandy who live on a yacht in Port Elizabeth.

The four cases had one thing in common: Upon reporting the crime to police, each victim was harassed by privates.

One girl was followed home by an off-duty officer who tried to force his way inside her home.

Another woman allowed a policeman to come to her home to investigate. She'd woken up in the middle of the previous night with a man on top of her, trying to rape her. She struggled out from beneath him and was able to buy him off with the money in her wallet. Then she screamed and the man fled in the night. When the officer came to investigate, she seated him in her living room, then walked into the kitchen to produce the wallet he requested to see. When she returned the officer asked to have a cigarette. She offered him one, and he withdrew from her pack a hand-rolled joint of marijuana, which she had never seen before. He reminded her of the penalty for possession of narcotics and threatened to throw the book at her unless she took care of this little problem he had, which she could see from the bulge in his uniform. She called his bluff by ordering him to leave, which he did.

Of the four women, only Melinda and Sandy remained on Bequia.

I made some notes and jotted down the addresses of the victims. I knew I hadn't seen the last of Bequia, and I hoped to look up the remaining two women when I was there next. It would be easy enough to corroborate their stories, and there might be a link to our assault. Then, I thought, if Sergeant Allen wouldn't call in the CID from St. Vincent on the case, there might be enough incriminating evidence against Bequia police to press for an investigation myself.

Failing that, perhaps the American Consul could help. By phone, Jim's father had advised Karl Danga, the American Consul in Barbados, under whose jurisdiction this part of the Caribbean falls, about our trouble in Bequia, and the consul had asked to be kept advised of any developments. All four female victims were North Americans; three of the four were Americans. Terry Miller agreed to tell her story to higher officials if asked, and felt the other three would do likewise. A shot in the dark, maybe, but it was information I was to use later.

The third person I met on the ferry was Father Adams, justice of the peace of Bequia, a small, retiring man with Occidental, cherubic features and a tawny complexion, who hid beneath a broad-brimmed hat. He was a prominent legal figure on Bequia. But he disappeared when I became embroiled in conversation with Dr. Columbo. I next glimpsed him on the foredeck, but again he ducked from sight until I confronted him at the rail just as *Seimstrand* pulled into the dock at St. Vincent.

I told him my name, and presuming that a man of his position would have knowledge of our assault, I identified myself as one of the victims. He made no reply. I told him I didn't believe Sergeant Allen's investigation was getting anywhere and asked him where I might go from there. But as soon as *Seimstrand* breasted the dock, he climbed over the rail and went ashore without answering

Either he's avoiding me, I thought, or he's the shiest man I ever met. I picked up my bag and followed him.

The *Grenadine Star* also was in, and as I caught up with Father Adams and began again to ask for his advice, the mate from *Grenadine Star* broke in with Son Mitchell on his arm.

We shook hands, and before I could finish my conversation with Father Adams, Son Mitchell took my arm and brusquely led me away. He brought me to a taxi driver he knew, and installed me in the back seat of the cab. Son professed deep concern about the incident and said he would do what he could to help, but his ferry was leaving for Bequia and he would get all the details from his wife Pat.

When Son left, the cab driver started to pull away from the dock without asking my destination. As he did so, he asked: "You know Mr. Jackson?"

"No, I don't think so."

He pressed on the brake. "Then come with me." He hopped out on the dock, pulled me out of the back seat and rushed me over to the back seat of a chauffeur-driven chocolate-brown sedan. He tapped on the rear window. "Allow me to introduce the Honorable Superintendant of Police, Mr. Jackson," said the cabby regally.

I offered my hand to an austere-looking man in a brown uniform decorated with gold braid. His solemn, brown face softened when I recounted my story. Though he didn't say so, it was obvious the incident was news to him.

"Is Rodriguez doing everything he can for you?" he asked.

"I don't know anyone by that name," I replied. "I've been talking with a Sergeant Allen in Bequia."

"Inspector Rodriguez is in charge there. Ralph Rodriguez. He should be handling the investigation—not some sergeant. I'll call him myself. He's new there, but I can't believe he doesn't know about it." Superintendant Jackson gave me his office phone number and promised to look in on the case.

"And I'll stop that rumor about the gold tooth once and for all," he assured me.

I thanked him, eased back into the back seat of the taxi, and we drove up the hill to the hospital. For a day that started out badly, things certainly were looking up, and I couldn't wait to tell Jim the developments. For the first time, I felt that Jim's attacker might just find himself behind bars.

The driver stopped in front of the clinic's modest portico, got out and opened my door.

"How much do I owe you, Mr. Brown?"

"You don't owe me nothing, Ma'am, not after all you an' your husband's been through."

"But I insist." I reached inside my bag.

He stopped me by placing his hand on mine. "I'll tell you honest, Ma'am. There's times I'm ashamed of my race."

"Don't say that."

"Yes'm, some days I'm ashamed of my own color." Eyes downcast, he shook his head.

"You mustn't feel that way. What happened to us has nothing to do with color, with race."

"He was a colored man, wasn't he?"

"Yes, he was black. But there's another black man right inside those doors who's doing a lot of good for people. It's men like Dr. Cyrus and yourself—good men—who set an example for the rest. Don't ever feel ashamed of being black."

"If you ever need a cab, you call me." He handed me his card. "When your husband's better I'm going to show you through the botanic garden. Then I'll take you up to see the volcano. No charge."

"We'd like that. Thank you, Mr. Brown."

Whatever racial prejudice I might have been harboring, consciously or subconsciously since the incident, dissolved with the words of that humble man.

Jim was sitting up when I arrived. The tube leading to his chest had been removed and he no longer talked in raspy monosyllables. He was full of questions about my trip to Bequia, and brightened visibly with the hope my meeting with Nolly seemed to offer.

"But I worry about you going to Bequia alone," said Jim. "For all we know the guy could still be there."

"I hope he is. Don't you see, Jim? That's our only chance of finding him."

"What I see is that this has become an obsession with you. What is it that's driving you so?"

"I'd like to think it's justice. Deep down I suppose it's revenge. The police are going to do nothing unless pressed. And I believe Nolly can find this guy."

"And then what? Do you really believe they'll convict one of their own?"

"Maybe not. But if this guy goes free, it won't be because we didn't try."

I returned to Villa Lodge with Jim's parents that evening. The mysterious Harry Maharaj was still lumbering about the dining room, uttering empty threats and busting knuckles when we retired early to bed.

CHAPTER NINE

Saturday, July 18

———————————— I was in one of those deep, lifeless sleeps when I heard an urgent knock at the door. I awoke not knowing where I was and instinctively reached for the gun under my pillow. It wasn't so much that I needed it—certainly not in my hotel room at Villa Lodge—but that I couldn't get to sleep without it there. Reaching for the revolver in my sleep had become a reflex.

"It's Bobby Brisbane," said the voice on the other side of the door. "Phone for Betsy."

I pulled a dress over my nightgown and followed Bobby, the hotel manager, outside and along a path to his apartment.

"What time is it anyway, Bobby?"

"Oh, after midnight."

He led me to the living room of his garden apartment, turned down the volume on the television set and left the room. I picked up the receiver.

"It's Nolly," whispered the voice. "Listen carefully. I don't have long. You're going to get a call in the morning from Inspector Ralph Rodriguez of Bequia. He's on the case now. Put off going to the hospital if you have to, and wait for that call. Can you do that?"

"Yes."

"Rodriguez has a suspect. If he knows you'll be here, he's going to pick up his suspect and bring him in for questioning in the morning. Can you take the ferry back here tomorrow?"

"If he's got the man? I'd swim back."

"That's the problem. His suspect is Gold Tooth."

"Aw, no. How many times do I have to tell them it's not Gold Tooth?"

"Listen. Rodriguez is alright. He's a damn sight better than Allen. I've worked with him on other cases under cover and he's not the moron Allen is. I told him it wasn't Gold Tooth, but he's got a line on a guy with a gold tooth and he's convinced he's the one. I can't dissuade him."

"So you want me to come back there to humor Rodriguez and look at his Gold Tooth?"

"That's right. I made a deal with Rodriguez. He knows you're steamed with Allen and ready to stop working with police. Super-intendent Jackson called him this afternoon, so he's under fire from St. Vincent. I told him I'd get you to return tomorrow to look at his suspect if he'd bring in mine."

"You found him?"

"Not yet. But I'm trailing him. I promised to have him for Rodriguez by eight tomorrow morning. If you tell Rodriguez you'll be on the next ferry when he calls you tomorrow morning, he'll pick up both men: Gold Tooth and my suspect. Look, I've got to go. Will you go along with Rodriguez?"

"Yes. I'll be on the next ferry."

"Good. You'll hear from me." Nolly hung up.

I went back to bed and pondered the bizarre call. It was a tall order to produce Jim's attacker by 8 o'clock the next morning. But I never doubted Nolly could do it, *if* his suspect was the assailant.

*   *   *

I was called away from breakfast with the Holmans to take a phone call at the hotel switchboard.

"This is Inspector Rodriguez from Bequia. I've taken over your case, Miss Hitz. We have two suspects and a couple of knives for you to see. You did tell one of my men the man had a gold tooth, didn't you?"

"No, I didn't," I said. "The man does not have a gold tooth."

"Witnesses often make mistakes, you know. I'm certain . . ."

"There's no mistake about the gold tooth except in the mind of the police officer who told you he had one."

Then I stopped myself. Play along, Nolly had said.

"I'll be there to look at your suspects, but I hope you'll keep looking for the man who fits the description in my statement. A man without a gold tooth."

"Very good. When can you come?"

"I'll be there on the *Grenadine Star*. She gets in to Port Elizabeth at one-fifteen this afternoon. Would you mind meeting me at the ferry? I don't feel comfortable walking around Bequia alone."

"Of course. One-fifteen? I'll meet you at the ferry."

I returned to the breakfast table and a few minutes later was again called away to the switchboard. It was Superintendent Jackson of Kingstown. Could I go to Bequia on Sunday? I told him I was going to Bequia today, Saturday, to look at two suspects Inspector Rodriguez had lined up.

"Don't go," he said. "Rodriguez is looking for a man with a gold tooth. I just spoke with him and told him to release his suspects and start from scratch. If you wait until Sunday, I'll send a CID man with you in plain clothes. You should have some protection."

My heart fell. "Can the CID man come with me today?"

"No, Miss Hitz. And if you go alone, we can't be responsible for what might happen to you."

"I want to go today to show Inspector Rodriguez I'm a cooperative witness," I said. "Let me go this time alone. I'll have to spend the night on Bequia because there's no return ferry until Sunday. Your CID man can come to Bequia on the Sunday morning ferry and keep an eye on me then."

Reluctantly the superintendent agreed.

Hastily I dialed Bequia police and asked for Inspector Rodriguez, hoping to forestall his releasing the suspects. He was not in. I had to take my chances and go to Bequia regardless.

At noon I boarded the *Grenadine Star* and paid my fare to the deck hand. A few minutes later the mate climbed down from the wheelhouse. "You'll never pay your way aboard the *Star*," he said, returning my red five-dollar bill. "Captain Hazel's orders."

Again Father Adams was among the passengers and again he seemed to go out of his way to avoid me. Just to make sure it wasn't my imagination, I led him in a little game of hide and seek. Out of a crowd I appeared beside him on the bow. He turned and found a bench in the passenger section. Later I found him there behind a newspaper, so I slid onto the other end of the same bench. A moment later he was gone. Approaching Bequia, I lost him in the men's head, where he remained until our lines were sent ashore. Why was he going to such pains to avoid me?

A large crowd milled about on the dock at Port Elizabeth that Saturday morning, but when everyone left, there was no Inspector Rodriguez. I waited a bit longer, then crossed the street and inquired for him at the front desk of the police station.

"Not here," said the uniformed officer at the desk. The officer knew not who I was or that the inspector had made any appointment.

I stepped outside and heard a crash of breaking glass coming from the back of the station. I peered around the corner as a bottle flew from the upstairs door and shattered on the rusted hulk of an old truck overgrown with weeds behind the police station. Three off-duty officers were perched on the back steps drinking beer and having a little target practice with bottles.

I felt someone staring at me, and turned to see a light-skinned Negro in his mid-twenties leaning against a wood pillar beneath the overhanging second story of the police station. He seemed to be waiting for someone. It was not a kind face that continued to stare at me with strange intensity.

I turned and faced him squarely. "Hello," I said awkwardly.

He cast his eyes downward. "Hello," he replied, his lips parting to reveal a gold front tooth.

It took a moment to dawn on me whose company I shared, then my impatience turned to anger. I picked my way up the back steps, through Bequia's Finest, to the office.

Sergeant Allen sat at the desk, fondling a steel-bladed dagger sharpened to a stiletto point. On the desk lay a similar knife, honed to slightly broader, but no less sinister point.

"I had an appointment with Inspector Rodriguez," I said. "Do you know where he is?"

"Nope. Did you see the man?"

"What man?"

"The one who stabbed your husband. That him outside?"

"You mean Gold Tooth downstairs?"

"Yeah. Is he the one?"

"Is that where you got those knives? From that man?"

"Yeah. You recognize either of these?" he asked, brandishing one in each hand. The long cruel daggers looked more like ice picks than the machetes from which they were made.

"What kind of police force are you running here? If you think that's the guy who knifed Jim, what's he doing hanging around outside the station with me? No, he's not the man, but he's obviously no saint either if you took those two knives from him."

"You see knives like these all over. They use 'em for cutting grass, opening coconuts. . . ."

"Like hell they do. No wonder he was giving me the evil eye. He thinks I'm fingering him for the job. I didn't come here expecting an FBI inquest; one-way windows and a police line-up. I came here to keep an appointment with Inspector Rodriguez and to look at two suspects. I've finished working with you; you and I are going to accomplish nothing. I want to see the inspector. Where is he?"

"Calm down, lady. I'll go look."

My anger hadn't subsided 15 minutes later when Inspector Rodriguez arrived. His face was a handsome mixture of Caribbean races, his proud cheekbones, straight youthful hairline and black curly eyelashes setting off his intense brown eyes.

"Sorry I'm late," he apologized.

We shook hands.

"I expected to see you at the ferry dock, over an hour ago."

"I got tied up. Look I don't blame you for being mad. Sergeant Allen was supposed to see that the suspect outside was kept under guard."

"I'd appreciate having nothing more to do with Sergeant Allen."

"I'm on the case now," he said. "I was on St. Vincent the first few days after the incident and only learned when I got back to Bequia that nothing was being done. I went to Friendship Bay myself this morning and searched the area."

"Did you find anything?"

"No evidence, but I picked up two suspects I'd like you to look at. I feel quite confident we've got the man downstairs."

"I saw your Gold Tooth—the one standing outside."

"Is he the one?"

"No, he's not even close."

"Don't you want another look? You can question him if you like."

"I don't need another look. He doesn't resemble him in any way."

"But he's got a gold tooth."

"Isn't that my statement," I pointed, "there, on your desk?"

"Yes."

"I wish you'd read it. It's all there, the sequence of events, a description of the assailant, everything I know."

"I'm sorry. I haven't read your statement. I know that sounds bad, but I've been up all night chasing down suspects. Maybe we can still come up with something before you leave. Would you be willing to take a drive with me around the island?"

His apology sounded genuinely embarrassed, sincere.

"Of course. But what about the other suspect you say you have?"

"He's downstairs, too, but I doubt he's the man we're looking for. This is a little irregular, but it will save the time and trouble of organizing a parade if he's not the one. Follow me. We're going to walk downstairs and come through the station the back way. I'll walk to the front desk, open a ledger and pretend to show you something inside. The suspect will be sitting on a bench just inside the door. He'll be facing you. Look at him, but don't say anything. Then follow me outside to my car. Got it?"

"Got it."

I did exactly what he said. I followed him down the steps and through the back of the police station. Rodriguez paused at the open ledger. I glanced over his shoulder at the entries, then raised my eyes to the figure seated on the bench. He sat stoop-shoul-dered, head bowed, wringing his hands nervously.

But there was no mistake!

It was him!!

I felt at first a flood of intense relief that the long search was finally over. A moment later it was all I could do to keep from attacking him with my bare hands.

He never looked up, never saw me.

I followed the inspector out the door to his car and slid in the passenger seat. He closed his door and started the ignition.

"Well?"

"It's him."

His surprise was as great as my own.

"You're sure?"

"Yes. But I want a better look, so there's no chance I'm mistaken."

"We'll arrange a little parade. As far as anyone's concerned, you never saw this man at the station until the parade."

"Is that like a line-up?"

"Parade, line-up, same thing," he said, stopping the car in the center of town. "Can you come back just after four? It'll take a little time to find three or four approximate look-alikes for the parade. I'll pick you up if you like."

"That's all right, I can walk back. But thank you, thank you very much, Inspector."

I booked a room at the Frangipani, walked up the hill to my room in a secluded guest wing, and turned on the shower. As the cool spray pelted my back, my initial feeling of exultation gave way to a heavy burden of responsibility. In exactly one hour I would make a decision that would make or break another man's life. I had to be certain—dead certain—that the man I identified was indeed the assailant. I dried off, dressed and walked to the police station at the head of the harbor.

"Are you ready," asked the Inspector in his office. I was aflutter with anxiety. "Yes," I replied nervously.

"There are nine men. You can talk to them, ask them any questions you want. Ask any of them to take off clothing if that will help. Get them to strip if you want. If you see the assailant, touch him on the shoulder and say, 'This is the man.' Take as much time as you want, but be certain."

"I could question them all, but if the assailant is there, I'll recognize him immediately. Will the record indicate how long it took me to identify the man?"

"Yes."

Then I'll not waste time, I thought.

The Inspector led me to a large, second-floor room that had been entirely emptied of furniture. The deadly silence was broken by the hollow echo of my own footsteps on the linoleum floor as I walked with measured steps past the row of nine men and stopped in front of the first.

I looked down the straight row of men. Eight of the nine stood tall, their shoulders back and heads raised. I walked down the row, pausing to look carefully at each face. Eight of the nine withdrew their eyes in shyness or chuckled self-consciously at my piercing stare.

Only one man—he was was somewhere near the middle of the row—was obviously under extreme stress. His head was tucked onto his chest and his rumpled shirt and brow were soaked in sweat. From his fingertips clear down to the soles of his feet, he shuddered and twitched like a puppet coming unglued. He was the only man to whom I spoke.

"Step forward, please," I said.

He only shuddered the more.

"You. Step forward, please," I repeated.

He took a small step, his eyes still glued to the floor.

"Look at me, please."

Without raising his chin from his chest, he cast a fleeting glimpse ahead in my direction.

"I want to see your face. Please look at me."

Cautiously, he raised his head and tried to look beyond me to the open window in front of him without meeting my eyes.

I looked at the face and was filled not with fear or even pity, but again with blinding rage at the sight of this man who one week ago had watched with cool dispassion as the very life ran out of Jim, but who, now that the tables were turned, was reduced to a whimpering coward at the prospect of answering for his deed.

Clenching his teeth, he flexed the muscles of his jawbone, struggling to gain composure, to look like the others. The whites of his eyes were obscured in a nest of red blood vessels.

"Take off your shirt, please."

He unbuttoned the buttons with his left hand and removed his shirt.

"Where did you get the red eyes?"

"My eyes not red," he stammered.

"Your eyes are very red. Why are they so red?"

His head began to shimmy and the tendons in his neck stood out. Rivulets of sweat ran down his chest.

"Where were you last Saturday night?"

"Home," he said, staring again at the floor.

"You boarded our boat last Saturday night. You stabbed the captain and you robbed us, didn't you?"

He shook his head violently. "No."

"This is the man," I said, touching him on the bare shoulder. "I'm one hundred per cent certain. This is the man who robbed us and stabbed Jim Holman."

"*Me?*" he shrieked, feigning disbelief. "Not *me! Me?*"

"Yes, you."

I looked at the inspector. He nodded and I followed him back to his office.

"That was a positive identification you made," declared Rodriguez with quiet pleasure.

"Now what?"

"That's it. That should be enough for a conviction."

"On what charge?"

"I don't know. That's for the prosecutor to decide."

"Don't you want me to make a statement or something?"

"You identified him. That's enough."

"I'd like to make a statement."

"Sure, if you want. Sergeant, take down her statement," he said to Allen.

The sergeant wrote down in my words what transpired at the line-up, including my questions and his answers, then I signed it.

Inspector Rodriguez summoned the suspect, placed a compassionate hand on his shoulder and led him downstairs. When he returned he told me the man I identified was Calvin Hunte, 26, of Friendship Bay. He'd been in and out of trouble all of his adult life, but this was his most serious offense.

I showed the inspector the blood-caked vial of mace and again offered it as evidence, thinking it would quite importantly link the assailant's hasty, pained exit from our boat with the suspect's severely bloodshot eyes.

The inspector agreed that Hunte had obviously suffered severe eye trauma, but declined to keep the mace, feeling that the case was already sewn up. "All we need now is Jim Holman's I.D.," he said. "The suspect will be remanded to custody in Kingstown Monday morning. Do you think Jim will be well enough to attend a police parade there?"

Before I could answer, the phone rang and Inspector Rodriguez gave Superintendent Jackson the news that the assailant finally was in custody. Jackson asked to speak to me, said some reassuring words and also asked if I thought Jim could identify Hunte in St.

Vincent. I told him I believed he could and would ask Dr. Cyrus's permission for Jim to attend the line-up. Then I returned the receiver to the inspector.

"Bail?" Rodriguez exclaimed after a long pause. "Yes, Sir, I realize it's not a capital offense. But I feel strongly he should be held without bail until the preliminary hearing. First of all, I've got a lot of scared people on this island. There's been a real uproar over this incident and no one's going to feel safe if this guy's out on bail. Second, what's to keep him from jumping bail—getting on a boat and going to another island?" Another pause. "Right. That's my recommendation, sir. No bail."

When they hung up, Rodriguez turned to me. "Well, I guess you heard. Jackson asked me how much I thought they ought to set bail at."

"I heard your reply. Do you think he'll take your advice?"

"I think so. I think he can appreciate what the cruising boats mean to this island. This is going to be a hard thing for Bequia to overcome. How can I ensure the safety of my people and of visitors if Hunte's out on bail?"

"If they do set bail," I asked, "how much would it be?"

"Oh, two thousand dollars maybe. That's a guess."

Eight hundred U.S. dollars, I thought. "Do you think his family could come up with that much?"

"I don't know his family. I've only been on the island a couple of months myself," he confided. "But judging from the crowd that turned out for the parade, I'd say Hunte's got more enemies than friends. I went out to bring in three men for the parade. Word spread and I couldn't keep them away. You saw—there were eight volunteers, two of them I know have been burned by Hunte before."

"What's next?" I asked. "Will our sworn statements be enough for a conviction or will we have to testify in person at his trial?"

"No, you'll have to testify at his trial, otherwise he goes free. The preliminary hearing will be in Bequia. The trial will be in St. Vincent. The earliest date the magistrate can hear the case will be . . ." He flipped over the pages of his calendar. ". . . about September 10—a little more than two months from now. The trial itself could be any time after that. You'll be here for the trial, won't you?"

"Hurricane season already has begun, so we've got to take our boat west. Jim and I have talked it over. As soon as he is well enough to be flown to the States, I'll find crew and sail to Curaçao, where we'll stay until November. Isn't there some way to expedite matters—to convene the preliminary hearing in the next few days?"

"You can talk to Superintendent Jackson about that. I know he wants to clean up this case, and if he knows you're leaving the islands, maybe he can hurry it up."

Outside the police station, hordes of Bequians of all ages milled about gossiping, whispering and rejoicing. I felt a little like Dorothy whose house had just landed on the wicked witch. They opened a path as I walked among them to the Frangipani, and then two young men came forward to shake my hand. I recognized one, maybe both, from the line-up.

"Hunte took me for fifteen hundred dollars," said a husky youth of about 20. "Before I was tending bar at Frangipani I used to have my own taxi. Make pretty good money, too. Hunte's made a mess out of his life, but he wanted to make something of hisself by starting over with his own taxi. He talked me into co-signing a loan for him at the bank. Then he wrecks the car, defaults on the loan and leaves me to pay it off. I didn't know what I'd got myself into. I lost my taxi and still owe the bank over a thousand dollars."

"While he was driving the taxi," said the other, "my girlfriend gave him an envelope to bring to me. He drives away, opens the envelope and finds my passbook inside. Then he drives to the Barclay Bank, throws down the book, signs my name and withdraws all my savings—everything I worked for."

"Was he charged?" I asked.

"Sure, the bank went after him. But Father Adams repaid the money for Hunte. That preacher won't get his boy off this time, though."

Returning to Frangipani, I found Nolly waiting at the same secluded table we'd shared the day before. A broad grin and heavy eyelids were all I saw of his face. I bought us both a drink and took a seat beside him. Son and Pat Mitchell stopped by with congratulations and left us alone to talk.

"How, in eighteen hours, did you find Hunte when he eluded police for a week?"

"You about told me who I was looking for," he said elusively. "All I had to do was find him."

"How did you find him?"

"If you think like one of them, the rest is easy. From talking to you I had a pretty good idea the man was from Friendship Bay. You said you anchored there about four-thirty. An off-islander would have left in time to get back to his island before dark. Or, if he was staying on Bequia, he'd have to have a friend and a place to stay. In that case there would have been two of them. But only one man came to your boat.

"The only times both you and Jim appeared on deck were when you entered the harbor and when you ate your dinner in the cockpit. It was dark when you ate, so he must have seen you when you sailed in.

"He watched you without being seen, and he knew there was one man and one woman on your boat. If he hadn't seen you sail in, he would have to assume from the size of your boat that there could have been more people—maybe another couple—and I don't think he would have tried what he did, armed as he was with just a machete. He saw lights through the port holes of the forward cabin, so even though he knew you were awake, he could assume you were in bed and he figured he could take you."

"So," I said, marveling at the accuracy of his logic, "you knew you were looking for a man from Friendship Bay. Then what?"

"Then I had to establish a motive. I got three men I might have looked for if I thought the motive was rape. You're careful how you dress and you hadn't been ashore. There are easier targets living alone on shore—girls who go topless right on the beaches here—so I could pretty rule out rape as a prime motive. Murder? I don't think there's anyone on this island's going to kill just for the sake of killing. That leaves robbery. Who's got more money than tourists? He could see from your flag you're American and your boat looks expensive.

"The harbor was quiet and your boat was a sitting duck, especially for a man who knows his way around boats. I remembered the dinghy painter. You said he tied a round turn and two half hitches—the next best thing to a bowline for a man who's in a hurry or tying a knot in the dark.

"He got about two hundred from you. He should have split right then, not taken the chance of sticking around and getting caught. But he needed more money than that. I was looking for a man who's desperate for money, big money.

"I knew about a guy they call Little Boy—that's Hunte. I guess it's a nickname from the time he was a kid. He fit your description, all but the skin color, which is the one feature you blew. Hunte's a good two shades lighter than you described. He's been in plenty of trouble—usually money trouble—but I knew about one other serious assault.

"Hunte shipped out on a freighter once a few years back. Son Mitchell helped Hunte and some other men from Bequia get jobs as deck hands. A few days out, he told one of the officers he wanted to be put off in the next port. He didn't want to work anymore. He'd signed a contract and the officer reminded him he couldn't be released from it without a good reason. Hunte got hold of a lead pipe, went up to the wheelhouse and gave them a reason. He beat two of the officers nearly to death. They put him off in the next port, but they couldn't afford to stick around and press charges.

"I knew Hunte was capable of the kind of cold-blooded assault you described. Not long ago Hunte was out lobstering with another guy about a mile offshore. Hunte was supposed to stay in the boat and follow the bubbles while his friend gathered lobsters with a Scuba tank. Hunte knew his buddy had a big bankroll in his knapsack, so what does he do but leave his friend to drown. The diver made it back to shore somehow, against a hell of a current, then he beat the bejeezees out of Hunte.

"I talked to young Roderick Mitchell and found out he and his brother knew more than they were letting on. I was pretty sure they knew who did it.

"But how?"

"They came out to the harbor for their dinghy, just like they said. But they told me they were carrying a shotgun. You don't just carry around a loaded shotgun if you find your dinghy missing, do you? So they had to have seen something. I think they saw the man go aboard your boat. The moon was just about full."

"Then why didn't they come sooner? In time to help?"

"That's what I wondered. They were well enough armed to take him, and they were three men against one. The fact that they were carrying the gun indicates that they were prepared to intervene. But for some reason they stopped and called the police instead. Now it's possible they found Hunte's clothes near where the dinghy had been tied and that's how they knew who it was. But it seems clear they chose not to confront Hunte themselves."

"Why not?"

"Any number of reasons. They're all Bequians. They're neighbors. Hunte's father helped build *Wave Dancer*, Mitchell's father's boat. That may be hard for an off-islander to understand, but it counts for a lot around here. So they called the police. When the police didn't come, they called them again. Finally, when they heard you scream, they felt they had to help, and that's when they launched the skiff and came out to your boat.

"After they got you and Jim to the hospital, they returned to Friendship Bay and saw a man hiding under the pier. Still they wanted the police to be the ones to find him, so again they called the police. Still the police didn't come and in the morning the man was gone.

"Then the Mitchell boys heard the rumor that you said the assailant had a gold tooth. They weren't about to point the finger at Hunte, when they thought you were naming a different guy. Eventually they might even have believed they were wrong. I even told them myself that Gold Tooth did it," Nolly chuckled.

"What for?"

"Hunte disappeared the Saturday of the stabbing and he wasn't seen all the next week. I wanted him to relax and come out of hiding. There actually is a guy on the island with a gold front tooth who's been in some trouble. Rodriguez was convinced he was the culprit."

"I know," I said, "I saw him at the station this afternoon, before the parade."

"Poor ol' Gold Tooth," laughed Nolly. "I paid him a little visit last night while I was tracking Hunte. All week long that man's been shaking like a dog passing chicken bones, ever since he heard about the gold tooth. He wanted to split for another island, but I told him to play along with Rodriguez by coming down to the station with him. If Hunte learned Gold Tooth had been picked up, I figured, he might come out of hiding. Rodriguez picked up Gold Tooth at eight this morning and by noon we had Hunte.

"Ah, but Gold Tooth was some scared. 'Better get rid of that goatee,' I told him, 'unless you want a trip to the slammer.' "

"He was clean-shaven when I saw him," I said.

"I don't wonder," Nolly laughed.

"Tell me something, Nolly. If Hunte didn't come out to our boat with rape on his mind, why was he naked?"

"What better camouflage than dark skin at night? He's been in trouble before, and he knows white folks can't hardly tell one black man from another. Now any black man can pinpoint another Negro's skin color precisely, but he can't, for example, tell you the color of his clothes. A white man, on the other hand, can tell you an assailant wore a burgundy shirt and olive-green trousers, but he'd be hard put to tell you whether the man's skin was the color of clay or charcoal.

"If Hunte wore clothes, they might have been spattered with blood and he'd have to destroy them, then sneak around naked. But by going naked, he can wash the blood off, then climb back into his clothes when he's finished. He probably doesn't have more than a few shirts and pants. If you live to describe those clothes, chances are somebody will know who they belong to."

Nolly finished his drink. "I've got to go," he said. Then he smiled and added "Remember, Rodriguez found Hunte."

He disappeared.

*   *   *

I phoned Jim at the hospital that evening. "Guess who's spending the night in jail?"

"You?"

"No. Calvin Hunte."

"Who's Calvin Hunte? No! They got him?"

"Nolly found him. I picked him out of a line-up. It's him alright. Rodriguez and Jackson want to arrange a line-up so you can do the same. They seem to think they'll have an ironclad case if you can identify him, too. Think you can do it?"

"You know me and faces. But sure, I'll try."

"When do you think you'll be up to it?"

"As soon as Dr. Cyrus will let me. I'll talk to him."

"You sound almost like the old Jim."

"I'm doing better. My lung's reinflating slowly and I can draw longer breaths. I walked out on the patio today."

"I wish I could be there. I can't get back until the evening ferry tomorrow, but I'll call you in the morning."

"Keep the gun with you at night, Betsy."

"Alright, but remember—he's in custody."

"I still don't like your being on that island alone. He might have friends."

That night I sank into a soft double bed at the Frangipani and pulled down the mosquito net canopy.

I felt we'd won this round. Hunte was in custody and Monday morning he would take the ferry ride to St. Vincent in handcuffs. The rest should be mere formality.

He matched my description. He had a record—no convictions, but a long history of troublemaking. Even if he can find somebody to alibi him, I thought, any prosecutor should be able to poke holes in it. I picked him out of a nine-man line-up; Jim could do the same. The Mitchell boys could be subpoenaed to testify. The vial of mace had obviously caused the bloodshot eyes; I would try again to have it admitted as evidence. Rodriguez had promised to search Hunte's house in the morning. He might turn up more incriminating evidence—the machete, my billfold or credit cards. But even without more evidence, Hunte's conviction seemed assured.

Why then did my gut ache with doubt?

It was another night of fitful sleep. The wind piped up shortly after midnight and the flowering hibiscus beat furiously against the thin louvered walls and door of my room. Time and again I awoke in a tangle of mosquito mesh, clutching the revolver with both hands. If there was anyone who had no business carrying a loaded gun, it was I.

I thought of *Cheers* straining at her lines out in the harbor and wondered what Bill Little had set for a mooring beneath the surface. There was no way inside my room to gauge the wind strength, so cautiously, with gun in hand, I slid open one of the expansive wood doors that opened onto the harbor. I estimated the wind strength at a steady 30 knots, with higher gusts, and wished I'd thought to row out one of our plow anchors as a back up. I consoled myself that *Cheers* would ride out a blow better at a mooring than tied to a dock, but blamed myself for trusting without question another man's ground tackle.

SUNDAY, JULY 19

Before daylight, I was up and dressed. I hurried down to the waterfront just at sunup and drew a sigh of relief upon finding *Cheers* plunging through the white caps sweeping the harbor, but still in her same relative position. The wind seemed to have dropped but was still a steady 25 knots out of the northeast, and a few early risers had begun setting additional anchors.

How strange it seemed that this boat, which had been the center of our world in the year since we'd moved aboard had entirely lost our attention amid all the excitement following the accident. We were into hurricane season now and could expect more frequent blows as tropical depressions began forming over the warm tropical Atlantic and sweeping northwestward across the Caribbean. There was no telling how much longer *Cheers* would have to remain here unattended.

I hurried around to Bequia Slip, rowed out to *Cheers* and put heavier chafing gear on the mooring pendant. I flipped on the depth sounder and read 15 feet. I tied the dinghy painter up short to the bowsprit and lowered the main anchor, a 45-pound plow, and six fathoms of chain into the bow of the dinghy, then flaked down another 12 fathoms of nylon rode into the stern. It was hard work, but it felt good to be doing something.

Cheers now was headed northeast, and since the prevailing winds are usually from an easterly quadrant, I rowed the anchor out to windward and dropped it over the side at a 45-degree angle to the mooring rode, toward the east.

Drifting with the wind back to *Cheers*, I climbed up the bobstay, took a few turns around the windlass, then cranked in on the rode until *Cheers* rode entirely on the anchor, setting it well into the sandy mud. Then I slacked off the rode until she rode equally to both the anchor and the mystery mooring.

The flying jib had been left loosely lashed to the bow pulpit in our haste to leave the boat. In last night's high winds the sail had torn free from its lashings. So I bagged it and stowed it below. Then I checked the bilges, started the engine and charged the batteries while searching again for my wallet. Clearly Hunte had jumped with it, and if he hadn't made it to shore with the wallet, he must have dropped it somewhere between our boat and the shore, so probably it lay at the bottom of Friendship Bay.

Feeling I had done all I could for *Cheers*, I returned to the Frangipani for breakfast.

Afterwards, Pat Mitchell unlocked the door to the mail room and I shuffled through packages searching for the parcel containing our long-awaited charts. I found nothing addressed to us.

Then I walked to the police station where Inspector Rodriguez was just returning from a search of Hunte's home.

"Nothing," he shrugged. "No knife, no money, no billfold. Jim's identification is going to be important to the case," he reiterated.

"I spoke with Jim last night," I said. "He's willing and needs only Dr. Cyrus's permission. But why is his identification so crucial when you already have mine?"

"You're only the witness," he replied. "A victim's testimony weighs heavier with a jury. We want both."

Before noon I was back at the Frangipani. Pat Mitchell pointed to a short, middle-age man who was seated at the bar wearing blue jeans, a faded denim work shirt and one of those blue Greek yachting caps so popular with balding American cruisers.

"He says his name is Bill and he's looking for you," she said.

Bill, I learned, owned one of the two multihulls anchored at Friendship Bay the night of the incident. He was alone aboard his boat that night and turned in early. He hadn't heard or seen anything out of the ordinary, he explained, but came to see if he could help in any way.

"Damn it, if only I'd known," he exclaimed, shaking his head. "I've got a friggin' arsenal 'board that boat. I know I could've taken him. I got a twelve-gauge pump action shotgun, a thirty-eight revolver, a big old World War II Very pistol, a police siren and flood lights mounted on my spreaders. If I smell trouble, all I got to do is reach for a gun, roll over in bed and press a button. Those goddamn lights come on and that siren wails like a bitch kitty. Jesus, I wish I'd known."

Bill even offered me a bunk on his boat. "At least let me take you out and show you my set-up," he urged. "You and your husband can't be too prepared if you're going to stay in the Caribbean. It's not like it was twenty years ago, you know."

I thanked him, declined his kind offer of lodging, and asked him to deliver a message to the Mitchell boys, whom he said he knew.

I wrote them a quick note of thanks for their help and asked to hire them to find my billfold by snorkeling between the shore and the spot where we'd anchored that night in Friendship Bay.

Bill promised not only to deliver the note, but to lead the excursion. He left in haste now, a man with a mission.

Without credit cards and identification, I had no way to get cash, short of borrowing more from the Holmans, to whom I already was indebted deeply. For a couple on a tight budget who rarely even ate a sandwich out, we'd become pretty high rollers in the last week. I made overseas calls to the States at the drop of a hat, stayed in expensive hotels, rode taxis around St. Vincent at $15 a crack and ate all my meals in restaurants.

But my expenditures were nothing compared with Jim's hospitalization at the Cyrus Clinic. Still there would be a charter flight for him back to the States, more hospitalization and a return flight to Curaçao. We still had to find crew for the sail to Curaçao, whose expenses and airfare we would pay.

Our expenses and those of the Holmans already exceeded $4,000 U.S., thanks to a man who took from us only the equivalent of $80 U.S. Still I was grateful we had enough money in reserve to get the best medical care we could for Jim, and family who cared enough to see us through.

Our dwindling savings weighed heavily in my thoughts as I asked Pat Mitchell for my bill.

"There's no bill," she replied. "You're our guest."

I protested, but she refused to accept any payment for my lodging, dinner in the patio restaurant at her family's table, breakfast and phone calls.

"Son and I are deeply troubled by what has happened," she explained. "We realize this will be a serious blight on Bequia for a very long time. You cared enough to come back to set matters straight and we're just extending to you a little island hospitality. Come see us again as a customer and a friend," she said. "You will come back for the trial, won't you?"

I assured her we would return to testify at Hunte's trial, thanked her warmly, and boarded the afternoon ferry for St. Vincent.

*   *   *

It was past hospital visiting hours when the ferry pulled into Kingstown, so I caught a cab to the Lodge, where the Holmans were waiting for me in the dining room.

"Word's reached your friends at home," said Jean passing me a stack of telegrams. "The switchboard's been hot for two days with calls for you and Jim. You're supposed to call your sister in Alexandria, your father in Annapolis, Murray Davis at *Cruising World* and Don Brown in St. Croix."

"Jim's doing much better," said Doc. "Dr. Cyrus says that if he continues making this kind of improvement, he can come home with us before the weekend."

I heard an eerie, familiar crack, and saw Jean look up from her menu and wince. I turned to find Harry Maharaj shadowing me, working over the knuckles of his left hand.

"Oh, Harry. Yes, yes they have. He's in custody. Open and shut case, Harry."

"Give me his name."

"His name? Right, his name. I don't know his name, Harry." I lied.

"I need to know his name. . . ."

"Look, Harry, the police are taking care of it. He's in jail."

"You think I can't get to him, even in jail?"

I was saved this time by the waiter, who summoned me to take a call at the switchboard. It was Don Brown, an old friend who, like Jim, had been a yacht captain for the last nine years. He'd just this season given up skippering other men's boats for a living and had moved to St. Croix in the Virgin Islands, where we had visited with him when we passed through on *Cheers* two months before.

Don's name had come immediately to mind when we talked of moving the boat west without Jim, and he's probably the only other soul to whom we would have entrusted the delivery, with or without me aboard.

Don had heard about our trouble and wanted to help me get *Cheers* to Curaçao. "I've talked to your sister Susan," he said, "and she wants to come, too."

"Jim should be well enough to fly to the States by the weekend, his father says. How soon can you get here?" I asked.

"We both can get flights on Sunday, a week from now. We'll

meet in Barbados and be in St. Vincent Sunday morning. Is there still no airstrip on Bequia?"

"No. You'll have to catch the noon ferry. Get a cab from the airport on St. Vincent to the dock, then get on the ferry *Grenadine Star.* I'll meet you at the ferry dock in Bequia. *Cheers* will be provisioned, fueled and ready to depart on Monday. The sail to Curaçao shouldn't take us more than four days, so you can be back at work the following Monday if you want to."

Then I called my sister Susan, who had planned to take two weeks off from her job at a graphics studio to cruise with us through the Grenadines. That was before the accident, but she had the time and wanted to come on the delivery.

"I'm sorry it won't be piña coladas and calypso music," I apologized, "but I sure could use your help and your company."

Susan said she had sent the charts airmail, as promised, 13 days ago, so we had to count on their arriving during the coming week. "See you Sunday in Bequia," she said, "and no, you won't pay my expenses. There's something you should know, but we didn't want to alarm you. Dad's been in the hospital again. Dr. Hochman suspected a heart attack, but it looks like it was just another attack of angina. They kept him for a few days, but he's home now, so give him a call."

Our father, at age 72, was as strong and fit as many men half his age. He retired early from a career as a U.S. attorney in Washington and moved to a modest home in Annapolis, from which he can see his 27-foot Tartan sloop in her slip.

In earlier days he was known as a racer to be reckoned with on Chesapeake Bay, and he would instill the fear of God in his crew —my mother, sister and myself—as we gybed spinnakers round the buoys and generally struggled to avoid the skipper's wrath.

But like good whiskey, he mellowed with age and when he took old *Windfall* out these days, it was usually just to putter around the bay or enter a solo race for the fun of it. His beloved mate, my mother, had passed away and his crew had moved away.

Growing up under the watchful eye of a prosecuting attorney father who without a doubt had sown some pretty wild oats in his day seemed a lifelong lesson in honesty, humility and chastity. Never had an eligible beau passed Dad's hawk-eyed scrutiny until, at the age of 23, I offered up Jim. His fondness for Jim was immediate and grew to deep affection over the years. It saddened me to think how badly Dad must have felt, confined to a hospital bed himself, to learn secondhand of our trouble and Jim's injury. I'd been so busy between the hospital and the investigation, I hadn't thought to call him.

I placed my call and after an anxious wait, the long-distance operator rang back. "You're party's on the line."

I choked up the moment I heard my father's strong, familiar voice. We both talked at once, then no one talked at all for what seemed a very long time. My eyes filled with tears.

After I assured him that Jim was going to be fine, he confided his grand plan that would ensure that the whole of the West Indies would quake in the wake of our little disaster. "I've talked to the State Department," he said. "Now write this down: Karl Danga. He's the U.S. Consul in Barbados."

"I know, Father."

"Be still and listen. His number is 63574. I've talked to Murray at *Cruising World*. He said the magazine is behind you."

"I know. I have a telegram from him."

"Are you going to listen or talk?"

"Listen."

"I called your cousin Fred at the CIA. He says you've got to call this Consul Danga and . . ."

I began the call as a 30-year-old woman, his intellectual equal, but by the time I rang off I was again his infant daughter who could say only, "Yes, Dad."

Yep, the old fire was still there. Not only was Dad going to be all right, he'd probably outlive Jim.

MONDAY, JULY 20

Seeing Jim Monday morning confirmed his professed improvement. He was eating a full breakfast when we arrived and though he was still pale and painfully thin, there was nothing wrong with his appetite.

"Dr. Cyrus says I can attend a line-up tomorrow," he said, "and he'll even throw in a wheelchair."

Dr. Cyrus entered the room, clad in a white coat and followed by his pretty, Irish-born wife.

"I must ask that when you attend the parade tomorrow, you not climb any stairs, Son," said Dr. Cyrus. "And ask the police to limit their procedure to one hour. I sincerely hope you are able to recognize the person who did this to you, young man," he said serenely. "Those prison guards are a rough bunch," he continued. "While at the general hospital where I practiced for many years, I was frequently called upon to administer care to some of the prison inmates. Many had been beaten beyond all recognition and I can assure you it was not at the hands of their fellow prisoners. The animal who committed this act belongs in a cage," he concluded blandly. "I have an idea those boys will take care of your assailant, Son."

When the doctor left the room, I phoned Superintendent Jackson and told him that Jim could attend a parade. I told him there were additional matters I wished to discuss with him and was given an appointment for 1 o'clock that same afternoon.

Then, remembering Son Mitchell's advice to leave no stone unturned, I telephoned Hudson Tannis, the minister of tourism, foreign affairs and home affairs, under whose auspices the whole of the police department falls, and was given an appointment by his secretary for 3 o'clock that same day.

I had several objectives in mind when I met with the police superintendent. Ostensibly, I wanted to make sure that the line-up would go smoothly and ask that he enter the vial of mace as evidence to underscore the significance of Hunte's red eyes.

That afternoon I met with Superintendent Jackson in his office. He was a kind, personable man who, without his gold braid cap and shoulder boards, seemed to have lost his stiff military austerity. He scheduled the line-up for one-thirty the following day, Tuesday, and would send a car to transport Jim. He eagerly accepted the mace as evidence in the case.

With those details out of the way, I broached the subjects of still greater concern to me. First, I wanted to ensure that Hunte would be held without bail, at least until my crew arrived, so I could safely remain aboard *Cheers* in Bequia until we sailed. Second, I wanted to be sure Jim and I were doing everything in our power to assist the prosecutor with the case. Third, I wanted to know on

what charges Hunte would be arraigned. And finally, I wanted to
see if the prosecutor could expedite the trial so that the case was
called before the magistrate before I sailed for Curaçao.

Whether by plan or by accident, I was my father's daughter after
all. I hadn't grown up under the thumb of a thorough, sometimes
vindictive lawyer for nothing. If Hunte went free, I was determined it wouldn't be for any shortsightedness on our part.

The mellow, middle-aged superintendent leaned forward in his
chair and placed the fingertips of both hands together.

"Both Inspector Rodriguez and I have recommended to the
magistrate that Hunte be held without bail until the preliminary
hearing. Bail usually is set for any crime short of a capital offense
—any crime short of murder. But with Mr. Holman still confined
to a hospital bed, this could develop into a capital offense at any
time, as far as the magistrate is concerned. You say you are leaving
the islands with your boat in one week?"

"Yes, next Monday."

"Then I give you my word that Hunte will be kept in custody
without bail at least until you and your boat are safely out of the
Grenadines.

"As for the trial, there is nothing I can do to have the case heard
before a prescheduled court date. The dates are set many months
in advance and there is no way to change them. Both you and Mr.
Holman will have to return for the preliminary hearing and for the
trial, and my government will pay your airfare and expenses. Plan
to hear from us in September.

"As for the charges against Mr. Hunte, I believe he will be
charged with malicious mischief."

Malicious mischief! It sounded like a kid tipping over outhouses
on Halloween night!

"What sentence would that carry if he is convicted?" I asked.

"I believe seven to fourteen years, but I'm not certain."

"Mr. Jackson, I know little about law, but I was thinking he
might be charged with armed robbery. How about assault with a
deadly weapon or attempted murder? Attempted rape?"

"Miss Hitz, as a former British colony, we still follow English
law. There are no such charges as attempted murder or attempted
rape under English law."

"So a guy can keep trying, until he gets lucky, under English
law?" I asked.

"Well, I guess you could look at it that way." he laughed. "Monica Joseph will probably be prosecuting the case," he said. "She's sharp and I can assure you she will go for the maximum sentence she can, which I think will be for charges of malicious mischief."

I was early for my 3 o'clock meeting with Hudson Tannis, so I stopped downstairs at the tourist office and picked up some travel brochures to read while I waited. As St. Vincent and the Grenadines is a newly-independent nation of more than a dozen separate islands, I was not surprised to find cruising yachtsmen the target audience for several of the bureau's colorful flyers. And there I found the tack for my conference with Hudson Tannis.

After a short wait in his outer office, I was greeted by a man of great stature with a highly-polished baritone voice. He was dressed casually in conservative gray trousers and a blue multi-pleated dress shirt, no tie. He showed me inside his large, air-conditioned office and invited me to take a seat at one of several black leather club chairs surrounding a huge coffee table.

I was beginning to doubt my humble mission was worthy of his time when he excused himself to take a call of some importance, I judged from the way he preened his voice before speaking.

"It's the president of Korea," he whispered as he held the line. "They're anxious to engage in trade with my country, and I'm visiting with him next week."

North or South Korea, I wondered, certain now that I had no business troubling such an important man seated at such an expansive, high-gloss desk. The coffee table was littered with slick North Korean trade publications featuring automobiles, mining, and travel.

When Tannis finished his phone call, he summoned his equally eloquent aide, O. S. Barrow, who shared that same, educated baritone voice with a hint of a British accent.

My mission in seeing Tannis suddenly seemed rather hairbrained but, on quick reassessment, it still seemed a good idea. I went for it.

Nolly Simmons had helped me to an extent I could never repay. I sort of fancied that Bequia's future lay in the hands of people like Nolly Simmons, Son Mitchell and Inspector Rodriguez. Despite what happened to us on Bequia, I was still very fond of the island and its people, and did not wish to see Bequia shoulder the blame for the deed of one man. I knew I would write something about the incident someday, and I looked this day to Hudson Tannis, the minister of tourism and himself a native Bequian, for an upbeat slant.

Carefully I laid my groundwork, relating briefly our mishap in Bequia. I added how beautiful we found his islands, then touched on the trouble we'd had in the Tobago Cays and other ports, adding my theory that the same few bad actors who were working over the same harbors year after year were giving the Grenadines a bad name among yachtsmen. Then I explained that I was a freelance writer and would be working up a piece on our experiences in the Grenadines. I had no desire to condemn his islands as a dangerous cruising ground, if I could only point to something constructive being done to clear the waterfront of its troublemakers. Finally, I offered what I thought would provide a workable solution to the problem.

With Nolly's prior consent, I identified him as the homegrown Sherlock Holmes who had found our assailant as well as the last dozen or so men charged with crimes on Bequia.

Then I told him about a husky fiberglass lifeboat that Nolly salvaged when it washed ashore after Hurricane Allen last year. "It's a strong and able sea boat," I explained, "which would make an ideal harbor patrol boat in Admiralty Bay. Nolly Simmons is willing to donate this boat to the island of Bequia, as well as his time in fitting it out for harbor patrol service. He will stay on without pay to oversee its use and recruit and train operators. The boat needs a small inboard diesel engine, then capital of about three thousand E.C. to begin operation. I know some of the people at a couple of the charter companies which operate in the Grenadines—Stevens Yachts and CSY—and I think they could be persuaded to donate some equipment they may already have as spares for their boats—a VHF radio, fenders, docklines, life jackets, that sort of thing.

"We think a volunteer crew can be recruited from among Bequians and visiting yachtsmen to man the patrol boat, while only one paid operator need be employed full-time under Nolly. We believe the operating capital, including one salary, can be raised from local businessmen with a vested interest in maintaining a safe waterfront."

A similar plan was successful during the past summer in Newport, Rhode Island, I told him, to stop a rash of yacht break-ins.

"I hope that by the time word of our mishap in Bequia gets out, a plan to safeguard its future visitors already will be afoot, before Bequia becomes another St. Croix, shunned by tourists ten years after a well-publicized incident of violence which involved American tourists."

"With all due respect, Miss Hitz, I think we have here an isolated incident of a nature that is not likely to be repeated now that this man is in custody. I certainly thank you for bringing it to my attention, however."

"I don't believe what happened to us is an isolated incident. Do you remember the name Carl Schuster, the American yachtsman who was murdered aboard his boat *Zig Zag* two years ago?

"That was determined to be the result of a homosexual lover's quarrel with his own crew member, I believe. Nothing could be proved."

"That's the story police put out," I said. "Schuster was murdered with a machete aboard his boat in the presence of his crew, a Grenadian named de Lisle, who hid in another cabin during the incident. A Grenada man was arrested long after the murder. Some of Schuster's documents were found among the man's belongings and de Lisle identified him as Schuster's murderer."

"You concede, then, that the murderer was a man from Grenada, not from these islands."

"The murder took place on St. Vincent—that's what people remember. Still, two years later, you don't see any cruising boats in Cumberland Bay. Think what that would mean to the economy of Bequia.

"I've read your *Visitor's Guide to St. Vincent and the Grenadines*, Mr. Tannis. Have you seen this cruising guide?" I produced my copy of Chris Doyle's *A Sailor's Guide to the Windward Islands*. "It's the one used by most cruisers, and it covers the islands from St. Lucia through Grenada. It's updated each year and is well-thought-of. Fifty-two pages—nearly one half of the text—is devoted to the anchorages of St. Vincent and the Grenadines. You can see I've underlined some of the trouble spots Doyle details: 'Cumberland Bay, where well-liked American yachtsman Carl Schuster was murdered. . . . Kingstown, whose local kids are

some of the most annoying in the Windwards . . . tough youths
. . . unsafe to leave your boat unattended . . . Petit Martinique,
the center of smuggling trade. . . .' We can add to those Friendship Bay and the Tobago Cays. That doesn't leave many safe ports.

"I'm not talking just about offenses in which yachtsmen are the
victims. I can name you four women—three Americans and one
Canadian—living on Bequia's waterfront who have been sexually
assaulted and/or robbed in the last six months. Police don't have a
suspect, but Nolly is convinced the crimes were not committed by
the same man."

"Then why doesn't your friend do something about it if he
knows who did it?"

"He's an architect, not a police officer. That's why this harbor
patrol is a good idea. It would give police live communication with
the waterfront, transportation, and the means to make an arrest."

"Miss Hitz, I can appreciate what you're saying. I'm from Bequia myself. I've always thought St. Vincent and the Grenadines
were the closest thing to heaven. But attitudes are changing. Fifteen years ago no one locked up. Cinema and television are part
of the problem with young people. They see it's so easy to make a
few dollars through crime."

"Do you mind if I make some notes?"

"Please do. Young people these days have no control at all.
Tourists dress to whet peoples' imaginations; some do not seem to
understand that some of us get ideas into our heads at the way
they dress."

"Do you agree, then, that some sort of harbor patrol would help
keep these youths under control?"

"Yes. This year's budget is five hundred E.C. for a boat from
Cannouan to clear out the Tobago Cays. Yachtsmen who are
litterbugs, most of them, throw their garbage everywhere. Yachtsmen are not careful about fires ashore. They are spoiling the very
thing that attracts them. I was in Tobago Cays just last month. In
that clear water I saw ham cans and beer bottles everywhere."

"Litter may be a problem, but it's not the problem I came here
today to talk to you about. What can I tell cruisers who wish to
visit your islands?"

"Tell them to stay away from the bad places," said Tannis.

"Exactly right," underscored Mr. Barrow, "exactly right."

"Tell them don't go to Kingstown," continued the minister of tourism. "Don't anchor in Friendship Bay. There have been four incidents there; it's too isolated. If you go there, don't anchor overnight. Leave by six p.m. If you go to the Tobago Cays or to Cumberland Bay, leave by six p.m. Anywhere you go, haul your dinghy out at night and chain it somewhere on deck. Hide your outboard below for the night."

"That may be good advice," I said. "but it doesn't really address the problem."

"Remove the temptation and you solve the problem." Mr. Tannis rose to his feet, indicating our interview had reached its end.

"As long as any person has more than another person," I said gathering my things, "there will be temptation."

"Miss Hitz, thank you for bringing this matter to my attention."

I left his office feeling I had the makings of a great article: "Yachtsmen, Litterbugs of the Grenadines." or "Minister of Tourism Says, 'Stay Away from our Harbors.'"

*   *   *

I caught a taxi from police headquarters to the hospital. There, in Jim's room, I met Barbados' chief surgeon, Dr. Jordan. At Dr. Cyrus' request he had flown to St. Vincent to examine Jim. He was a handsome black physician of about 45, with a distinguished mustache, of medium height and strongly built. After listening to Jim's chest he placed his stethoscope in his black bag and began a tale of bizarre coincidence. I realized before he finished that he was the man I once suspected was Jim's assailant, for he was the only man we'd seen on shore the night of the incident.

"I was in Bequia the weekend of July 11," he said. "My young son and I were fishing from the pier at Friendship Bay Hotel until just after dark. I guess it was about eight o'clock when we went on home. I wish I'd known. By the time I heard what had happened that night, you had already been treated at the clinic in Bequia. and were on your way to St. Vincent. It didn't occur to me at the time that you would be sent to the general hospital instead of here."

He was the final missing piece. Now the puzzle was complete.

When he left, Dr. Cyrus announced that Jim could be released on Wednesday, July 22, two days hence, to fly with his parents to the States. His father reserved a bed for him at St. Joseph's Hospital in New Jersey, while his mother tried to arrange flights. But Carnival was in full swing now in Barbados, through which all flights to and from St. Vincent must pass, and all seats were booked for the next two weeks. Finally, a private plane was booked for a charter flight to Barbados, connecting there with a regularly-scheduled flight to New York. The airline was alerted that one of the three passengers was a convalescent and would require special boarding and seating arrangements.

My work was finished. There remained only for Jim to identify his attacker on Tuesday and the case would be out of our hands until the trial.

Tuesday, July 21

Jim was shaved and dressed early, feeling more than a little apprehensive about the line-up. "What if I can't remember his face?" he asked, searching the bureau drawer for a belt.

"You'll remember," I assured him.

"But what if I make a mistake?" He tugged at his trousers, but they only slipped off his emaciated hips.

"You won't make a mistake. It's not just the facial features you'll recognize, or even his build. There's something about him and you'll feel it at once, just as I did. You'll know immediately which one it is."

Then in silence we sat together on the edge of his bed waiting for the police car to arrive.

At 1:25 the phone rang in Jim's hospital room. It was Superintendent Jackson.

"We won't be needing Mr. Holman's identification," he told me.

"But he's willing to go," I insisted. "He's dressed and ready."

"No. We've got a positive ID from you and that's enough. We don't want the defense attorney to suggest to the jury that the police doubted your ID."

"I can understand that, but I feel confident Jim can pick him out of a line-up now, today. If you ask him to do so two months from now, when we return from the trial, without his having seen

the man since that night on our boat, I'm not sure he could identify him then."

"He won't be asked to identify him at a later date."

"You're sure?"

"I'm sure."

"Alright then, good-bye."

So adamant was Superintendent Jackson that Jim attend a line-
up only the day before, I couldn't accept his abrupt change of
sentiment without wondering if he had some ulterior motive.

It was in these few minutes before the scheduled parade that the
superintendent would have been summoning Hunte and a handful of look-alikes for the line-up. Why did he wait until the final
moment before calling it off? Then I thought of Dr. Cyrus' words:
"Those guards are a rough bunch. I can assure you they will take
care of your friend."

Maybe Hunte wasn't presentable. He was due to arrive in St.
Vincent yesterday. Perhaps Jackson was hiding the fact that Hunte
had been worked over by the guards. It was a tantalizing prospect
to ponder.

*   *   *

Wednesday morning I rode with Jim and his parents to the airport where we said a very difficult good-bye. Jim handed me two
envelopes.

"This one is for Don," he said. "I've written him some details
about the engine and navigation along the Venezuelan coast.
"This one's for you—sixteen hundred in cash for boat expenses,
which I was able to draw from the bank here with my credit card.
Have a safe trip and don't forget to call as soon as you get to
Curaçao. Be careful in Bequia and promise me you'll lock yourself
in the boat each night.

"Speedy recovery and hurry back, darling."

I boarded the schooner *Friendship Rose* for the final ride to
rejoin *Cheers* in Bequia. As the peaks of St. Vincent fell astern, I
never looked back.

CHAPTER TEN

WEDNESDAY, JULY 22

——————————————— The decks of *Friendship Rose* as usual were thronged with passengers carrying heavy burdens of fruit from the market, sacks of flour and rice, and burlap bags that bulged with clothing. Whereas once I thrilled to every grunt as deckhands swayed on the manila halyards, sending heavy folds of patched canvas aloft, the trip to Bequia, after five crossings of the five-mile cut, had become mundane. I paid little attention to either the working of the vessel or the all-too familiar scenery.

I was longing to be on my own boat once more, for though I was alone in an alien part of the world, the security of home bobbed at the end of the day's run. I took a seat in the back of the crowded passenger section and began scribbling a work list to get *Cheers* in shape for the voyage: get charts, tune rig, check stern tube, bleed fuel line, scrub waterline and propeller, pick up staysail and Walker log, hide cash in safe, do laundry, fill fuel and water tanks, meet crew, stow dinghy, grease steering vane, buy fresh batteries for RDF, get weather report.

The *Friendship Rose* pulled into Bequia at 2:30 Wednesday afternoon and I was one of the last passengers to step ashore. At Frangipani I again inquired about the long-awaited package of charts and there found a postal slip directing me to the post office which adjoins the police station. I presented the slip to a cheerful young woman behind the wood counter.

"*Cheers*," she read. "So, you're the one. I wish I could have helped. I live over there, in Friendship Bay. Soon as I heard what happened I thought it was Little Boy—Calvin Hunte—who did it."

"Why did you think he did it?" I asked.

"He's always in trouble—always cheating people out of money or stealing it. Soon as this happens, Little Boy disappears, he goes and hides. I told police I thought he did it, but they wouldn't listen."

"Who did you tell this to?"

"That Sergeant Allen," she whispered contemptuously. She walked over to the door, stopped and turned. "He was standing right here. I told him Monday morning after it happened. I re-member 'cause it was the first day I was back to work after the weekend and I was waiting to tell him what I knew.

"Sunday Little Boy just disappears; even his family say they don't know where he is. He was seen hiding out in an abandoned house in Friendship Bay looking real bad."

"Can you tell me where this house is?"

"It's Miss Jane's house. I could show you better."

"What's her last name?"

"I don't remember. It's some Polish-sounding name, but folks just call her Miss Jane. She's South African and only spends va-cations over at her house. She's away now and that's why Little Boy could hide there."

"And what's your name?"

"Antoinette Cozier."

"Thank you, Antoinette, for trying to help. Maybe this infor-mation will help me to get my wallet back," I added, crossing the threshold to the police station.

"Wait a minute, Mrs. Cheers. Don't you want your package?"

"Almost forgot!"

I asked at the front desk for Inspector Rodriguez. He was out, so I left a written message for him to find me at the Frangipani.

It was 3 p.m. when I reached the Frangipani, where I borrowed a paring knife from the bartender and slipped open the cardboard box. Inside were two dozen folded charts that had launched this adventure.

I unfolded a small-scale coastal chart covering the waters between Bequia and Curaçao, including the northern coast and off-lying islands of Venezuela. The rhumb line course to Curaçao was about 265°, almost due west. With the easterly tradewinds on our stern and the help of a ½ to a 1½-knot current setting us toward the west-northwest, the trip should be fast and comfortable.

Three obstacles lay on or perilously close to our route, and it was about these island groups that Jim had penned the note of caution to Don.

The first was Isla la Orchila, site of a Venezuelan military prison, whose surrounding waters are restricted for a distance of 12 miles in all directions. Yachts passing too close to Orchila have been fired upon by night, and taken into custody by day, so we would give Orchila a wide berth.

Next were Islas Los Roques, an archipelago of 60 low-lying sandy cays sprinkled over 350 square miles of sea. For the cruiser with time to stop and explore, Los Roques is an alluring playground of myriad reefs and shoals, teeming with underwater life. But for the cruiser making his way west in their vicinity, Los Roques is a graveyard of wrecks, to be avoided at all cost. We would deviate course, if necessary, to pass well north of Los Roques.

The final obstacle in our path was a pair of parenthesis-shaped islands called Los Aves, or the bird islands. I knew little about them, except that they were low-lying, uninhabited and uninviting.

Three thirty and no word from Inspector Rodriguez, so I unfolded a large-scale chart of the Aves Islands, which, on closer examination, appeared to be coral atolls, more typical of the South Pacific than the Caribbean. Spread over 150 square miles of sea, their eastern shores each were guarded by a ten-mile submerged fringing reef, with only a sprinkling of coral islets defining their western extremities.

At 4:30 I folded up my charts and was about to row out to *Cheers* when the inspector found me at the Frangipani.

"I learned about a possible hide-out of Hunte's," I said. Then I asked if he would search the house of Miss Jane.

"I think it's too late," he said. "If he left any evidence there, he'd have destroyed it by now. He'd have gone straight there from the ferry."

"What ferry?"

"The *Rose* I guess. Didn't you see him?"

"Who? Hunte? What are you saying?"

"Hunte's back on Bequia. I guess he followed you on the *Rose*. I thought that's why you called me here—I thought you knew."

I sunk into my seat, too stunned to speak.

"I couldn't believe it myself," he said. "Four people have come to the station asking what Hunte's doing out. Two of my officers saw him get off the afternoon ferry."

"I can't believe that's true. Superintendent Jackson gave me his word just two days ago that Hunte would be held without bail until I left on my boat. Do you think Hunte escaped?"

"I think he's out on bail."

"Doesn't Jackson have the authority to hold him?"

"Should have. That was his opinion and that was mine: no bail. You heard me."

"Then there must be some mistake. Besides, wouldn't Superintendant Jackson tell you if he was setting Hunte free?"

"He should have," he shrugged.

I glanced at my watch. "It's after four. I want to confirm this with Superintendant Jackson before he goes home. Will you try to find out positively whether Hunte's on this island or not? I'll wait here. Please call me as soon as you know something."

Twenty minutes later I had Superintendant Jackson on the line. He was astounded at the rumor and assured me it couldn't be true.

"Hunte was transferred here only Monday," he stressed. "Today is Wednesday. Things just don't happen that fast around here. The magistrate would have to call the case, then he'd have to overrule my objection to bail, then he'd have to set bail. Hunte would have to find someone who wanted to see him free bad enough to come up with the cash. They would have to appear before the magistrate, pay the bail and return on a ferry. Even if that could be done in two days, which it can't, I would have been told, which I haven't. No, Miss Hitz, I can assure you, Calvin Hunte is still in prison."

"I want to believe that's true," I told him, "But according to the inspector, four people say they've seen him on Bequia this very afternoon. Is Hunte confined to a cell in that same prison compound where I visited you on Monday?"

"Yes."

"Would you please do me the favor of sending one of your men down to his cell to see if he's there? You see, I'm alone now and I'm afraid to stay on my boat if Hunte's free. I'd like to know before dark if he's on this island."

"Very well. If it will make you rest easier," he said, "I will check and call you back."

Feeling a little foolish for bothering him, I thanked him and waited. Of course he would have been consulted before the magistrate set bail.

At 5 p.m. Pat Mitchell summoned me to the phone.

"Superintendent Jackson has left for the countryside," said the voice of a subordinate. "He told me to tell you that the prisoner you asked about has been released."

"But how?" I asked. "Who bailed him?"

"I don't know anything about it, Ma'am. I'm just following Mr. Jackson's orders."

"What do you mean, 'he's gone to the countryside?' Does that mean Mr. Jackson has gone home for the evening or away for a few days?"

"I don't know, Ma'am. He only said to tell you he's gone to the countryside."

"It's true, then," sighed Pat Mitchell when I hung up the phone. "Well, I can't say I'm surprised."

"I'm very surprised. I went to a lot of trouble to see that the right man was apprehended. Then I followed through with meetings with Jackson and Hudson Tannis, just as Son suggested. They only held him there two days, Pat. Two days and he's free again. Jackson and Rodriguez weren't even told he was released."

"Someone must have wanted him out very badly. Someone with money and influence," she said. "But I don't think you have anything to worry about," she consoled me. "I doubt very much he'd try to harm you."

"I know very well what that man is capable of doing," I snapped.

"Aren't you overreacting, just a little, Betsy?" she asked.

I didn't answer. Maybe she was right. I tried to swallow my outrage . . . and my fear.

Nolly Simmons would know what to do. Though several people on Bequia had helped me a great deal, there was no one except for Nolly I felt I could call on the way you would a trusted friend. The rest maintained a comfortable distance without becoming in any way involved and I didn't wish to impose on them. Yes, Nolly would know what to do. If I was overreacting he would tell me, and if I was in real danger he would sense that, too.

I dialed a number Nolly had given me and spoke with his brother, Mac. He would tell Nolly to find me at the Frangipani when he returned.

The phone rang and again it was for me.

"I can see you're going to have a busy night," whispered Pat. "Feel free to use our phone. Just keep a record of your calls." She handed me the receiver and left.

"Yes, it's true," said Inspector Rodriguez. "Hunte's back on Bequia."

"Do you know who bailed him?" I asked.

"I shouldn't tell you this, but it was Father Adams. He was seen in town with Hunte's father over the weekend trying to get up bail money. He knows the magistrate and he can get results fast."

"And what am I supposed to do now that Hunte's free?"

"When are you sailing?"

"My crew arrives on Sunday, four days from now. We planned to leave on Monday."

"Well, I wouldn't worry. I don't think he'd try to harm you again."

"I'm the only witness. What makes you think he's not going to come for me when he knows I'm alone on the boat?"

"He'd be stupid to try it."

"He'd be stupid *not* to."

"I really don't think you have anything to worry about."

"How can you say that? No one thought such a thing could ever happen on Bequia. It did. Couldn't have been a Bequia man, they said. It was. 'He won't harm me?' Well, I'm not going to stay on that boat just to prove you wrong."

"I'm sorry," he said, "but there's nothing I can do. It's out of my hands."

"It's out of your hands, is it? Well you just lost your only witness," I said and hung up.

I was now more angry than frightened. I wanted to be alone to think, but there was no place to go. It was dark now and the last place I wanted to be alone was on *Cheers*.

Four days to wait for Don and Susan. Even if I stayed ashore and moved to a different hotel room each night, I couldn't feel safe. Without the mace, which I'd given to Superintendent Jackson, I had only the gun, which I still carried in my purse. But I was in no condition to make split-second decisions with a loaded gun.

Then I found a slip of paper Doc had given me before he left: Karl Danga, U.S. Consul 63574, the same name my father had given me. Brian McNamara at the U.S. Consulate in Barbados had told Jim's father to have me call him if I had any further problems. I figured this qualified and asked the overseas operator to connect me.

It was after working hours, and most of the consulate staff had gone home, so I spoke with Nick Robertson. He seemed genuinely concerned, but felt that any intervention by the consulate would probably do more harm than good by ruffling feathers of St. Vincent officialdom. I had to agree.

"If I were you," he warned, "I'd get off that island as quickly and quietly as possible. Fly to Barbados," he advised.

"I don't want to leave my boat unattended here," I said. "And besides, all flights to Barbados are booked until the end of Carnival next week."

"Oh, right," he said. "Then why don't you sail your boat to Barbados?"

"I'm trying to get west," I explained, "out of the hurricane belt. Barbados is a hundred-mile beat eastward, the wrong direction. The harbor is poorly protected and it's hurricane season."

"I want to help you," he assured me, "but I just don't know what to tell you. If you're really worried, and it sounds like you have plenty of reason to be, get off that island until your crew arrives, or stay well hidden on Bequia. I wouldn't go near your boat again. Please call us again when your crew arrives. In the meantime, I'll talk this over with the consul and get back to you. If you leave the island, let us know where you are."

I was glad I'd called. It was comforting just to hear another American's voice, and I felt that if something did happen to me, at least the consul might order an investigation. One thing was clear: I had to get off the island and not come back. I could not leave tonight, so I asked Pat for a hotel room, "This time as a paying customer," I insisted.

Tomorrow morning I could get underway alone for nearby Young Island, just off the southern tip of St. Vincent, where I could anchor and wait for my crew. My sister had to work until the weekend, but maybe Don Brown could come on ahead and the two of us could take *Cheers* to Curaçao. I phoned Don in St. Croix, but he wasn't home. I phoned the airlines, but all flights from the Virgin Islands were booked through Sunday, the day of his reservation.

Then I remembered all the loose ends. Our taffrail log was ashore at Ken Walker's machine shop and Nolly's father, Lincoln Simmons, was making a new clew for the staysail. I could pick up the sail as it was and manage with just the mainsail and flying jib for the sail to Curaçao, but Ken Walker was off the island until Saturday and the broken log was locked in his shop. The taffrail log would accurately measure our speed and distance run, and I could not leave it behind.

I'd been gathering names and phone numbers for more than a week and among them was Magistrate Nolan Jacobs' home number. I wondered why he had overruled Superintendent Jackson's objection to bail and also wanted to hear from the horse's mouth who had bailed Hunte and at what price. It was 8 o'clock when I spoke with a very irritated Magistrate Jacobs.

"The case was reviewed this morning," he said. "If the police do not come to court to object to bail, there is nothing we can do."

"I am concerned for my safety as the only witness," I explained.

"Call us in the morning. Good evening, Madam," he said and hung up.

At 9 p.m. Nolly found me. "I came as soon as I heard," he said. "You asked me once why I didn't pursue a career in law enforcement. Do you understand now that you've seen how these fuckers work?"

"Nolly, who do you think bailed him?" I asked.

"Father Adams," he said.

"The justice of the peace?"

"That's the one. He's been getting Hunte off for years."

"But why? Is he such a bleeding heart liberal that he doesn't care who Hunte hurts next?"

"A bleeding heart? I don't know," Nolly laughed. "The good fatha likes to pork young boys."

"But he's an Episcopal *minister*," I exclaimed.

"Minister, lawman and head of the school."

"Does he have so much money he can just throw it away on guys like Hunte?"

"Seems to. Hunte's basically a coward," he said. "He's in big trouble and my guess is he'll run rather than come for you. The magistrate made it easy enough for him to jump bail. I think he'll get on a boat and get off the island."

"Is he bound by law to remain on Bequia until the trial?"

Nolly seemed preoccupied with something at the bar and didn't reply.

"Nolly, can he leave the island without violating bail?"

"He's free to travel anywhere in the Grenadines," he said, staring at the bar. "He just has to return to Bequia on the appointed trial date.

"Stay here," he said. "I'll get us a drink. Don't turn around."

"What's up?" I asked when he returned.

"Hunte's brother is over there at the bar. The guy in the red shirt."

"Is he a troublemaker, too?" I asked.

"No. But he doesn't come here much. It's funny he should turn up tonight. I hope it's just coincidence."

I slumped down in my chair.

"Well, about all I can do is keep an eye on Hunte till you leave. You're not going to stay on the boat, are you?"

"No, I've taken a room here for the night."

"I hope you got a different room this time."

"Yes."

"Good. And I'm glad you called the American Consul. It's time someone told them what's going on down here. They're there to look after the interests of Americans in the Caribbean and it's their duty to help you. You shouldn't have to fly to Barbados to talk to them; they should send someone here to talk with you. If your case isn't reason enough, I'll give you details of half a dozen others involving Americans I've seen get a shafting here. Rodriguez could tell them plenty, too."

"You'd talk to someone from the American Consulate?"

"If you can get someone to come here, sure I'll talk to them. Have you told Jim that Hunte's out?"

"Not yet. He's still in the air on his way home. His flight doesn't arrive in New York until midnight. I know this will upset him and he's supposed to go into the hospital, maybe have more surgery. I'll call his parents in the morning and let them decide whether or not to tell Jim."

Nolly walked me to my room in a secluded guest wing of the hotel, behind the main building. He entered first and searched the room. Then he stepped outside, had me lock the door and he tried to get in.

"You'll be all right tonight," he consoled me. Then he walked up the hill to his house.

THURSDAY, JULY 23

Again I was unable to sleep that night, only dozing off after the sun came up.

Later that morning I spoke with Jim's mother in New Jersey.

"We didn't get home until two a.m.," she yawned. "Bob gave Jim the choice of going directly to the hospital or coming home with us for the night and seeing the thoracic surgeon today in his office. He's right here. I'll put him on."

Jim listened while I explained that Calvin Hunte was free and back on Bequia. He was worried and angry.

"Betsy, when will you realize that they're not playing by your rules? You're Whitey, you're a woman and you're an off-islander —that's three strikes against you from the start. When will you realize we don't count with them? Hunte's never going to answer for this, so just do what they want and get off that island before you wind up with a machete in *your* chest."

"Please don't worry, Jim. I'm going to take *Cheers* to St. Vincent today, to Young Island, where I can wait for Don and Susan. Only Nolly knows I'm leaving and where I'm going. When I get there I'm going to call the American Consul and try to get someone to come and talk to me."

"I don't want you to be on that boat alone for one night. If he wants to get you, he can find you in St. Vincent or anywhere else. I want you to get on the ferry today and get off that island. Go to St. Vincent, to Villa Lodge. Tell the Brisbanes what's happened, get a room there and wait. I'll contact Don and Susan and see if they can come on the next available flight; maybe there'll be a cancellation. I don't want you getting underway alone and I don't want you picking up crew in Bequia. Boats are replaceable, but I'll never get over it if you're harmed. Now promise me you'll be on the next ferry to St. Vincent."

"It's after eleven o'clock here. I already missed the morning ferry and there isn't another until tomorrow morning. I can be anchored at Young Island with *Cheers* this afternoon."

"I want you to stay in a different hotel room on Bequia tonight, and take that ferry tomorrow morning. Now promise me you'll be on that ferry."

"I promise," I said reluctantly.

"And don't go running off on any more harebrained escapades. No more cops and robbers, understand?"

"Okay."

"I'm going to phone you at Villa Lodge tomorrow night and you'd better be there."

"I'll be there, but you should be in the hospital."

"I'm not going anywhere until I know you're safe."

I hung up, feeling guilty for interfering with Jim's medical program, but I knew from the tone of his voice there was no point in arguing.

The sun was nearly overhead and a gentle breeze promised a good day to air out the boat. Admiralty Bay was swarming with dinghy traffic, so I wasn't worried about returning to *Cheers* by day. At Bequia Slip, I picked up two sacks of clean laundry and rowed out to *Cheers*, where I spent the rest of the day readying the boat for the trip west.

The cabin smelled dank and musty. A furry blanket of blue-gray mold covered all the oiled wood surfaces of the cabin; sooty black mold speckled our books; everything leather was enveloped in mossy green fur. The usually shiny brass looked more like dull pewter and the head was blocked with salt crystals from disuse.

It was satisfying to have a long list of mindless chores and most of all, to be back aboard *Cheers*, preparing to leave behind this chapter of our lives. I scrubbed the woodwork with a vengeance, pushing from my mind all but the most rudimentary thoughts about my immediate task.

I loosened the drawstring on the laundry bag and emptied the laundered cushion covers onto the forward bunk. The slipcovers were clean all right. I'd sewn them only six months before, and they now were nearly threadbare from the laundress' diligent efforts to remove the blood stains, without success. But anything was better than bare foam, so I dressed the cushions and flipped over the symmetrical ones to hide the stains. The other I wrapped in sheets.

Then I pulled on a face mask, snorkel and fins and scrubbed the long green tresses of algae from the propeller and wiped the scum from the waterline. I tuned the rig, checked the batteries and swabbed the deck. Doing these chores, which were routinely Jim's, I realized how much I missed him.

I was enjoying a wonderfully mindless day until evening when, as I was about to row ashore, a sailing dinghy approached carrying Nolly Simmons and Inspector Rodriguez. Nolly tacked the small double-ender with skill, then shot up into the wind and coasted alongside *Cheers.*

"Just a social call," said Nolly.

I took his painter. "Please, come aboard," I invited.

The inspector apologized right away for our misunderstanding over the phone, and I for my short fuse.

I mixed a round of drinks and we talked well into the evening. I always had been careful never to use Nolly's name in the presence of the inspector. As far as anyone knew, I believed Rodriguez to be the one who apprehended Hunte. This was the first time I'd shared their company together, and in the privacy of the dark cockpit, away from the eyes and ears of the waterfront, there no longer was reason to conceal Nolly's involvement in this case and others. The pretense was over.

They spoke openly and candidly not only about this case, but about a long history of police corruption in the past. I listened attentively as Rodriguez spoke about his 16 years with the force in St. Vincent, his mission to quell the "revolution" on Union Island last year, and impressions of his nine weeks on Bequia.

Stories flew as they compared perspectives on a group of four undercover agents who for at least two years conducted raids on yachts and shoreside residents—mostly American expatriates—living on Bequia. According to them, it was widely known that CID men canvassed yachts and homes of foreigners on the pretext of checking passports, visas and cruising permits, while planting drugs on the unsuspecting travellers. Upon "discovering" the drugs, the agents would typically demand on-the-spot payoffs of $300 or more, or sexual cooperation from women, threatening their victims with exposure and stiff fines if convicted. Their innocent victims, some of whom had business interests at stake, either paid them off, fled Bequia in fear, or stayed to fight charges. Those who stayed found their sworn affidavits mysteriously disappeared from the police files.

"And you say most of their victims were Americans?" I asked.

"Americans and Canadians," said Nolly.

"If I tell this to the American Consul, will either of you back me up?"

They looked at each other without speaking.

"I will," said Nolly.

"My days on the force are numbered," said the Inspector.

FRIDAY, JULY 24

At 11 o'clock I boarded the *Grenadine Star* for St. Vincent. Just as the battleship-gray landing craft was idling away from the pier, I spotted Nolly making his way through the crowd toward the *Star*. I hurried to the rail. He leaned over the bulwarks and whispered to me. "You can relax. Hunte left this morning for Tobago Cays."

"I can't turn back now. I promised Jim I'd be in St. Vincent tonight. Thank you, Nolly."

He evaporated into the crowd.

On the passage to St. Vincent I thought of our experiences two weeks before in the Tobago Cays and chilled at the thought of unwary cruisers stumbling into the lair of not only the unsavory pair we'd encountered there, but a potentially-lethal band that now included Hunte.

Shortly after noon, I checked into a new room at the Villa

Lodge. If I was a menace with a loaded gun, I was only a little less dangerous with a telephone and plenty of time on my hands. In the privacy of my room, I placed a call to the consul in Barbados.

"Mr. Danga is in a meeting now," said the strong male voice, "but I'm Ronald Kramer, the vice consul. How can I help you?"

He knew nothing about the incident, so I retraced the case briefly.

"But if you're off the island," he observed, "it doesn't seem like you're in any immediate danger."

I had to agree he was right, but said that I wished to have an audience with a representative from the consulate, here in St. Vincent, to discuss this and other incidents of police corruption involving American visitors to the Grenadines. I outlined some examples and offered to provide names, details and witnesses who would corroborate my information.

He listened attentively and said he would talk it over with Karl Danga, who would call me back.

I found the number for Caribbean Sailing Yachts (CSY) in the St. Vincent phone directory and advised Alan Hooper of the potential danger in the Tobago Cays. He was grateful for the information and said he would pass it on to his charterers in person or by VHF radio.

"There's someone here in my office you should talk to," he said, passing the phone to Chris Doyle, author of *A Sailor's Guide to the Windward Islands*.

"We're updating the guide all the time," said Chris, "and I want to be able to tell cruisers about the places to avoid. Problem is, the trouble spots are beginning to outnumber the safe ones in the Windwards. Nolly Simmons is a personal friend of mine. I don't even talk to the police anymore because they do and know nothing. The Grenadines need some sort of local patrol to keep the harbors safe for yachtsmen. Son Mitchell can see this, but the rest of the reps in Parliament are too stupid to realize just how much revenue comes to the Grenadines from yachting. I'll be in Bequia next week. I'll talk to Nolly and find out what's going on in Friendship Bay and Tobago Cays."

After lunch Consul Karl Danga returned my call.

"I think you should understand that proceedings in the Caribbean are very slow by American standards. Let me also assure you that no prejudice exists toward you in this matter. I have called Police Commissioner Jackson and advised him of your problem. He promised me that he would call you before he goes home this evening.

"Now if you're not satisfied with the way the case is being handled, I would suggest you engage an international attorney to look after your interests in this matter. I can give you the names of several: There's Sir Frederick Philips of Philips and Philips, and a Mr. Hughes . . ."

"Thank you, Mr. Danga, but this is a criminal case, not a civil one, and I don't wish to go to the expense of hiring an international lawyer to carry out the work that should be that of the prosecuting attorney."

Like my meeting with Hudson Tannis, much was said, but I got nowhere. The American consul was courteous and reassuring in a vague sort of way, but clearly he was not interested in digging any deeper into my case or others involving Americans whose rights had been violated in Bequia. Reluctantly, but without argument, I gave up.

When by 4:30 Police Commissioner Jackson had not called, I got his number from the switchboard operator and called him, hoping to catch him before he went home for the weekend. The police commissioner was the cousin of Superintendent Jackson and his superior.

When I finally got the police commissioner on the line and told him who I was, he blew up. "Your embassy told me about your charges of police misconduct," he shouted. "What are you? Some kind of spy? I said I would call you if I learned anything. Now what do you want?"

"I want to know why Calvin Hunte was released despite Superintendent Jackson's assurances to me that he would be held without bail."

"He could not possibly have assured you of any such thing," he declared.

"He did. I want to know why Hunte was released. I want to know when the trial will be held and whom I should contact about returning for the trial."

"I have another call," he interrupted.

"Will you call me back?"

"Yes," he agreed reluctantly.

Police Commissioner Jackson called again at 6 p.m. "The magistrate decided to set bail after he learned that Hunte's victim was released from the hospital."

"Hunte was released and on a ferry to Bequia within an hour of the victim's leaving the hospital."

"I can't help that. The trial will be in early October. Probably October 6. The preliminary hearing in Bequia will be one week before that. My government will advise you of the exact date and will send both of you plane tickets."

"With whom should I speak about the arrangements?"

"I give you my personal assurance it will be done."

"With whom should I leave my Curaçao address and itinerary?"

"With me."

I gave him our address in Curaçao, then added, "We will stay in Curaçao for three months and will leave the Caribbean in November for the Panama Canal and South Pacific. If the trial takes place before then, we will return to testify. But after November we will be at sea and there will be no way to communicate with us."

"You will hear from me," he assured me.

*　　　*　　　*

"I'm afraid I've made a real mess of things here," I told Jim when he telephoned me that night. "I told the vice consul those things in confidence, hoping he would organize an investigation, but instead he or the consul repeated them to the police commissioner. Now Jackson thinks I'm some kind of subversive spy, and it's Jackson we have to deal with from here out."

"This is never going to come to trial," Jim said, "so don't worry about it. I reached Don and Susan. They're both on their way to Barbados now on separate flights," he said. "Expect them to meet you at the Lodge tomorrow morning."

"Thanks. I'll call you when we get to Curaçao. It shouldn't take more than four days. Now please go to the hospital."

"I'll see the doctor tomorrow."

"You belong in a hospital."

"I'll be waiting for your call from Curaçao."

Part Three

The night is clear, windless, warm. A ceiling of stars shines overhead and a heavy blanket of dew has settled on the pale blue deck of the Australian ketch. Cabin lights on other yachts anchored nearby in Spanish Water have long been extinguished, and only *Walu* is brightly lit as the four of us sit in the corners of the snug center cockpit, recounting lost times.

"Now I've heard it all," declared Richard with quiet indignation. "I don't suppose Calvin Hunte's been convicted."

I shook my head. "There's been no trial."

"And never will be," added Jim.

"I'm not so sure," I said. "I've been writing letters—two to Police Commissioner Jackson, two to Inspector Rodriguez, one to Son Mitchell—pressing them to convene the trial date so Jim and I can return to testify."

"And?"

"They haven't replied."

"Welcome to the Third World." Richard turned to Jim. "I'm with you, Mate, sounds like a bloody whitewash to me. Three previous offenses, no convictions. Betsy, what makes you think Hunte's going to answer in court this time?"

"Whitewash or not," said Robyn, "why testify? Why go back to Bequia at all? Haven't you two been through enough already? Why don't you just put this behind you and get on with your own lives?"

"Can't do it, Robyn," I sighed. "Until Hunte is behind bars where he belongs, he *lives* in our forward cabin, in my mind anyway. And what about the next cruiser who stumbles in his path? I lie awake some nights, wondering, *who's next?*

The crescent moon slipped behind *Walu's* stern.

"More coffee?" offered Robyn.

"Thanks, no," said Jim. "Let's call it a night. Tomorrow morning we grind and glass the rudder."

Early the next morning I rowed out to *Walu*.

Robyn was diapering Joelle when I coasted alongside *Walu*.

"Jim's had an accident. He was fairing the rudder when the grinder slipped and caught him in the thigh. Robyn, you were a nurse. Think you could stitch him up?"

"Let's have a look."

Robyn tucked Joelle in a wicker basket and passed her down to me. Then Richard and Robyn climbed in my inflatable and I rowed briskly for shore.

"The grinder cut right through his coveralls and gave him a nasty gash just above the right knee. He won't go to a doctor. Says he's sworn off them. He tried to con me into suturing the wound and when I refused, he insisted on doing it himself."

"I'm pretty rusty," confessed Robyn. "It's been, what, Rich? Four years since I sutured a wound? Betsy, you're looking at my last patient."

Richard gripped his stomach and grimmaced.

We tied up the dinghy, scurried up the ladder and found Jim stretched out on the settee, his medical supplies laid out on the table beside him, sipping an iced rum and studying the photographs in *First Aid Afloat*.

Richard and I took up posts seated on the galley counter while Robyn and Jim practiced suturing the upholstery.

"This calls for a tot of rum, don't you think?" asked Richard. He reached for the open bottle of navy rum. "Robyn's a pro," he consoled his friend. "Why, I remember the time she stitched my thumb when I nearly severed it clean off in the middle of the Indian Ocean. Terrible wound, terrible wound, but I hardly felt a thing."

"Richard!" Robyn glowered. "Why you hypocritical coward! Your thumb took four tiny stitches and you fainted!"

Richard knocked back his spot of rum. "Yup, Mate. It's all part of life's rich pageant."

"So tell us, Betsy," said Robyn, drawing the skin together. "When Jim flew to the States to recuperate, you returned to Bequia, found the attacker was free and then fled to St. Vincent. Hurricane season was on and you had to get *Cheers* west."

"Ah, yes, the trip to Curaçao." I filled our four glasses. "Even Jim hasn't heard the entire story in detail. Two weeks after the stabbing my crew met me in St. Vincent . . ."

CHAPTER ELEVEN

SATURDAY, JULY 25

——————————————————— I rose from the breakfast table at the sound of my sister's voice and hurried to the lobby of the Villa Lodge, where Susan was rummaging through her udder-size shoulderbag for local currency with which to pay the cab fare, while Don Brown removed their duffles from the trunk.

"Boobah!" she exclaimed, giving me a gruff bear hug.

The dreaded childhood name jolted me back 25 years to my apprenticeship under the thumb of a domineering older sister who'd become a cherished friend now that we were grown. Somewhere between pimple days and crow's-foot years, Susan had emerged, without my really noticing, into an exceptionally beautiful woman of 31. The piano-stick legs had filled out to shapely, slender calves, and the knees no longer knocked when she walked. Her naturally blonde hair fell where it pleased, in wind-tossed waves framing her face.

I tussled her hair. "I'm so glad you came."

Don Brown, 34, was an old sailing friend with many Caribbean miles under his belt. Like Jim, he was a professional seaman, one of the rare ones not given to telling sea stories. One of a huge Catholic Cape Cod family with whom he retained close family ties, Don was pure New Englander from his short hair and Ivy League dress to his habit of clipping the R's from his speech. Soft-spoken, humble and kind-hearted, Don Brown was for a decade a well-known, well-liked yacht skipper along the Eastern Seaboard. But he was a settler at heart, so it was no surprise when he gave up skippering other men's boats and set up stakes in a paint business ashore in St. Croix.

Over strong coffee, the three of us laid plans to sail for Curaçao the following day, Sunday, and when the pot was empty we struck out for the Kingstown marketplace to do the provisioning.

This was Susan's first trip to the Caribbean, and she reveled in the curious new sights, smells and sounds. And strangely, as we threaded the familiar streets that Saturday morning, I was discovering through her eyes a side of St. Vincent I had missed.

Chickens and goats scurried out of the way of passing trucks, and donkeys carrying great burdens of fruit and coconuts ambled by toward the marketplace.

Susan's drab khaki fatigues and camouflage Army-issue cap failed to conceal a woman's shape. Tough youths at every corner voiced boyish adoration with lustful cries of "Sssst!", which succeeded each time in getting her goat.

Outside the odoriferous fish market sat the charcoal ladies, their hands and clothes black with soot, selling the cooking fuel for the outdoor braziers used by most of the locals. The great black lumps they peddled looked more like souvenirs of the great potato famine than charcoal.

If the waterfront district was an eye-opener for Susan, our spree through the open-air market was a colorful pageant of West Indian life as scores of rural Vincentians who'd been up picking the fields since before sunrise left their plots in the countryside to take up stands from which to barter their wares in the city. Out front, the street was choked with gaily-painted wood-planked buses whose names—*Peace and Plenty, Godspeed Express, Divine Pride*—offered a thumbnail sketch of island life.

Beneath the roof of the open-air market, plump, brown-skinned matrons in flowered dresses wearing calico kerchiefs or wide-brimmed straw hats sat spread-kneed behind wood tables heaped high with produce.

"Papaya, three for a dollar!"

"Dasheen!"

"Want some mangoes?"

"Cinnamon, dollar a bunch."

"Best nutmeg, right here!"

Behind them hung stalks of bananas, from the tiny cigar-size green ones a hundred to a stalk, to giant plantains 30 to a stalk. The variety—yellow pumpkins, coral carrots, crimson tomatoes, mottled melons, shiny gourds, and furry brown kiwis—could grace an impressionist's canvas in a study of texture, color and shape.

Whether it was the artist in my sister or the bartering that so stimulated her I'm not sure, but she rose to the challenge. In no time her arms—and mine—were piled with copious amounts of ripe fruit, vegetables, dried herbs and flasks of hot pepper sauce. I emptied my armloads on Don and caught up with Susan at a table lined with neat rows of mysterious brown bottles.

"Love potion," Susan explained. "This woman makes it right in her kitchen."

"Come on. We've got to make the noon ferry."

I led her outside where Don was negotiating with two young boys. Settling on a price of two dollars, they loaded our provisions and duffles on two hand trucks and, trailed by a swarm of fruit flies, we hastened to the ferry dock.

Arm to arm we passed our cargo over the rail of *Grenadine Star* and took seats atop a pyramid of Heineken beer boxes in the bow, where the only other passenger was a rather distressed yearling calf, neatly diapered in a burlap sack.

When we pulled into Bequia, Don rowed the provisions out to *Cheers* while Susan and I rounded up loose ends in town. Our first stop was Ken Walker's machine shop, where the transplanted American sold and serviced outboard motors and his petite Belgian wife kept the books.

"Here's your taffrail log," he said. "The bracket's good as new." He took the invoice and tore it up. "No charge for the repair. I've read some of your articles. I hope you're going to write about what happened."

"I hope you scream bloody murder," intoned another customer.

"It's time someone told the truth about what's going on down here," said the machinist.

"I will, someday," I promised.

Next we climbed the steps to Lincoln Simmons's sail loft, where Nolly's half-brother was seated at a worn wooden bench completing the final touches to *Cheers'* staysail with a needle and palm. He'd renewed the entire leech tabling, had built a new reinforced clew, and was taking the final stitches in a handsewn clew cringle. Then he folded the sail accordion-style, rolled it into a tidy bundle and dropped it into the drawstring bag.

"I cannot take your money," he said handing me the bag. "My father says to wish you a good trip."

Time and again the people of Bequia showed me by their kindness and infinite generosity how badly they felt that their idyllic island had been spoiled by violence.

When we returned to *Cheers*, Don already had renewed some missing cotter pins in the rigging and was familiarizing himself with the engine room. I greased the self-steering vane and Susan bent on the staysail while Don bled an airlock out of the fuel line.

By sunset we were ready for sea and I brought *Cheers* into the fuel dock. I realized then that I'd never docked the boat under power. It was just one of those things, like so many others, that Jim routinely did, so willingly I'd hardly given it a thought . . . until he was no longer there.

I missed him sorely. After a few days in a port, he'd grow itchy to go to sea again, for passages were his lifeblood, his reason for cruising. Without Jim, it seemed unnatural that *Cheers* should be putting to sea at all.

Nolly came by the dock to say good-bye. The four of us went out that evening for pizza and Don and Nolly found many common ties and friends in the Caribbean.

Late Saturday night, Nolly walked us back to *Cheers*. We parted with a warm embrace.

SUNDAY, JULY 26

We were up at first light on Sunday. While Don deflated the dinghy, I gathered up our passports and cleared customs.

"Ready to leave?" asked Don when I returned.

"You're the captain. There can only be one, and besides old

captains make lousy mates. Because you'll be doing all the navigating, how about if Susan and I take care of the meals, clean-up and sail handling?"

We agreed on equal, single watches of three hours on, six hours off, and with a gentle breeze filling in from the east, *Cheers* powered away from the dock.

Once past the anchored yachts, we raised the mainsail, reacher and staysail and bore away on the port tack, able to lay the 265° magnetic course to Curaçao before we even cleared Admiralty Bay.

The barometer was steady, seas were calm and Radio Antilles was forecasting winds of 10 to 20 knots out of the northeast, with no mention of tropical disturbances.

By late afternoon we were well out of sight of land, which seemed like a good opportunity for some target practice if I was ever going to learn to shoot a gun with accuracy.

I blew up a 30-gallon garbage bag, cinched up the neck and trailed it 50 feet off the stern. I stood on the after deck, leaned into the backstay, and locked both hands around the revolver. With arms out straight, I sighted down the barrel, squeezed the trigger . . . and missed by a country mile. Certainly the boat had lurched. I corrected my aim, shot again and missed. Next Don fired and missed. We were quite a team. Five bullets were all we cared to expend on the exercise, so when our last two shots hit their target, we called the drill a great success and hauled in the bag.

"Farewell to the Grenadines!"

*　　*　　*

There's nothing like an ocean cruise to renew the soul, and I could hardly have asked for finer weather or better shipmates. Don was an experienced skipper and a good seaman who exuded quiet confidence and had a gentle manner in asking for anything. Susan, who's sailed all her life, was a tireless foredeck hand and always had a magic touch with a helm.

Trade wind sailing took on new meaning now that we were going *with* the trades instead of bashing into them. In making our way south and east from New England, Jim and I had battled headwinds much of the way, four hours on, four hours off, with little time for anything but navigating, cooking, steering and sleeping while underway. How he would have loved this trip, now that we'd finally turned the corner to enjoy the downwind run he'd earned.

MONDAY, JULY 27–TUESDAY, JULY 28

For two langorous days *Cheers* reeled off the miles as we tacked downwind, seeming to find her own groove in the moderate swells which rolled beneath her keel. Lee cloths to hold the off-watch in their bunks were a thing of the past as we surged westward at a comfortable six knots under the press of full working sail.

With hair piled loosely on top of my head, the warm breeze astern, I could steer by the feel of the wind playing at the nape of my neck. Though the sun never again showed its face after the first day, light sweaters sufficed for night watches and we never needed oilskins. Cooking was child's play, and we used the mild weather to good advantage, preparing sumptuous meals laced with freshly-pressed garlic and dried herbs, lavishing on the sherry.

The forward cabin, usually an untenable space at sea by virtue of its overlarge bunk and the extreme motion in the ends of the boat at sea, became a comfortable chamber for sleeping or just whiling away the off-watch hours with a good book. *Cheers* would occasionally dip her lee rail, but we took no green water on deck, so the forward hatch was left open for much of the passage.

Susan marveled at the grace and agility of the silvery-blue flying fish that skittered on their elongated tails, then spread winglike pectoral fins to soar out of harm's way hundreds of feet across the surface of the water. If by day they fled our path, they seemed by night attracted to the red glow of our compass light. Lying in the forward cabin, one could hear their fatal thuds as they flew head-long into the cabin trunk and plummeted to deck. Each morning we would harvest as many as 30 rigid bodies from the waterways and commit the remains to the frying pan or to the deep.

On watch, alone with my thoughts, I remembered the unforget-table night at sea many months before, when Jim and I were sailing south off the Little Bahama Bank. Overhead, the moon was full. Just at midnight we were showered with flying fish and engulfed a moment later by a throng of porpoises, who snapped the fish ravenously as they leapt and plunged beneath our bows. Jim roused me from my sleep and we ran to the bowsprit and tossed squirming fish to the porpoises who frolicked in our bow wave.

At sea we'd come to know each other in a way not possible ashore.

How I longed to look forward and see Jim perched on the cabin top, badgering the elusive sun as he chased it with the sextant while I kept time with the watch. For that's the way I saw him if I closed my eyes. His head of thick curly hair, eyebrows bleached an invisible blonde by the sun. Those wonderfully craggy laugh lines that framed blue, blue eyes that had looked at far horizons. His smile was a flash of piano keys that could light up a room, and when he laughed it was an infectious sort of laugh that came from deep within.

How strange it felt, our parting, for this time it was I who was going off to sea, promising to telephone when I arrived in port. For six years before we went cruising it was always I left waving good-bye as the black yawl he skippered pulled away from the dock.

It was a nomadic life, his former job as a yacht captain. Between spring in Annapolis, summer in Newport and Maine and fall again in Annapolis, we managed to see each other for six months out of each year. And there were always winters when *Malagueña* lay covered and cradled that we could be together. But before long the separations grew painful.

One day, six years ago—it was between Thanksgiving and Christmas—Jim climbed the stairs to my attic apartment in Newport, kicked my cat and set a cardboard shoebox atop my chest of drawers.

"This time I've come to stay," he said.

"I was hoping you would."

That Christmas I gave him a five-board pine sea chest I'd found in an antique shop, but he never outgrew that shoe box, Jim just wasn't a collector of things.

My longing to go to sea on a boat of our own fanned his own desire. I needed only to light the flame. The spark always was there.

Slowly the sea chest began to fill with the things we'd need for our voyage: my old star finder, *Ocean Passages for the World*, pilot charts for the South Pacific and Indian Ocean, binoculars and sea boots, marline, sail cloth and a pinch bottle of Scotch.

By the time we bought our first house, in 1977, the contents of the sea chest had grown to fill a room on whose wall was hung a giant color map of the world. Push pins were added, and from a pile of tinder a fire blazed.

"But how are we going to swing it financially?" Jim asked skeptically. "I've seen too many shaky operations like this—too many broken dreams. Sure, people cut loose and they go. Then the money runs out and the boat gets to looking like a garbage scow. The dreamers finish their days pickled in cheap rum while their boat rots beneath them in some exotic wasteland—Fort Lauderdale, Nassau, St. Thomas. You've seen them, barstool cruisers with broken hulks and not two cents to rub together. They don't know it but they died with their fortunes. I don't want that to happen to us."

"We won't let that happen to us. We can turn this house into a boat. We bought it right. We paid thirty. When the work's finished it will probably bring seventy, maybe eighty. Newport's a boom town; you've seen that. And we've done a first-rate renovation. We'll put all the proceeds from the house into a boat. Because it will be our primary residence, we'll be exempt from capital gains tax on the house."

"What kind of boat can you buy for that kind of money today?" he scoffed.

"A used boat. A well-built older fiberglass boat equipped with a lot of the gear we could never afford to add to a new boat."

"We'd have to have funds for at least a year of cruising," he said, "and a cushion in case something happens."

"Such as?"

"Such as illness, an engine overhaul, a new suit of sales. Just believe me, plenty of things will crop up."

"I'll sell my Stone Horse. There's a lot of interest in classic wood boats and Peter Duff's keeping the market alive—and high. I bet I could get seventy-five hundred, maybe eight thousand for *Williwaw*. We could cruise for a year on that alone."

Jim eyed me skeptically.

"With your savings, the small inheritance from my mother and the proceeds from *Williwaw*," I continued, "we'd have enough for maybe four years."

He produced a pencil and paper and played with the figures.

"You're right," he conceded.

"And we could work along the way if we have to."

"You'd leave Newport, leave everything just like that?" he asked.

"Just like that."

"But what about my sod farm? I've been running yachts for nine years. Commercial tonnage before that. The Coast Guard before that. I'd like to . . . What's that parable, about the Greek who turned his back to the sea, put an oar over one shoulder and walked inland until someone stopped him and asked, 'What's that you're carrying?' And there he put down his oar and lived out his remaining days.

"Sometimes I feel I want to just stop and feel the grass grow under my feet. Trade a rocking boat for a rocking chair on a big front porch of a sod farm and watch the grass grow."

"You'd hate it and you know it. Besides, I hear there's bigger money in worm farming."

He grinned.

"You were born for this and you know it. Look at that silly tattoo. What farmer you ever met has his name tattooed on his arm?"

"I was sixteen."

"It started before then."

"I guess."

"Your grandfather was a Sandy Hook pilot and his father went to sea before him. You're named for them. Your mother told me. It's in your blood, Jim."

"I guess."

For the next three years we talked with the greatest restraint about one day cutting loose, as though the plan would crumble if exposed to the cold light of day. Never consciously did we make the decision to cut the land ties and go. Rather, it was a longing that always played inside us both. We both were attached to Newport and we both felt fulfilled in our jobs, but we were biding our time, wanting a stronger hand in the shaping of our lives, wanting to see something of the world from the deck of our own boat.

Then one day the pieces simply fell into place.

John Nicholas Brown, the Rhode Island philanthropist and aging yachtsman for whom Jim had worked the last nine years died suddenly aboard his boat. He and his wife had just arrived in Annapolis, Maryland, for a fall cruise on Chesapeake Bay when it happened. Sitting in the main cabin, recounting to Jim a recent visit with his grown children, the breath simply went out of him. He died in Jim's arms.

Some have declared the passing of John Nicholas Brown in 1979 at the age of 79 heralded the end of yachting's golden era. Whether valid or not, it did spell a different life for Jim, who had been devoted to his employer and friend and had promised to stay with him as long as he continued yachting. Jim stayed aboard the black yawl *Malagueña* in the employ of Mr. Brown's widow, Ann Brown, for another year.

But scarcely a month had passed when Jim, still in Annapolis, got a ship-to-ship call on *Malagueña*'s radio. Friends Jim and Tootie Morris, who were making their way south from Annapolis to Florida, had decided to stop cruising and return to Denver. Though still attached to the cutter, *Cheers of Denver*, they'd decided to sell her. Did we want her before she went to the yacht brokers in Annapolis?

We knew the boat well and had visited aboard her often while in Newport the previous summer. A heavy-displacement, full-keel double-ender, there was no question that she was strong enough to sail any ocean of the world. But could she get out of her own way?

In my office at *Cruising World* I pulled an Alajuela 38 brochure from my overstuffed boat files. Her lines plan revealed what I had never seen of her underwater shape, a fine entry forward, full forefoot, ample beam and balanced ends. She was a double-ender descended from the type developed by Norwegian Colin Archer in the 1880's for use as rescue boats on the tempestuous North Sea. But if Archer's husky Redninskoites provided the inspiration, a more contemporary designer, probably John Atkin, had an even greater hand in her design.

Her hull shape had been refined and streamlined from the massive scantlings of Archer's heavily-framed, wood-planked work boats to a hull that could be finer, lighter, more weatherly and perhaps even stronger built in fiberglass for use as a yacht.

A tall mast, generous sail area and cutter rig confirmed that she could be very fast indeed, despite her heavy displacement. She wouldn't win any races around the buoys—not against the ultra-light displacement greyhounds popular today—but we cared nothing for racing. No, this boat would move respectably enough in light air and really come into her own when the wind pipes up and the lightweights head for the harbor. Give her a little sheet and get her to the trade winds and *Cheers* could take us anywhere quickly, safely and comfortably. And with a draft of just under six feet, she could navigate the Intracoastal Waterway, shallow Bahamas banks or South Seas lagoons with ease.

Jim telephoned me at home in Newport that night. "Well, what do you think?" he asked.

"I think I'll be down this weekend. Can we take her for a sail?"

"You bet. We'll go out on Sunday. Just you and I—we'll tell no one."

Cheers of Denver lay berthed at Annapolis Yacht Sales where a broker already was recording her specifications. We had been given first refusal and if we failed to exercise it, she would go into multiple listings within a few days.

As we stepped aboard the boat our excitement was tinged with sentiment at the absence of our friends. They'd taken off only their personal belongings and everywhere were signs of the painstaking care they'd taken of the boat. Her white hull was polished, stainless steel gleamed and teak woodwork was richly oiled.

The entire cabin was hand-crafted of clear-grained oiled teak with none of the salty, overdone embellishments of some of the imports, no stereo entertainment center, shag carpeting, turned wood taffrails or grotesque carvings. Just good honest woodwork whose joints fit together with surgical precision.

She had a conventional layout that would be hard to improve upon for one couple, in port or at sea. The owner's stateroom was forward with a large double bunk, ample stowage areas and a separate, enclosed head with shower. The motion at sea can be violent in the extreme ends of the boat, so the coffin-size port and starboard settee berths in the main cabin would be fine sea berths when sailing through the night.

Shafts of sunlight streamed through the louvered skylight overhead, illuminating an old-fashioned brass trawler lamp which hung over the drop-leaf dining table. Mounted on the main bulk-head was a handsome brass heat stove whose radiant warmth would dry the cabin and rejuvenate the crew on cold days.

The galley, aft, had a gimballed propane stove with oven and a deep stainless steel sink with foot pumps for both fresh and salt-water. The galley was just to starboard of the companionway, where fresh air would relieve the cook from the steamy aroma of food.

Opposite the galley was a navigator's station with a lift-up chart table, two powerful ship-to-shore radios, a depth sounder and radio direction finder. Beneath the cockpit was mounted a 40-horsepower, three-cylinder diesel engine, accessible through a door abaft the companionway ladder.

With fuel tanks filled, she would have a cruising range under power of better than 700 miles at six knots, range enough to transit the belts of windless doldrums under power alone. Every unseen cubic inch of space could be utilized to carry gear, clothing and food stores sufficient to last an entire year, or to sail halfway around the world. Freshwater could last four to five months—longer than we'd ever be away from port—and the cockpit awning doubled as a rain catcher, which would enable us to directly re-plenish the tanks by simply connecting a hose.

She was as basic and self-sufficient as any boat could be. But how did she sail?

We removed the sail covers, started the engine and cast off our lines. Jim swung the massive ash tiller and we coasted out into Chesapeake Bay.

There was a nip in the air that Sunday in November, and a light breeze had begun to fill in from the north. We headed into the wind and cut the engine. Jim hoisted the mainsail and high-cut flying jib and I sheeted them in from the cockpit. I nudged the tiller to port, the bow fell off to starboard and slowly *Cheers* heeled and began to gather way on a beam reach across the bay.

But what weather helm! Sitting to windward, my feet braced against the opposite seat, I pulled the tiller mightily, but the bow tried stubbornly to round up into the wind.

"This tiller's a bear!" I called to Jim who paced the foredeck looking aloft.

"Let me give you more sail forward," he said. He hoisted the staysail, then eased the mainsheet. The bow fell off a point, the tiller ceased its fight and we gathered speed.

I released the helm. "Six knots and she's steering herself!"

Back and forth across the bay, we put *Cheers* on every point of sail and tried out every conceivable sail combination: hard on the wind, wing and wing before the wind, mainsail reefed and double reefed, staysail up and down.

Little by little we got to know the boat and her temperament. When poorly trimmed, her sails waged war on the massive outboard rudder and the tiller could break a helmsman's ribs in heavy seas. But with sails sheeted properly and the tiller handled with an iron hand inside a velvet glove, she responded like a finely-tuned instrument, all parts in harmony.

Jim disappeared below to the bowels of the boat to search out telltale clues to the real integrity of her construction. For two hours he probed the bilges, insides of lockers, examined plumbing, electrical wiring, the hull-deck joint, chain plates, mast step, bulkhead tabbing, engine installation and through-hull fittings. There was no doubt from the look on his face when he emerged that *Cheers* had passed his scrutiny.

"Everything is first rate. And you should see the inventory of spare parts. There are back-ups for the back-ups. Incredible! Two rudders and three blades for the self-steering vane. Three sets of running lights. Throw in a case of beer and this boat's ready for sea right now."

The following spring we put our house on the market. It sold in four days and *Cheers* became ours free and clear. The entire interior would have fit inside the smallest room of our 14-room house, but we were coming to find how little one needs to cruise, not how much. Aboard *Cheers* there was a place for everything and everything had its place.

We were free to wander. To find the distant ports we'd pinpointed. To sample new foods, make new friends and try our tongues at new languages. To sail every day of our lives, to declare a Sunday in mid-week if we chose.

*   *   *

I wondered, that night alone at the helm as we sailed for Curaçao, how much of the dream could be salvaged. It would crush me to put *Cheers* up for sale and return to shore, but then I was more attached to this boat than was Jim. And more in love with Jim than with the boat.

What countless hours of enjoyment this boat had given us. If only we'd been assaulted somewhere ashore it might be easier to pick up the pieces. But that cabin—our forward stateroom—echoed the violence of that night. In Curaçao I would change all the fabric—get rid of the blood stains and try new colors. That would help. But we'd learned too vividly that an intruder could slip unnoticed on our boat. Could we ever again know a night of sound sleep?

I was learning to use the revolver and Jim could show me how to use the shotgun. We'd keep them loaded and close at hand. We could install some kind of alarm system, or we could install a fan and seal the boat each night.

But what a way to live.

When Jim was better we would leave the Caribbean. He could first recuperate in Curaçao, and when he was strong enough we would transit the Panama Canal and roam the South Pacific, just as we'd planned. Maybe in the South Seas, among the gentle Polynesians, we'd put the incident behind us and learn not to jump at each bump in the night.

But it had to be Jim's decision.

*   *   *

Of the three Netherlands Antilles—or ABC islands, as they are called—only boomerang-shaped Bonaire, the easternmost of the group, has no oil refinery and consequently is far less industrialized than its sisters, Curaçao and Aruba, to the west. We were intrigued by stories of an unspoiled oasis whose expansive salt ponds are the nesting ground for vast colonies of pink flamingos. Her gin-clear waters and underwater coral gardens make Bonaire a choice dive spot for adventurers the world over.

We were making good speed, and since Bonaire lay so near our path, we decided that if we raised it by daylight, we would stop and anchor there for a couple of days before going on to Curaçao. Susan and Don could afford the time, and I could just as well call Jim from Bonaire as from Curaçao.

On Tuesday evening, our third day at sea, I was an hour into my watch when Don came on deck at 7 p.m. and placed the radio direction finder atop the sliding hatch.

"You've been at the chart table since supper," I said.

"Yes, we're getting close."

"How about a cup of coffee?" I asked.

"No thanks," he said, flipping through *Reed's Almanac* looking for radio frequencies. "I want to get this bearing. But you go ahead. The steering vane's holding a good course."

I read the Walker log, went below and made my hourly entry in the ship's log. *Time 1900; Course 255°M; Log 312 n.m.* I drew a cup of coffee from the thermos and returned on deck.

Don sat in the companionway, the *Almanac* opened in his lap, tuning the antenna searching for a null amid the familiar tones of Morse code.

"Would you hand-steer a good compass course for a minute?" he asked. "Give me a mark when you're on two six zero."

"Ready?"

Dit da da dit, dit da da da, da da dit.

"Mark."

"Good, again."

Dit da da dit, dit da da . . .

"Mark."

"Good."

"Don, do you trust RDF?"

"Sure, but it's only an aid. Why?"

"We've had bad fixes from it this time of day. It's not the unit, Jim says, but night effect, a disturbance that occurs just before and just after sunset, which can give you a bad bearing."

"That's true. But Curaçao has a marine beacon and it's coming in clear, right where I want it. I'll tune it in again later."

"Can you get a cross bearing from Venezuela?"

"I've been playing with six aerobeacons along Venezuela, but the coastline is mountainous and I think there's some refraction. There's been too much cloud cover to get a shot with the sextant the last two days, so it's all I have to go on—that and my DR."

"The Curaçao beacon is nearly dead ahead. It confirms your heading, but it doesn't give your longitude, your distance off."

"True, and it's hard to gauge the current. The chart shows up to a knot and a quarter of current setting west. But then, there's that notation that sometimes a surface counter current is encountered, which sets *east*."

"I'm surprised we haven't seen Los Roques."

"My course should have left them 12 miles south, to our port. They're very low, you know."

"But there are two powerful lighthouses on Los Roques."

"They're maintained by Venezuela. They could be out or not as bright as specified on the chart."

"Sure, I forgot."

"Relax, Bets. I think we'll make Bonaire early tomorrow. We should pick up some lights by midnight." He packed up the RDF. "We'll have to be on our toes on watch tonight." He searched the sky and went below. "Sure wish we had some moon."

By 8 o'clock the wind was about 20 knots out of the east. Neither the moon nor a single star shone overhead. Ahead, opaque sky met inkpot sea with no visible horizon. The bow wave boiled with phosphorescent life which streaked past the hull in silver-green slivers. Astern, the free-wheeling propeller spun a contrail of bright, iridescent life.

Every 15 minutes or so I stood and looked around in all directions, scanning the horizon for a light, a loom—any sign of land. By 9 p.m., when Susan came on watch, the wind had increased to about 25 knots, dead astern. Frothing white coamers, comfortably spaced, marched down upon us, hissing as they tumbled beneath our keel.

Don came on deck for our change of watch. "See anything?" he asked.

"Nothing," I said. "I think we'd better reef."

While Don steered, Susan and I dropped the staysail, then double-reefed the main and vanged it to starboard to prevent an accidental gybe.

With plenty of apparent wind, I engaged the steering vane and Cheers settled down to a good course of 260°, yawing a little as she sluiced down waves, reeling off a steady 6 knots.

Suddenly I heard a flutter in the rigging, looked aloft and saw something hit the mainsail. A pile of flapping feathers fell in my lap in the cockpit and I nearly jumped out of my skin. Our visitor stood and shook himself off, trying to regain his dignity, too rattled to fly off.

A booby! By the red glow of the compass light, his feathers appeared white and his bill a beautiful robin's egg blue. His feet were webbed and the big bird plodded clumsily around the cockpit, taking it all in. He visited with us for perhaps 10 minutes, then hopped to the rail and flew away into the night.

"A good omen," I remember saying. "Land is near."

I went below to get some sleep while Susan stood watch and Don studied the log and brought his position up to date.

❋   ❋   ❋

Six bells roused me from a light sleep and I went on deck for my 3 a.m. watch. Susan was asleep in the forward cabin and Don was hand steering. The wind had dropped to 15 knots.

"How's it going, Don? See anything yet?"

"We've picked up Bonaire. Have a look. The five-second flasher far ahead to starboard marks the southern tip of Bonaire. We'll pass between it and that nine-second flasher way over there." He pointed to a light just abaft our port beam, far away.

"So you raised Bonaire just when you said you would. Good job, Don. I didn't mean to question your navigation. I guess I've just been nervous lately."

"Sure, I understand. I figure we're eighteen miles from Kralendijk Harbor. We should arrive about six a.m., so we can expect to enter in good light. You want to steer 240°."

Don lay down in the cockpit. I engaged the steering vane.

"You've been up all night, Don?"

"Yeah, I'm pretty bushed," he yawned.

"I'll enter your log reading," I said.

I read the log, went below and wrote in the ship's log: *Time 0300; Course 240°M.; Log 360.2 n.m. Sighted lights off Bonaire.*

I checked the batteries and found the voltage in the number two bank was below 12 volts, so I returned to deck, started the engine and began charging in neutral at half throttle.

"Might as well get some speed out of it," said Don, engaging forward gear.

"But don't we want to enter the harbor after sunup?"

"It's an open harbor. We'll be alright," Don yawned. "Let me know when we're abeam of the two lights."

I studied the two flashing lights. "But Don, they never will be abeam. One's far ahead off our starboard bow, the other's off our port quarter."

He was very tired and did not reply.

"Don, they never will be abeam. Do you mean to let you know when we're between the two?"

"Yes, let me know."

I was confused. I wanted to check the chart. The vane was steering a good course, so I looked around, then went below and switched on the red chart light. But the only chart that lay open on the table was a small-scale coastal chart which covered the waters from the Lesser Antilles all the way to Panama. No characteristics were given for lighted aids to navigation; they were simply numbered consecutively from west to east.

I switched on the depth sounder. The red blip flashed three fathoms! My heart lept to my throat. I switched to feet. It translated: 18 feet. I dove for the cockpit, pulled back the throttle and disengaged the steering gear. I threw the tiller hard to starboard, but it was too late. *Cheers* climbed a wave and raced headlong down its face. Coral crashed beneath her keel and a wall of water broke over us, filling the cockpit.

Don, stunned, grabbed the helm and gave the engine full throttle ahead. "We can't turn around. Our only hope is to drive her over it."

"No!" I screamed.

With horrible crushing, grinding, crashing *Cheers* bounced from one coral head to the next, surging ever shoreward as each frothy comber broke wholly over us.

Susan emerged dripping wet in the companionway. "God, what's happened?"

"Stay below!" Don ordered. "Close the hatches."

Before she could slide the companionway hatch shut, another coamer hit the cabin, knocking Susan down and swamping the galley. *Cheers* reeled over on her starboard beam. I grabbed the port cockpit coaming. "Hang on!"

Don clung to the tiller, trying to straighten out the boat as the tiller thrashed from side to side, trying to shake his grip.

There was no point in steering. The 15-ton boat was like a bath tub toy in the grip of each wave, which picked her up and flung her down with a horrible jolt.

I could not see the bottom or what lay ahead. The sky was opaque black and the water around us white with foam. It was difficult to tell what was up and what was down.

"Get below," Don shouted over the noise of booming surf.

I crawled below and passed my safety harness up to him.

"Clip on," I called. "If you wash over there's no way to get you back."

If the holocaust on deck was frightening, the pandemonium below was only a little less so. The din inside the hull was an agonizing cacophony of destruction as the boat bounced from one coral head to the next with crashing, splintering force.

I felt numb with the morbid realization that *Cheers* was breaking up beneath us. I thought of the life raft, but knew that its rubber floor would be shredded on the coral. But if *Cheers* broke up, we sooner or later would be forced to abandon ship, so I laid out three life jackets and started to round up survival gear.

Poor Susan. I wanted so much to reassure her that we would be alright, and I never doubted that we would survive. But I was so grieved about *Cheers* that I felt impotent to do much of anything.

Susan surprised me by putting an arm around my shoulder and assuring me that we would pull through. "And when we do, you'll have every cent that's mine to save your boat. Now tell me what to do."

The boat lurched violently and we had to crawl from handhold to handhold. Even simple jobs seemed to take forever.

I turned off the refrigeration and all unnecessary circuit breakers to conserve battery power for the radio. Susan dogged the hatches and sealed the ports while I checked the bilges. The bilges were half full of water, but there was no way of telling whether it had come through a hole in the hull or through the companionway.

I dropped two of the three boards in the companionway and closed the sliding hatch. Don was still wrestling with the tiller and straining to see land. The binoculars lay in the bottom of the half-filled cockpit well. I located a spare pair and passed them up to him.

"Do you have a searchlight?" he shouted.

I passed up the 200,000 candle power lamp, which he plugged into a socket in the cockpit. He scanned the horizon.

"Nothing," he called.

"If this is Bonaire, why aren't there any lights—or a loom?" I asked.

"If we are where I thought we were, we wouldn't be on a reef. Quick, close the hatch! Here comes another."

I crouched on the companionway ladder and waited for the next wave to strike. When it did I slid open the hatch, passed Don the bilge pump handle and cut the lashings on the plastic tub that housed our survival gear and brought it below. Then I filled two heavy canvas tote bags with additional things we would need if we had to abandon ship: flashlights, a blanket, first aid kit, additional flares, a portable VHF radio, a dozen D-cell batteries, our passports, cash, ship's papers, the .38 revolver and 45 rounds of ammunition. The life raft and plastic tub contained everything else we would need, including food, and there was 10 gallons of freshwater in two jugs lashed on deck.

Then Susan and I wedged ourselves below and waited. I was wedged between the navigator's station and the galley, my back on the cabin sole, knees bent, my feet against the galley sink. With each crash of the keel, the cabin sole pushed against my bottom, and as the hull flexed, the galley bulkhead beneath my feet strained to tear loose from the hull. I was overcome with grief for my tortured boat and could only think how she seemed to me like a beached whale in the throes of death. Susan and I held hands without speaking, impotent to help her.

The hatch slid open and Don crawled below, drenched and weather beaten. "There's nothing more I can do until sunup," he said. "That's just an hour and a half away." He sat beside me. "God, I'm sorry," he said compassionately. "After all you've been through."

"I was on watch," I reminded him. Then I muttered something about the flashing lights, the depth sounder, if only I'd turned it on sooner.

"We'll get her off, Bets," he said, squeezing my hand. "I promise."

Then he turned on the VHF and broadcast a mayday message.

CHAPTER TWELVE

──────────────────────── **D**on repeated the mayday message twice every 15 minutes through the hours of darkness. He dialed through all 55 channels on the VHF radio, but there was no traffic, no other human sound outside our small cabin. We decided against using our more powerful single sideband radio until we were more certain of our position.

It was possible, of course, that a ship was picking up our mayday but that we were not receiving its reply. Until we could determine and broadcast our true position, we could expect no assistance. Except by using the two Emergency Position Indicating Radio Beacons aboard, which would alert a plane and enable a pilot to locate us by homing in on our signal. Activating an EPIRB in this part of the world, with airports on Aruba, Bonaire, Curaçao and along the Venezuelan coast, would most certainly initiate a search and rescue mission by air.

It was hard to believe that twice in one month mayday messages were broadcast from *Cheers* when never before in our lives had Jim or I ever called for assistance. With the attendant risk and expense to the aiding party, such broadcasts are not to be made lightly.

Dawn cast new light on our situation, and with light came new hope.

161

Just before 6 a.m. Don slid open the hatch and strained to see land as the sky's blackness gave way to blue. He was on deck for what seemed a very long time, then the hatch slid open and he hurried down between waves.

"Nothing," he scowled. "I can't see a blessed thing."

"No land?"

"Nothing but breakers on both sides of us, deep water ahead and far behind us."

"Betsy is the boat insured?"

"No."

"Not even for total loss?"

"There's no insurance at all."

"Shit!"

Don scanned the charts once more and finally the pieces began to fall into place.

"I think we're here," he said, pointing to a large coral reef east of Bonaire. "Aves de Sotavento. If we had less current than the chart indicated—say a quarter of a knot instead of a knot and a half—that would put us in this area. Two aerobeacons off the Venezuela coast confirmed my DR position, but the signals were weak and maybe distorted."

"I remember reading a little about Los Aves—the bird islands. They're Venezuelan and they're uninhabited."

"If this is Aves de Sotavento and we're somewhere on this reef," said Don, "the chart shows a low island just three miles southwest of here. The lagoon is shallow and we could make it to the island by life raft or the inflatable dinghy if we have to."

"We could take supplies from the boat and set up camp on shore," said Susan.

"And leave *Cheers* here?" I snapped defensively. "This is my home, you know. She's everything we have. Do you really think I can just move ashore and leave her bones on this reef?"

It was Susan's voice that snapped me out of my morose state. She had climbed over me and was perched on the companionway ladder, poking her head through the hatch between waves.

"There's a ship!" she exclaimed, pointing north.

I pulled myself into the companionway and saw a cargo ship two or three miles distant.

"She's headed this way," I said. "Susan, quick, take a bearing on her."

I scurried to get the flare gun and passed it up to Don, who tried firing several rounds, all duds.

"Her bearing hasn't changed," said Susan, puzzled.

"She must have seen our sail and she's hove-to," I explained. "I better get on Channel 16."

Don slumped in the cockpit. "Her bearing hasn't changed because she's on the reef, too. She's a wreck."

We stared in silence at the ship, tracing in our minds the breadth of the formidable submerged reef that claimed the two vessels.

Just as I slid open the hatch to take the flare gun below, Don spotted a second ship to the north, about four miles out to sea.

"Looks like she's heading away," Susan observed. "It's hard to tell without the binoculars."

"She's probably bound for Venezuela," said Don excitedly. He reloaded the flare gun and fired. The last round raced just 50 feet into the air and dropped a few seconds later into the sea.

"We've got some hand-held flares," I offered, "and a signaling mirror."

"Get the flares."

I charged below and passed up two orange smoke flares. Then I tried to raise the ship on Channel 16, but heard only static silence.

"They're not monitoring the radio," I said, discouraged.

"They're not monitoring because there's no one aboard," said Don. "This one's on the reef, too."

How had they struck the reef, I wondered. Had they blown ashore in bad weather? Had their crew survived? If no one had succeeded in salvaging these valuable ships, what were our chances for saving *Cheers?* And if this was Aves de Sotavento, where was the land we should find to leeward?

"Betsy," Don said, "why don't you activate one of the EPIRBs. Susie, your eyes are better than mine. Look for birds, a cloud, a jet contrail—any sign that might point to land."

I passed up a second safety harness for Susan, then broke the seal on the plastic survival tub that housed one EPIRB unit. We had bought it 10 months earlier and had sealed it in an airtight plastic bag to keep it dry. I pulled the orange activating tag, but the red lamp that indicates the unit is functioning did not light.

I had to assume that the EPIRB was not transmitting, so I then removed the other EPIRB from its bulkhead bracket, erected the folding antenna and flipped the switch. The red pilot light came on; the EPIRB was transmitting. It should operate for eight days with a range of 200 miles.

The sun was now fully visible above the eastern horizon, and from his perch atop the jib halyard winch, Don discovered a low spit of land to the southwest. As the sun continued to rise, the land became faintly visible from deck. It was a cloudless day and the wind-rippled water ahead of us sparkled pale green, graduating to shades of turquoise, the characteristic colors of shallow water. Though the wind had dropped to a gentle 10 to 12 knots, the waves spawned by last night's boisterous trades continued to buffet our port quarter. We were now beyond the line of breakers, so waves no longer broke wholly over us; instead their wash cascaded past us, filling the air with spray as *Cheers* shuddered and bounced over coral rubble.

If this was Aves de Sotavento, as we now believed, the chart showed that water was a deep 100 fathoms to within a mile of the reef, then a minimum of 20 fathoms right up to the line of breakers. Perhaps it was the slightly different motion—the feeling of a ground wave beneath our keel—that led me to turn on the depth-sounder when I believed us to be far off soundings.

If only we'd left Bequia three hours later, I lamented. If only there'd been a moon. If only I hadn't started the engine. If only I'd turned on the depth-sounder a minute sooner. I'd always felt so attuned to this boat, so at one with her at sea. How could I have driven her so blindly into this obvious danger without knowing?

Cheers lay perhaps 500 feet from deep water to windward, astern of us. But surfing with the waves was one thing. No vessel, it seemed, could survive a trip back out through the huge breakers, even if a rescue vessel came to offer us a tow.

Ahead, the shallow lagoon appeared no more than waist-deep for perhaps 1,000 feet, and in patches the reef lay completely dry. Beyond that, where pale green water gave way to aquamarine, the bottom was studded with menacing brown coral heads as far as the eye could see. They reared from the lagoon like a field of moguls, presenting an impenetrable barrier to an exit through the lagoon.

There was little we could do for *Cheers*. We talked of gathering together all the berth cushions, fenders, horseshoe ring and Coast Guard cushions and securing them to her starboard side at the turn of the bilge to cushion the hull from the beating it was taking from the coral. Wearing his life harness, Don put on a face mask and slipped over the side to examine the keel and starboard bilge area for damage.

Cheers lay at an extreme angle of heel, her starboard rail a foot awash, moving steadily further onto the reef.

"I know it's hard to believe," Don said when he surfaced, "but the hull's perfectly sound. All the noise we've been hearing—the grinding and crashing below—is the coral breaking up under the keel. I saw it through the face mask. We've left a path of pulverized sand where we broke a trail through coral."

"You don't have to say that for me," I said, even though the unchanging water level in the bilge supported Don's assessment. "I'm all right, really. I felt the hull flexing. Felt the bulkheads working. Felt the keel hammering up the cabin sole. I can feel her breaking up right now, so don't tell me it's just a flesh wound. I don't buy it."

I wanted so much to think positively, to reassure my crew that we would be rescued and pretend we could save the boat, but I was worn down. This time I couldn't seem to bounce back. I decided the best I could do was to keep my mouth shut and keep busy.

For all my wasted efforts trying to clear cabin debris and raise help on the VHF, I did do something purposeful that morning. I found in the icebox six frosty bottles of Heineken beer. Joyously, we put an end to them before they grew warm. Never before or since has a beer tasted better. If our future was not brighter, it looked no worse after we drank them down.

It was just after 10 a.m. when Susan saw them. Don had flaked down 10 fathoms of anchor rode on deck and was about to lower the 45-pound plow anchor with 35 feet of chain when we heard her cry.

"A boat! Look there!" She pointed out to sea. "They see us and they've come to help!"

Three hundred yards to windward, just beyond the line of breakers, hovered an outboard-powered orange inflatable with several persons aboard. They coasted up and down along the line of surf seeming to look for a pass. We flapped our arms high over our heads. They waved back.

Help had arrived.

But who were they? From where had they come? Our EPIRB could be received only by aircraft; we had seen no plane. Our VHF transmission might have been picked up by a ship, but we had seen no vessels other than the two wrecks. We might have been spotted by someone on the island, but a small boat from shore would have tried to reach us through the lagoon; this boat hovered out to sea.

Each time the boat rose to the top of a swell, we could plainly see four black figures against the bright orange rubber of the inflatable boat. They were either dark-skinned or they were wearing dark clothing or wetsuits.

As desperately as we wanted to be rescued, we waved them away. There was no way for them to negotiate the surf breaking on the reef, so we tried to motion them around to the south and then west, where six miles distant, just off the west point of the island, according to the chart, there was a deep-water entrance into the lagoon. All this we tried to communicate by hand signals while waving them out of danger.

But when next the boat rose to the crest of a swell, there was only one man aboard. The others had slipped over the side. But why? Why had they taken such a chance?

I went below and got the gun, loaded it and slipped it in the waistband of my shorts.

"I don't like this," I said to Don.

"I don't either," he said. "What have you heard about pirate attacks off Venezuela?"

"Nothing about Venezuela," I said, "but a few in Colombian waters. Drug smugglers mostly, smugglers who hijack yachts. Do you think they've come to loot the boat, Don?"

"Let's hear what they have to say."

"Don, how's your Spanish?"

"Zip. How's yours?"

"I don't speak a word. Susan, remember any Spanish?"

"A little. Relax, you two. And for God's sake don't let them see the gun."

We watched for the figures to appear in the surf, but when next we spotted them, two were alongside Cheers's high port side clambering to get aboard while the third stumbled toward us in turbulent, waist-deep water. Don motioned them around to the starboard side. Without waiting for a hand, they pulled themselves aboard by the starboard shrouds and together they swung the third man aboard.

They lifted their face masks in unison. All three had raven-black hair and dark complexions. I searched their faces for a hint of their intentions, but found only cold, dripping stares.

"Buenos dias," said Susan.

"Buenas," they replied, trying to catch their breath.

We shook hands all around and said our first names, to which they said theirs: Pepe, Fernando, Pablo.

"Americanos?" asked Pepe.

"Sí, Americanos," said Don. "Thank you for coming."

"Thank you," we echoed. "Gracias, muchas gracias."

"Habla usted Español?" asked Fernando.

"No, I'm sorry," said Don. "You speak any English?"

"A leetle," said Pablo. "You capitán?"

"Sí, capitán."

"Just you and the two señoritas on the boat? Any others?"

"No," said Don. "Yes," said I simultaneously.

Two of the men looked at each other in puzzlement, but let it pass.

"Are we . . . " stuttered Don. "Is this . . . I mean, where are we?"

"Aves de Sotavento," said Pablo. "You didn't saw the light?"

"Yes, I saw the light. How long's it been blinking five seconds?"

"Two years, maybe more. Light keeper on Barlevento supposed to fix it."

"I'd like to talk with him," Don said tensely.

"No, Barlevento is too far. You come with us," said Pablo.

"Where?" asked Don.

"Sotavento."

"Do you live on Sotavento?" I asked.

"Sí," said Pablo. "No," said Fernando. Then they talked in Spanish.

"You come with us," repeated Pablo.

"But how?" asked Don. "We can't swim out through that surf."

"You have no small boat?"

"Yes," said Don. "I mean sí, we have small boat. Betsy, Susan, blow up the Avon."

I was reluctant to inflate the dinghy because I was afraid to leave *Cheers* stranded where only they could get to her with their more seaworthy outboard-powered inflatable. But Susan seemed to trust them as much as I mistrusted them, and she dug the billows out of the lazarette.

There would be no harm in readying the dinghy, I decided. But what if they cast us adrift in it so they could loot the boat? But I couldn't unroll the collapsed dinghy, much less operate the foot pump, without dropping the gun. I'd lost a lot of weight in the last few weeks and my clothes hung on me. I inched over to the companionway and slinked below. I put the gun on the shelf in the icebox and returned topside, where Susan and I wrestled the inflatable into shape.

"Do you want something to drink?" asked Don.

Pablo nodded.

"Susie, aren't there some sodas in the reefer?" he asked.

"I'll get them," I broke in.

I hurried below, passed up three colas and moved the revolver to the chart table. Then I returned topside and inflated the dinghy.

"Maybe one of you could pay out this line while I walk the anchor out," Don said to Pablo.

Pablo and Fernando looked at each other in amazement. Anyone who had put his boat on this reef, which everyone around knows is dangerous, couldn't be much of a navigator. And a skipper who would anchor his boat which is irrevocably aground on a reef can't be much of a seaman, either. They shrugged their shoulders and paid out the rode. But when Don began walking the anchor shoreward, toward the lagoon, rather than seaward, they protested.

"Deep water is that way, Capitán," said Pablo, pointing toward the breakers.

But Don had ideas of his own. "We've got to move her out of the wave action," he said.

Pablo shook his head.

"If I had two weeks and twenty men I could bring her over this reef and into the lagoon," Don declared when he had set the anchor.

"Never hoppen," said Pablo. "No boat will last two weeks here. When this reef take a boat she never give it back."

I mulled over those words as I went below, gathered up our two bags of survival gear and prepared to leave *Cheers*. My eyes filled with tears. My grief at the thought of never seeing her again in one piece welled up as a lump in my throat. But I knew I could not stand her cries of agony as she broke up.

With bags in hand, I climbed the first step of the companionway ladder. The clock struck 10 o'clock and a familiar eerie chill ran up my spine at the sound of the four bells, jolting me back in time to that horrible night in Friendship Bay when, standing at the rail, I was gripped by the same indecision as my mind teetered between fleeing for my own safety and standing by something I dearly loved.

I put down the bags and rummaged through the tool box for a screwdriver.

"What are you doing?" Susan called from deck. Her voice was urgent. "We've got to go!"

"I'm taking the clock. And the half model of *Cheers*. I'm taking them for Jim."

"Don't you understand we've got to wade to the dinghy?" she said. "They'll be ruined. You'll see your boat again. I'll come and take them off tomorrow if you want. Come on."

Don and the men hatched a plan. Pablo, who spoke quite good English, would take Susan and me ashore to their camp on the island. We would launch our dinghy and row through the lagoon until we reached deeper water. The other two men, Fernando and Pepe, would remain with Don aboard *Cheers* to stow gear and close up the boat. The fourth man, who had remained behind in their inflatable out beyond the breakers, had been given instructions to wait for Don and the other two, who would swim to their inflatable. They then would proceed around the reef and meet us inside the lagoon. They had a large Zodiac with a powerful outboard, and would tow us in our small dinghy to the island, where we would be welcomed at their camp.

The four men were fishermen, as I understood it. Two were Venezuelan, one Chilean, and one a Spaniard. They had a powerful radio ashore on which they talked three times a day to someone in Puerto Cabello, on the Venezuelan mainland. They promised to radio the Venezuelan Guardia Nacional, which they said would dispatch a rescue boat immediately to tow *Cheers* off the reef.

There was no perceptible tidal range on Aves, no chance of moving her to deeper water without outside help. The rescue boat could be there by late afternoon, they said, and by dark *Cheers* could be afloat again. They had some plywood ashore with which to patch the hull if she holed, so we could at least busy ourselves readying gear to refloat her.

I was apprehensive about the three of us splitting up, and I did not like leaving *Cheers* with strangers aboard, even with Don. But Don seemed to trust them and he was the captain. I dismissed my misgivings as paranoia, the result of tensions following our assault in Bequia. I started to bring the gun, just in case, but left it behind when I realized we would have to wade through strong current before we could climb into the dinghy. A gun that had been dunked in saltwater would do us no good anyway.

The dinghy was launched over the starboard side and our two bags and the oars were placed inside. Pablo jumped in the water and coaxed the inflatable to a spot free from surface coral heads. Then Susan and I half-waded, half-swam to the inflatable and climbed aboard.

I kneeled in the inflatable dinghy, and rowed toward the point of land to the south, in no particular hurry since it would take the Zodiac an hour or more to power around the reef.

Susan sat in the bow and Pablo, a burly, dark-skinned Venezuelan with a ready smile, sat in the stern. He was a full head shorter than I and portly, I thought, until he peeled off his wetsuit. Then I saw he was powerfully built with a bulldog neck, broad shoulders, muscular biceps and forearms, robust thighs and calves. What he lacked in stature he more than made up in brawn, and though his face showed a man of about 40, his physique was that of a young athlete.

Pablo peered over the stern of the dinghy and pointed with amusement to a silver-gray shape that shadowed our progress across the lagoon.

"Many barracuda in the lagoon. They follow you like a dog." He bared his teeth to illustrate a barracuda's fang-filled mouth. "They are curious, that's all."

Our progress was aided by a little current and a gentle wind, so we made good speed over the bottom.

Three hundred yards from where *Cheers* lay, where we were to meet the others in the Zodiac, the water deepened from aquamarine to brilliant sapphire. I shipped my oars and we drifted, waiting.

"Row!" said Pablo.

"Aren't we supposed to wait here?" I asked.

"Row," he insisted, pointing to the southwest, where there was no visible land.

"But the island is there." I pointed due south. "You said you would take us to your camp."

"Row," he insisted.

"We're supposed to wait here for Don and the others."

"Okay, I row," he said impatiently.

Abruptly he took my spot amidships and tried vigorously to propel the boat toward what appeared to be open sea. He held the blades at the wrong attitude, scooping water on the backstroke and finding only air when he pulled. Our friend couldn't row a stroke.

It doesn't take a degree in marine science to know that fishermen the world over are supposed to know how to row, nor a degree in psychology to sense when your life is in danger. Their plan became clear to me now. It was so simple, so obvious. How could we have been so naive?

Pablo had lured Susan and me away on the pretense of radioing for help, leaving Don on the boat with the other two. They would kill Don, ransack the boat, then amuse themselves with Susan and me before killing us, too. They could leave this remote island and never be discovered. After awhile someone might find the stripped wreckage of *Cheers*, but eventually even her hull would become part of the reef.

We had made it so easy for them. How could we have been so stupid? Of all people, I should have known better. Poor Susan. I could see she still suspected nothing. Why hadn't I brought the gun? Even if it wouldn't fire, they couldn't be sure of that. It might have given us time to escape. The gun now lay in the chart table where even Don did not know where it was. The others would find it when they looted the boat.

Having twice fallen backwards in the dinghy, feet flying, Pablo paddled the dinghy with one oar, canoe style. We moved gradually southwest, where we could see no land.

We were defenseless. I tried to think of a ploy—any way to get back to Don and the gun, but Pablo continued to paddle with iron determination to wherever it was he was taking us. His back was turned to me, so I tried to get Susan's attention in the bow by making grotesque faces and pointing to Pablo. She thought I was clowning and shot me a look that said, "Cut it out, you jackass."

I clamped my hands around my throat, popped my eyeballs, then made a throat slitting gesture with my index finger. She got my message and turned away to ponder the implications. Then she turned back and shot me a look that said, "I think you're wrong."

Maybe she was right. I tried to feel Pablo out by asking him questions. About his wife. Did he have a family? Did anyone live on Barlevento, nine miles east?

He responded by asking which of us is Don's wife? Where is the other man? How much money is our boat worth?

Even Susan began to come around.

"An airplane will come for us today," I blurted out. "We have a special radio that tells airplanes we are in trouble. It sends a beacon that tells the airplane where to find us. They will fly over the island and see our boat and see your boat and find us here. The radio is on and it will bring us help today."

Pablo nodded and paddled.

Several times we asked what had happened to Don and the others and why they had not met us, but always his answer was the same: "They come." He grinned and paddled.

When *Cheers'* mast was no more than a frail toothpick inclined against the azure sky behind us, more land appeared on the horizon ahead. It was low and barren of trees, but it was plainly attached to the land we had first sighted that morning. Pablo was taking us to the island, as promised.

The sun was high in the afternoon sky when we rounded the island's western point, three miles from *Cheers*, and sighted a rickety wood pier that stuck out from the scrub-covered land. A wooly mongrel with handsome black and fawn markings grew wild at the sound of Pablo's voice and ran up and down the length of the pier thrashing her tail so excitedly I thought she would fall in. Already tied to the dock were a beat-up 20-foot fiberglass launch and a needle-nose, 28-foot Magnum speedboat with the name *Phantom* emblazoned in foot-tall letters on both sides of her light-blue hull.

At the head of the pier was a cement walk that led past a tall flag pole from which snapped a bedsheet-size Venezuelan flag, and at the end of the walk, a white fiberglass igloo. I had to rub my salt-stung eyes to be sure the shiny white dome was indeed someone's abode and not the extra-galactic space craft of a surrealistic dream. But there it sat, a structure of futuristic technology upon a land that seemed utterly forgotten by time.

Aves de Sotavento is more reef than dry land. The lagoon's bottom was a bed of living coral; the beach was composed entirely of broken fragments of dead coral bleached white as bones; even the very earth beneath our feet was reclaimed coral. There are only two colors on Aves, starkest white and blinding blue-green. Every fragment of coral, every grain of sand, the lagoon and the sky is either eye-searing white or a kaleidoscope of dazzling blues and greens.

The only animals indigenous to this punished land are coal-black lizards that scurry underfoot, sinister scorpions and countless hermit crabs with shells the size of tennis balls. Heat rises from the land in rippling waves that distort one's vision. Even the white coral of the beach is too hot to walk on without shoes. Sweat is a way of life on Aves. The island is stark, desolate, parched and menacingly beautiful.

Pablo swung open the squeeking screened door to his prefabricated fiberglass igloo and led us inside. He seated us and set down two long glasses, a pitcher of ice water from the refrigerator and a tube of salve for our sunburnt skin. Minutes later we heard the whine of an engine and saw Don and the other three securing the Zodiac to the pier.

Our hosts swarmed up the dock carrying five enormous spiny lobsters, headed for the kitchen. Pablo wrestled them into two cauldrons and boiled them in shifts over the propane stove.

While Pepe, the young Spaniard and Fernando, the handsome Chilean, returned to their fishing, Pablo and Rafael, our Venezuelan hosts, killed us with kindness. Rafael more than made up for his lack of English by conversing with us in comical pantomime. Rafael's plump, animated face *was* his vocabulary. There was no question that we three needed their kindness, but we were more anxious to organize a rescue party for *Cheers*.

Aves, we discovered, was an outpost of the Venezuelan Exterior Department, and Pablo and Rafael were not fishermen but government employees who were relieving Bartolemey, the legendary keeper of the reef, for three months while he broke his island isolation by serving on a mainland outpost. Since it is easier to defend occupied land against foreign intrusion than abandoned soil, Pablo explained, their job was essentially just to "keep the reef"—to monitor and report all traffic, with the Guardia Nacional at their disposal if needed. *Cheers* was the first yacht to "call" at Aves since their arrival in May, and Susan and I were the first women they'd seen in nearly three months.

While the lobsters simmered in the pots, Pablo took our passports, then logged our arrival in his ledger. Where a visa would be stamped in our passports, he wrote in the most careful calligraphy:

Aves de Sotavento
Mar Caribe
Venezuela –S.A.
29-7-81
Pablo Antonio Silva M.

"A souvenir," he explained.

I assured him it was unlikely we would ever forget our stop at Aves de Sotavento—or him.

I saw a black box with two knobs on a shelf against the wall and was told that yes, it was the radio. I examined it and Don agreed that it was an old double sideband AM radio, useless for contacting commercial ships or yachts.

I asked Pablo to make his call on our behalf, but he explained that he can communicate with his headquarters on mainland Venezuela only three times a day at predesignated times: 7 a.m., noon and 3 p.m. As it was 1 p.m., we were too late for the first two broadcasts.

Despite Pablo's assurances that help would arrive tonight, it seemed impossible that even their swiftest vessel could reach us before morning.

Pablo called us to a table elaborately spread with platters and covered dishes. One by one he lifted the lids and heaped our plates high with baked grouper and lobster tails sautéed in garlic butter and herb rice. It was a sight to make a shipwrecked sailor cry, a banquet indeed.

At 3 o'clock a voice came on the air. I heard Pablo give our names and that of *Cheers*, but understood none of the Spanish. He signed off and assured us again that a rescue vessel would arrive that night. At daylight we could attempt the tow.

At 3:15 I walked outside to search our surroundings for gear with which to cushion *Cheers* and patch her if she holed. We had manual drills, self-tapping screws and plenty of caulking compound aboard the boat, so I looked for plywood, tires, crowbars, a jack and anything else we could use to get a bit of leverage and protect the hull.

Noblé the dog was understandably unaccustomed to strangers and plainly did not cotton to other women on her turf. She tailed me suspiciously, sniffing my trail, and bared her teeth when I tried to enter one of two open outbuildings.

Beyond the house I found a stagnant salt pond choked with a mysterious red algae on whose surface swarmed the island's other indigenous creatures—mosquitoes. Though our hosts screened every orifice of their house and burned scented mosquito coils around the perimeter of the rooms, the mosquito had dominion over man on Aves.

Beyond the salt pond was a long flat plain that looked like a small airstrip where sparse grass struggled to gain a foothold in the coral rubble. Beyond that, a few dwarf, crippled mangroves dotted the brittle land.

I remember reading in some cruising guide that Curaçao port authorities consider themselves the guardians of small craft in this part of the Caribbean and regularly track down missing yachts by helicopter, airplane and patrol boat anywhere within range of their equipment. Our lives were in no way now in jeopardy, but the EPIRB had been activated and to turn it off might only make them search the harder, presuming we had sunk.

Rafael found me and gestured that yes, a small plane could land there. He carried around his neck a pair of eight-power binoculars and led me to a cinder block outbuilding, which formed a base for their electricity-generating windmill. We scurried up the ladder, crouched out of range of the cavitating blades and steadied the binoculars on the edge of the roof. There, if I closed one eye and held my breath, I could just see *Cheers*, her mast leaning at 40 degrees, four miles across the lagoon to the northeast. From this high vantage point I could watch the weather and keep a lookout for a rescue vessel. How long before a storm arrived and the waves dashed her to pieces on the coral. I returned again and again to this perch to watch for help.

That evening, before the sun set, Pepe and Fernando brought their Zodiac to the dock and unloaded their catch. They were not commercial fishermen, we learned, but adventurers who'd come from Caracas to spend a few days at Aves snorkeling and spearfishing for sport.

It had taken them just over two hours to cover the 90 nautical miles from Caracas north to Aves in *Phantom*, their rocket-fast speed-boat with two powerful outboards. Once here, they left *Phantom* at the dock and worked both sides of the reef from the Zodiac, diving four hours in the morning and four hours again in the afternoon. It was early on their morning foray that they spotted *Cheers* on the reef and returned to get the others before swimming out to us. Had they not been there, it is doubtful that Pablo and Rafael, who seldom wander far from their igloo, would have found us before we finally abandoned *Cheers* and made for the island.

Though Fernando and Pepe spearfished for sport, they could feed all seven of us amply and pay for their trip by selling the remainder of their catch in Caracas. They were the hunters and Pablo and Rafael the cooks. Given a clove of fresh garlic and any sort of fish, they staged culinary extravaganzas. Pablo, married to an English-speaking wife from former British Guyana, passed many evening hours composing pretty fair love sonnets to her. Twenty-six-year-old Rafael, a bachelor, was counting the days until the ship came to return them to the mainland. There was no news, no recorded music, no commercial radio, no letters from home or newspapers during their three-month isolation on Aves.

The seven of us took all our meals together in the house. Evening suppers were jovial occasions preceded by a drink of Scotch and Coke and followed by Pablo pining away at his ukelele. At night Susan, Don and I shared their bedroom, the three of us sleeping together on a single mattress on the floor, while Pablo and Rafael snored from their single beds. Fernando and Pepe slept on *Phantom*.

THURSDAY, JULY 30

I ran to the dock before dawn to look for running lights or an anchor light indicating that the Guardia Nacional boat had arrived. Pablo guessed that she would proceed straight here to the point and anchor off the pier. I scanned the lagoon then searched the rim of the sea, but even as the sky turned blue, there was no ship. I climbed the windmill and peered through the binoculars. There was no other vessel besides *Cheers* and the rusting hulks on the horizon.

When the others were up, Susan and Don climbed in the fiber-glass launch and Rafael sped them across the lagoon. They waded out to *Cheers* and climbed aboard. They took all loose gear from deck and locked it below and returned to camp with the remainder of our fresh food and dry clothes. Unbelievably, they found the bilges dry.

At 3 p.m. Rafael called me to the windmill, where we saw a ship approaching from the south. By four o'clock a gray-hulled steel vessel of about 65 feet overall dropped anchor off the point in front of the igloo.

Don, Pablo and I jumped in the launch and Rafael ran us out to the vessel, which looked like a poorly-maintained World War II relic. A pivoting gun was mounted on her foredeck.

"She looks like a PT boat," observed Don, "but she's built of steel instead of plywood."

"Do you think she has the muscle to pull *Cheers* off the reef?" I asked.

"I think so. She should have plenty of horsepower. It's just a question of whether she can get a strong enough cable around the boat. She'll have to work from a distance of six or eight hundred feet, and on a lee shore at that."

"The wind's dropped," I said hopefully.

"Yes, and the waves are down from yesterday. The conditions are as good as they'll ever be."

Two men appeared and climbed down into our launch. Rafael powered across the lagoon toward *Cheers*, carefully conning his way through coral heads. Neither man wore a uniform, but I was told by Pablo that the middle-aged one was the captain. He was a slight man, brown and wrinkled like a raisin from the sun. He wore no shirt, had no front teeth and spoke no English. The stub of a hand-rolled cigarette dropped from his lower lip.

Sensing the captain's cold indifference, Pablo explained to him with dramatic gestures that my "husband" had been stabbed in the

Grenadines and that in fleeing west we had struck a reef during the night. It was a great performance, but the captain remained coldly aloof. When we got as close to *Cheers* as we could, Rafael idled down and pointed to the boat, but the captain, who was facing aft, did not turn around.

I began to work on the captain and Pablo translated. Helpless, humble and grateful was the way for a woman to play it. When that failed to raise a response I asked him point blank if he would try to pull my boat off the reef. He turned, looked briefly at *Cheers*, spat in the water, then said something to Pablo in Spanish.

"The captain says your boat is too far on the reef. It is too late to help."

"Tell him she is strong. She's not even holed. Ask him please if he will try."

"The captain says he will not risk his ship on the reef. He says your boat is finished."

"If we can pull out some of these coral heads, ask him if he will bring his boat into the lagoon and try to drag *Cheers* over the reef and into the lagoon."

His final reply needed no translation: No. Period. He gestured Rafael to return him to his ship.

When the captain and mate were back aboard their ship I spoke frankly to Pablo.

"It seems strange to me that the captain would bring his ship all the way here, then refuse to try to save my boat when he's hardly looked over the situation. Why did he even bother to come? Do you think he's waiting for a bribe?"

When we returned to the dock, Fernando and Pepe were cleaning their catch at the water's edge. This time, in addition to fish and lobster, they'd speared a sea turtle. Rafael returned to the Guardia Nacional boat and invited the captain to share our dinner, but he declined, saying they would be getting under way immediately for Puerto Cabello. That answered our question.

With no chance that the Guardia would help us, we had but one resort to save *Cheers*. Fernando and Pepe's holiday was over and they would leave in the morning for Caracas in Fernando's speedboat *Phantom*. They were our only link with the outside.

I mixed up a half gallon of rum punch and put the pitcher in the freezer to chill. When Pepe and Fernando had iced down their fish, Susan brought them inside and I made them comfortable. We listened eagerly to their stories, commended them for their hunting prowess, fussed over their fish spine wounds and plied them with drinks.

We learned little about Pepe, an affluent Spaniard in his late 20s who spoke no English. He was pleasant company—quiet, intelligent and very expressive with sign language.

Fernando, we learned, was an equestrian who showed and jumped horses professionally throughout South America. He was fortyish with an athletic build, toothy smile and continental sophistication. He had an affinity for fast horses, fast boats and fast women.

"What will you do," asked Fernando, "now that the Guardia is leaving and your boat is still on the reef?"

"You're our only hope of getting help," Susan explained. "We have no other way to get off the island."

"I understand you have one broken outboard and the other motor is sick," I added. "Rather than limp ninety miles south to Caracas with a contrary current, how about taking us to Bonaire to get help? It's just thirty-eight miles west. The wind and current will be with us, so if we lose the other engine, there will be land to leeward where we can get help. I'll hire a mechanic to fix your engines. I'll fill your fuel tanks and pay all the expenses while we're in Bonaire."

"But we have no passports," Fernando protested.

"I'll explain that to the officials."

"No chart."

"I'll navigate."

"What about all our fish?"

"We'll sell them for you or I'll buy them myself."

"All right," he said. "But understand one thing."

"What's that?"

"You must be ready to leave at six a.m."

"We'll be ready."

CHAPTER THIRTEEN

——————————————— At daybreak, the Guardia Nacional boat was still anchored off the point. At first I felt comforted that their presence would tend to discourage looters, but somehow I didn't entirely trust them, either. Why hadn't they left?

Don remained behind on Aves to watch over *Cheers*. Using her own ground tackle and winches, he hoped to nudge her further out of the wave action and would try to get a buffer under her bilge area. Fernando had kindly offered to leave behind his Zodiac and outboard so Don could be free to come and go to *Cheers*.

Susan and I had only the clothes on our backs, the same salt-stiff clothes in which we'd fled *Cheers*, but fortunately I'd thought to bring from *Cheers'* safe all the cash Jim had given me when we parted in St. Vincent.

Even on one engine, Fernando felt we could make the 38 nautical miles to Bonaire in less than two hours, so conceivably we could arrive by 8:30 a.m. While Susan looked after repairs and fueling of *Phantom* in Bonaire, I would canvas the commercial port. One more aborted rescue attempt could result in losing *Cheers*, so I decided not to waste any time or money on anything less than a tug, which I knew would have the horsepower, expertise and the long hawser to tow *Cheers* out through the breakers.

I felt fortunate even to have this second chance to save *Cheers*, and I was determined to return to Aves as soon as possible with a full-blown harbor tug, whatever the cost. Then we would cross our fingers and pull *Cheers* out through the breakers and hope she held together.

"We'll try to let you know what's up, Don. Can you monitor Channel 16 and 2182 on *Cheers* every even hour on the hour? We'll radio you as soon as we line up a tug."

"Good luck," he called as we idled away from the pier.

Though I knew Fernando had no large-scale chart of Bonaire, I assumed he would at least have had a small-scale chart for his trip from the mainland, which would include Bonaire. But no, he didn't.

"What exactly do you have?" I asked.

"Nothing," he said, punching a casette in the tape player.

"You mean you came to Aves without a chart?"

"Yes."

"How did you find it?"

"A fisherman told me what course to steer."

"What about the current?"

"What current?"

Distasteful as it was, we idled alongside the Guardia Nacional boat to ask for a compass course. Fernando was unabashed, for this was his usual practice. He rattled off the question to the mate in Spanish and after a moment came the reply: 275°.

Magnetic or true? I wondered as we raced away. Was that a course to the center of the island or the southern tip, which we wanted to round?

Outside the lee of Aves the wind was Force Four, a moderate breeze. The seas were directly on our stern, running about five feet—normal, well-spaced seas for the trade wind belt. With the starboard engine out of commission, we were making nine or 10 knots on the port engine alone—not the 20 knots Fernando had hoped. But 20 minutes away from land, the port engine also died. With no thought of keeping her stern to the swells, Fernando left the wheel and fiddled with the outboard, but could not unlock the secret to removing its cover. No matter, really, for he had no tools aboard. The next wave tossed *Phantom* beam to the seas. I took the wheel and tried to straighten her out, but with no headway, I had no steerageway and we wallowed precariously between seas.

Pepe turned the key in the ignition. The motor whined and

droned, then suddenly sprang to life. I put her in gear, straightened her out and we were on our way once more, with American disco blaring from the open cabin.

They were happy to have me steer, which required increasing diligence as Aves disappeared astern and the wind began to build and the seas grew larger.

When we were about 10 miles west of Aves, a great twin-engine military plane dropped out of the clouds and ran down our exact reciprocal course. It dipped its wing as it swooped so low overhead I could feel the thunder of its engines reverberate through my chest. Finally our EPIRB beacon had been picked up. I wondered if the plane would land on the tiny grass airstrip, but there was no way of telling, for we never saw it again.

The wind built in strength throughout the morning. The waves first became topped with whitecaps, then gradually the space between them began to close, producing shorter, steeper seas. Steering became a full-port-to-full-starboard rudder operation.

I grew apprehensive of the large cockpit. How could the enormous, scupperless, eight-by-12-foot basin drain the water if we broached and took a sea overboard? I could see no electric bilge pump switch on the steering console, or any access to the bilge or manual bilge pump. We could, of course, bail with buckets. But there were none.

Soon *Phantom*'s stern began lifting out of the water and the propeller would whine in thin air. The engine would race and die.

We tried different speeds and Fernando adjusted the remote-control trim tabs in every conceivable plane. Still the engine would race, then stall as we crested the steepest waves. Soon it became necessary for Susan to stand with me at the console, her hand on the key, to try to restart the engine each time it stalled, while I steered and manipulated the throttle.

"Fernando, what kind of safety equipment do you have aboard?" I asked nonchalantly.

"What do you mean?"

"You know, life jackets, flares, pumps, that sort of thing."

"Nothing. *Phantom* is a new boat. I bought her two months ago."

"I see. No life jackets?"

"No. I can swim. Pepe can swim. You girls can swim, yes?"

"Sure, we can swim. Do you have a radio?"

"No, just the tape player. You like this music? I have some BeeGees if you like to hear. . . ."

"No this is fine. Did your boat come with a bilge pump?"

"Bilge pump? What is that?"

"How do you empty the water out?"

"I don't. There never is any water in the boat."

"Will she float if she's full of water.

"I don't know. Are you worried, my love?"

I was not worried so much as I was acutely aware that a false move could invite a sea aboard. Though the cabin door was now closed, there was nothing to keep water from seeping into the cabin from the cockpit. Never again, I vowed, would I get underway on a Friday.

By nine o'clock I estimated we were midway between coasts. The wind peaked at about 22 knots and the seas, swept by white horses, grew no more. The engine continued to stall, but we limped on, still averaging seven knots.

By 11 o'clock sandy bluffs appeared on the horizon to starboard. We bore off to port, steering for a tall white lighthouse which seemed to rise right out of the sea. A flight of flamingos soared high overhead in formation, their necks outstretched and long legs trailing behind like winged escorts to their island.

By noon we rounded Lacrepunt, the southernmost point of boomerang-shaped Bonaire and turned at last into the lee of the island. Once 'round the southern point and into sheltered water, it was an easy hour's run north to our destination, Kralendijk Harbor. Even without a chart there was no mistaking the harbor. If you think like a sailor, it was right where you would put it: nestled in the crook of Bonaire's elbow, sheltered from the easterly trade winds by four miles of hilly island, and protected from blustery fall southwesterlies by Klein Bonaire (tiny Bonaire). Like so many colonial island seaports that played host to sailing ships, the entrance was wide open and the water deep.

Colonial Dutch influence was unmistakable in the fortress and tidy stone buildings lining the waterfront like a tropical Amsterdam. Inside the harbor, all was neatness, order, efficiency. Outside lay the muscle to do the job: three husky oceangoing tugs berthed abreast a pier just north of town, American flags snapping smartly from their stacks.

Entering the harbor, we believed the rescue attempt would fly or fail depending on what arrangements could be made in the next few hours. Fernando deposited me at the cement pier.

"Stay here and please don't go ashore until I've talked with customs," I said, grabbing our papers and running for the customs house. I began to tell my story to a Mr. Austin, a customs agent who spoke perfect English. I expected at least a stern lecture for arriving in his country aboard a boat with no papers which carried two aliens with no passports. When he rose from his desk and excused himself in the middle of my story, I was sure he was sending his strong men to the dock to apprehend the illegal aliens. But he returned a moment later with a chair for me and a pitcher of icewater.

"Now," he said, "just get your breath and tell me how I can help you."

After I finished the story and drained the pitcher, he locked the two passports and *Cheers'* document in his desk drawer, picked up his hat and took me in his car to the pier where *Phantom* was tied.

"Tell your friends they will be more comfortable at the marina," he said. "It's just three kilometers north of town. Tell them they can find a mechanic there. They are free to go ashore. Someone from customs and immigration will come later to take their names."

Mr. Austin drove me along the waterfront to size up the commercial tonnage and then to Bonaire Marina to look over smaller boats. All told, there were three huge oceangoing tugs and three tiny line boats, with no tugs in between. For work boats, there were two Korean fishing boats of about 140 feet overall, an inter-island gas freighter, a gaily-painted Venezuelan fruit boat of about 40 feet, a 28-foot fishing boat, a powerful-looking motor yacht of about 60 feet, and a handful of cruising sailboats and small runabouts.

"You're going to need the help of a shipping agent," said Mr. Austin. "There's only one man who knows about the ships that come and go from here. If anyone can help you, it's José Marchena."

He pulled up in front of the one-story red cinder block Kralendijk Trading Company, located on the waterfront just north of the main harbor. In a dark, air conditioned office, a man wearing black horn-rimmed glasses was seated in a swivel chair behind an expansive desk chattering on the phone in rapid Spanish. Everything about him, his animated gestures, his tall, lean frame, his stacatto speech and the nervous way he strummed the desk top with his fingertips suggested action, efficiency, results. As he talked, several secretaries filed in and out with papers. When he hung up the phone, he leapt to his feet, shook my hand warmly and offered me a chair

"You're in good hands," said Mr. Austin with a reassuring pat on my shoulder. Then he left.

José Marchena listened attentively as I told him my story, then he glanced at his watch, shoved aside the neat stacks of paper on his desk and cupped his face in his hands for a moment of meditation.

"So, you put your boat on a reef," he declared. "Jesus Christ, how are we going to get it off?"

Contrary to what I had read, he assured me that the Netherlands Antilles has no service comparable to the U.S. Coast Guard, which assists in the rescue of boats. We telephoned the airport and learned that our EPIRB had been received and that the Dutch Navy in Curaçao had dispatched a plane early that morning to investigate. It was their plane *Neptune* whose path we had crossed in *Phantom*. I reported that the crew of *Cheers* was safe and sent thanks to the Dutch Navy in Curaçao for responding to our call.

José Marchena then dialed a number from memory and spoke in lightning-fast Dutch, then slammed down the phone, rummaged through the card file on his desk and dialed another number. This time he spoke in a tongue I can only liken to the sound of a ricocheting Ping-Pong ball in an echo chamber.

"How many languages do you speak?" I asked when he hung up.

"Let's see, Dutch, Spanish, German, English, Papiamento. Five. The last was Papiamento. Sounds more like a disease of the mouth, doesn't it?"

He picked up his keys. "Let's take a ride."

I liked him immediately. There was a sense of urgency about José Marchena. He talked, walked and wielded a car like a man sitting on a time bomb. He was a one-man show, a marvel to watch. From his small office, served by a satellite crew of hovering male agents and female clerical help, he was the nucleus of shipping in the Netherlands Antilles, who had at his fingertips all the commercial tonnage in the islands and ports along the Venezuelan mainland. I'd come to the right place. José Marchena became my shipping agent and my friend.

He parked the car at Bonaire Marina. "Wait here," he said. "I'm going to talk with Don Marshall. He pulled a yacht off a reef once before."

He ran down the dock to a 60-foot powder-blue power yacht and returned a few minutes later.

"Well?"

"Don Marshall won't take the job, not without a visa and work papers. The Guardia Nacional almost grabbed his boat the last time he helped a yacht on Aves."

"There is more to this than you understand, young lady. Your boat is in Venezuelan waters. Bonaire confiscated a Venezuelan trawler earlier this year for fishing its waters illegally. They'd like nothing better than to even the score. No one is going to go there without working papers and visas."

"Can you arrange that?"

"The Venezuelan Consul here is a funny man. He probably will not give one of our boats the papers. For a thousand dollars you can fly to Caracas. They will run you around in circles for a week and anyway you will not be safe alone in the city."

"Then what are our choices?"

"We're going to talk with the Bonaire Petroleum Corporation. The three oceangoing tugs you saw are under Charter to BOPEC."

"They're bigger than we need. How much do you think they would ask for the job?"

"Ten, maybe fifteen thousand."

"Guilders or dollars?"

"Dollars. But they won't be interested in this job. They are businessmen. Salvage is dangerous business. They already have a good-paying contract bringing ships in right here."

José parked the car. "Here we are. Fix your hair. That's better. Now how badly do you want to save your boat?"

"To save my boat, I would do anything."

"That's very good. Use those sad green eyes. Let me do the talking."

We were shown to a modern, windowless office. Two executives listened, then explained the tugs were insured only for a 12-mile radius of Kralendijk Harbor.

I offered to pay for an insurance rider to increase their range of operation to include Aves for this job.

They led us to a chart on the wall. I showed them the spot on the reef where *Cheers* was stranded.

But again there were hitches. Even if they could get a work permit, they had a contract and could not spare a tug for one day. The sad green eyes didn't change their minds. They were sorry, but they couldn't help. Business was business.

We drove next to a freight dock where the two rusting Korean tuna boats were berthed. We jumped aboard the *Dong Won Busan 801*, a 140-footer. We scurried up a ladder to the bridge, left our shoes next to others outside the wheelhouse and were shown inside by the mate, a young Korean who spoke some English. He fetched Captain Kim Jung Nam, a soft-featured Korean of about 35 with deep black eyes and a shock of straight black hair that stood out in every direction like a haystack. He greeted José Marchena in broken Spanish and they spoke as old friends. He led us to a chart drawer from which he produced a chart of the two Aves islands.

I examined the chart and on the widest part of the reef, where the legend reads "heavy breakers," I touched my finger to indicate where *Cheers* lay. The captain studied the chart and drew a deep breath. He shook his head dismally, then he and José spoke in Spanish.

"Please tell him my boat is very tough." I took the pencil and sketched a profile of the boat. "Tell him she is like the old rescue boats of the North Sea. Fifteen tons. Very strong. Big keel. Solid fiberglass, two inches thick at the keel. She can survive a tow through the breakers."

They spoke again in Spanish, then the captain showed us to the wheelhouse door. I shook his hand and thanked him.

José drove me back to his office.

"What's wrong with you American girls you cannot cry?" he asked, pointing me to a chair.

"Did I blow it, José?"

"I think you did fine. If it were up to me I would put your damn boat on my back and swim with it here." He turned and placed an overseas call.

The overseas operator rang back and José conducted the call in Spanish. I gathered that it was about me and picked up from José's wildly flailing arms that he was imploring someone to help.

When he hung up the phone a burly young man of about 35 entered and spoke with him in Dutch. I introduced myself to Jack van der Eem, an intelligent, powerfully-built man with Dutch features who spoke perfect English. He was blonde with a ruddy complexion, dark close-set eyes and large calloused hands. Next Captain Kim entered with a chart rolled under his arm and his mate in tow.

Things were evidently beginning to take shape, though I had no notion of the details because the conversation was in Spanish. I was only beginning to realize my handicap. Speaking only English and limited French, I was a linguistic cripple. I might as well have been deaf and mute.

Finally José spoke. "Captain Kim wants to help you. He wants to save your boat to the extent that he has radioed the owner of the *Dong Won* in Venezuela and asked his permission to assist in the salvage of your boat instead of fishing for tuna. I also telephoned the owner in Venezuela and said that as your agent, I would put my company behind the effort. The owner offers the services of *Dong Won Busan 801* for 24 hours beginning tomorrow morning."

"What is the price?" I asked.

"Only one thousand five hundred U.S. dollars," said José. "That is very cheap. The ship will steam for Aves at eight a.m. She will try to tow your boat off the reef, but regardless of the outcome, she must return to Bonaire by eight o'clock the following morning to fish for tuna in northern waters. After your boat is freed from the reef, she cannot offer to tow you, escort you to Bonaire or assist you in any way. What do you say?"

"Please tell the captain I gratefully accept his offer. My sister and I will be aboard his boat before eight o'clock tomorrow morning. Would you please ask the captain how much his ship draws and what speed she can average?"

Captain Kim replied that the *Dong Won* drew 13 feet and could average seven-and-a-half knots. Figuring the contrary current, I calculated we could make Aves by 2 p.m. tomorrow. *Cheers* could be off the reef, patched if necessary, and anchored safely by sundown that same day.

Again we shook hands and the Koreans left. Then I spoke with Jack van der Eem. "What I need now is an escort vessel with enough power to tow my boat, if necessary, back to Bonaire."

Jack headed up the government-funded fishing co-op on Bonaire and had in his stable of fishing boats a 28-footer that could assist us.

"There is a good chance *Cheers* will be holed when she comes off the reef. We have all the materials we will need for a patch, but my crew has been through a lot and I will need them aboard my boat to man the pumps. I'd like to hire two divers to stand by and patch the boat if she holes. We have three pumps on *Cheers* that can handle a total of fifty gallons a minute. I'd like to get one large-capacity portable pump as a backup."

"That's no problem," said Jack. "Tomorrow is Saturday, so I can come with you on the *Dong Won*."

"That's very nice of you," I said. "I could sure use an interpreter."

It was 5 o'clock. Our work was done for the day. I looked at José's phone and wanted so much to call Jim. It was five days since we'd left Bequia, and I knew he was expecting my call. I knew he would be concerned, but I doubted he'd be worried yet. I knew only that he was in the hospital and might have had further surgery. It would do him no good and perhaps a good deal of harm to hear at the stage in his recovery that *Cheers* was on a reef. I hoped by the next day to get her off and bring her to Bonaire, so I put off calling him until then.

It was amazing what had been accomplished in three hours. José kindly drove me to the Bonaire Marina, where *Phantom* was berthed at a choice front slip.

"José, you've done so much for me, I hate to think of you missing all the excitement. Trade your city clothes for a swim suit and come with us tomorrow. I could use a good diver."

"Jesus Christ," he said. "I hate the sea. You bring your boat to this marina and I will drink a toast on your boat."

✳   ✳   ✳

My sister the fishmonger had sold *Phantom*'s entire catch—over 150 pounds of fish—on the dock. A mechanic was working on both outboards and I introduced myself to Lino Craane, a husky Bonairian of European descent who was up to his armpits in black grease. The 35-year-old jack of all trades immediately put down his tools and led me down the dock to a bright red half-ton racing sloop from Sint Maarten, which listed heavily in her slip.

Lino spoke only the native tongue, Papiamento, a curious mixture of archaic Portuguese, Spanish and Dutch. He seemed convinced that if only he spoke loud enough, I surely would get his meaning. Then with sign language he explained that the boat had gone up on Aves four months earlier. Lino and a small crew had pulled her off the inside lagoon reef, patched her and towed her to the marina. Lino was apparently the brains behind the salvage effort and showed me the boat as proof that my boat, too, could be saved.

Lino worked well into the night on *Phantom*'s outboard engines, but lacking replacements for many of the parts he discovered were broken, he could only jury-rig it. He apparently held little faith in Fernando and Pepe's ability to return alone to Aves against wind and current, so he announced he would accompany them. Lino eagerly wolfed down the late supper Susan bought him, but would accept no pay for his work.

Two men from customs and immigration came aboard next. Try explaining to officials of any Caribbean island that tomorrow the Bonairian will accompany the Chilean and the Spaniard (sorry, no passports) on the Venezuelan boat (sorry, no papers), while the two American girls who came on the Venezuelan boat will leave with another Bonairian on a Korean tuna boat.

To my utter surprise, they simultaneously cleared us in and out of their country courteously and without a hitch, waving customary overtime charges. I must say they were quite taken with *Phantom*. Fernando played them a selection of earsplitting pop tunes while they completed the paperwork in the cabin, stopping only to caress and covet the pure white fake fur that carpeted the cabin sides and overhead.

"This must be how Jonah felt," Susan whispered when we were bedded down for the night in *Phantom*'s forward cabin. "In this case, though, I think we've been swallowed by a polar bear."

CHAPTER FOURTEEN

SATURDAY, AUGUST 1

——————————————— At 7:45 a.m. José rapped on *Phantom*'s hull and greeted Susan and me with bad news.

"The trip's off," he said flatly. "When the owner learned two señoritas were going he withdrew the ship."

"But why?" I asked. "So what if we're women?"

"There are twenty-two men in the crew, that's so what."

The implication raised Susan's feminist hackles. "Is he afraid for our safety, or does he think we'll corrupt the crew?"

"Corrupt his crew—that's very funny. Have you seen those guys? Whew! I tell you what really happened. The owner monitors the radio. There are big strikes in tuna northeast of Bonaire. His two ships have seined until their bait tanks are full with anchovy. Now that the fish are biting he wants a piece of the action. He only asked fifteen hundred of your dollars for the trip. But a boatload of tuna will bring him many times that. Greed, that is the problem. Not women. Let Captain Kim work on him. I will try to find you another boat."

I lit a cigarette and peeled back the heavy drapery covering the picture window on the sea. We would know soon enough what kind of a night *Cheers* had spent on the reef.

Nine o'clock, 9:30. In a medley of tongues, José searched desperately for another boat by phone. After each call he would slam the phone down into its cradle and curse in the tongue in which he had conducted the call. The odds of saving *Cheers* were growing slimmer as the daylight hours slipped away. I paced and waited. The ashtray filled with butts.

At 10 o'clock Jack van der Eem burst into the room.

"The trip's back on!" he exclaimed, catching his breath. "You've got *Dong Won* until tomorrow morning. But if they find tuna on the way to Aves, their orders are to stop and fish, then continue."

Jack led Susan and me to his car and with a screech we pulled up to the dock where the *Dong Won* waited. Captain Kim, standing on the bridge, beckoned us up to the wheelhouse.

Hastily, we scaled the high steel bulwarks, then dropped down to the low deck and threaded our way past a dozen crew members who looked disarmingly like a band of Shanghai pirates. Some wore only a skimpy loincloth, some a diaperlike swaddling cloth wrapped around the waist and loins in loose horizontal folds of white cotton.

Though few stood taller than either Susan or me, they all showed a wiry strength born of muscling tons of thrashing tuna over the rails with flimsy bamboo poles. They moved with the quick agility of boxers.

There was more curiosity than hostility in their piercing stares as we passed among them, and none of the lewdness I'd become accustomed to from waterfront West Indians. Though the features were Oriental, the faces were those you'd see on fresh recruits on any military base, those of young men somewhere between peach fuzz and whiskers.

Jack led me aft to the rail and pointed down to a fiberglass commercial fishing boat with a small enclosed cabin and large cockpit tied to the pier astern of us.

"That's your escort boat," said Jack. "Four hundred dollars for the day. What do you say?"

"For that boat? For one day? Why she can't be over thirty feet."

"She's twenty-eight feet and she's got an eighty-horsepower diesel. The price includes the two crew." Two black men, a Rastifarian youth and a middle-aged man in coveralls, looked up at Jack expectantly.

"Their price sounds pretty steep."

"Pedro can make that and more fishing."

"They'll stand by while we pull *Cheers* off, then escort or tow us to Bonaire?"

"Yes."

"All right. Four hundred dollars."

Jack gave a nod to the helmsman and the older man cast off, bound for Aves de Sotavento.

I had the unsettling feeling I'd just been fleeced.

But Susan's eyes, wide and full of excitement, mirrored my own feeling of exhilaration and expectancy as *Dong Won* sidled away from the dock with a guttural drone. The waiting was over; the rescue was under way.

The *Dong Won Busan 801* was 140 feet on deck. Built 13 years before, she was a spartan vessel that showed every hard year of her working life. Her black-trimmed green hull was pockmarked with multicolored patches of chipped paint like open sores which bled down her topsides in rusty streaks. The wheelhouse was vintage 1945. Inside it was painted pale institutional green, coat over chipping coat.

It was 11 o'clock when we reached Lacrepunt and turned from the lee of Bonaire into the wind on an easterly course for Aves. From the 40-foot-high bridge of the ship, it was difficult for me to judge the wind and sea conditions. The ship's motion was easy as she plowed into whitecapped waves.

Once clear of the point, the mate and two deckhands entered the wheelhouse and took up binoculars, which they steadied on the plywood console, and began patiently, methodically scanning the horizon for birds feeding on bait fish, chased up to the surface by tuna.

At our present seven knots, it would be 4 o'clock when we reached *Cheers*, leaving only two and a half hours of daylight to get a line on her, tow her free, inspect and perhaps patch the hull. Tonight's waxing moon would be too dim to give us working light past sunset.

At noon the mess cook brought a large covered platter to the wheelhouse and Captain Kim invited us to join him at his noonday meal. We sat cross-legged around the platter on the wheelhouse sole while the mate steered by compass. I'd never sampled Korean food, but figured it couldn't be too different from Chinese, Japanese or Vietnamese.

Now I like hot food as much as anyone. My jalapeño enchiladas have ignited whole dinner parties and one whiff of my sambal oelek could bring a conquistador to his knees. But sharing the captain's mess that day I was in rare company. I was wholly unprepared for my first explosive taste of really hot food.

I made a greedy show of heaping my stainless steel bowl with a little bit of everything before tasting anything. Susan and Jack did likewise. Taking a cue from the captain, we raised our bowls to our lips and began shoveling in copious heaps of food.

Jack was the first one down. He pursed his lips in a shrill hyperventilating whistle and tried to snuff out the fire with great rushes of air.

"Ha aah-aah-aah!" wheezed Susan, clutching her throat.

I swallowed, drew a deep breath and tried to blink back the tears. The burning sensation spread like a bush fire across the roof of my mouth, down my esophagus to my tender pink stomach lining.

The mate looked over his shoulder and snickered. The distressed captain leaped to his feet, reached in a locker and produced three drinking glasses, which he filled with instant orange drink and water, and a small tin of cocktail weiners. Susan and I eagerly sucked down the remedy, while Jack, evidently feeling there was a certain machismo at stake, continued the meal.

At 1 o'clock three deckhands returned to the wheelhouse, and resumed their lookout for fish. Moments later there was a great whoop of excitement as they spotted a hungry flock of white gulls circling a well-defined patch of water about a mile to the northeast.

"We stop and fish for tuna?" I asked dismally.

"Those are the orders," Jack said.

The captain looked intently at the feeding birds, then he glanced at his watch. I could sense him calculating the time, weighing the decision. Without speaking he walked to the radio shack. A few moments later he returned to the wheelhouse and spoke in broken Spanish to Jack, who translated:

"He's obliged to check in with the owner every two hours. He reported no fish. We're proceeding to Aves."

I had missed the 10 a.m. and noon radio schedules, so shortly before 2 p.m. Captain Kim led me to the radio shack so I could try to raise Don as promised. But because their VHF was broken and the *Dong Won* had only an old double sideband radio with no frequency to communicate with *Cheers*, we could make no radio contact with Don. I would have to wait until we were within shouting range, then communicate by loud hailer.

By 3 o'clock I could make out the faint line of the vast reef to which we were heading. The captain pointed to the radar screen where three distinct luminescent blobs dotted the outer line. Remembering the other two wrecks north of *Cheers*, I touched the radar screen to indicate that the southernmost shapeless blob was my boat.

We altered course five degrees to clear the northern stretch of reef, then turned southeast to close with *Cheers*.

Two and three at a time the crew filed up to the bridge to glimpse my boat through the binoculars. My palms grew sweaty. I began to chew my fingernails. How had she stood up to four days on the reef?

When we were two miles distant I saw her slim, fragile toothpick mast inclined against a halo of white water. My heart fell.

"Jesus," muttered Jack. "You really did it."

"Do you think we can pull her off, Jack?"

He pulled a pouch of shag tobacco from his shirt pocket, rolled two tapered cigarettes and passed one to me. "It's possible." He struck a match. "But I wouldn't give you very good odds."

I drew a deep puff of the harsh tobacco. A glum silence hung over the ship. It was now 4 o'clock. We maneuvered to a position one mile directly upwind of *Cheers*, keeping safely off the reef while the captain assessed the situation. Captain Kim studied the chart nervously, his face lined with indecision as we drifted in the groundswell. He gave me a long disconcerting look, then studied *Cheers*'s position on the reef. Then he squatted facing aft, his face buried in his hands, torn with the weight of his decision.

At last he stood and ordered the bosun to start heaving the lead line as *Dong Won* swung in a wide half-circle and edged forward toward the line of breakers. The lee shore of this reef was clearly no place for the lumbersome fishing vessel with her throaty old single diesel, 30-second delay between wheelhouse controls and engine room, and restricted rudder angle.

As we approached the breakers, *Cheers*'s position on the reef looked far more perilous than even I had realized. The sight was almost more than I could stand. She lay over on her starboard bilge, starboard deck awash, keel fully exposed, heading shoreward with her port quarter toward us. Pablo's fiberglass skiff was anchored inside the lagoon not far from *Cheers* and three bodies bounced up and down on the bowsprit, apparently trying to change her trim enough to move her.

Dong Won's old diesel resounded in eerie refrain as undulating blue waves rose, curled, then exploded in a flash of white foam across the vast plain of coral rubble. The bosun heaved the line and called the soundings as we crept toward the breakers. From the bridge I could clearly see the coral head-studded bottom. When only 200 feet from the line of breakers, the captain swung the ship into the wind and ordered the anchor set. The great rusty Northill splashed over the bows and a stud-link chain ripped through the hawsepipe with a stacatto chinking sound. With engine idling in reverse, *Dong Won* drifted back to within 100 feet of the curling waves and fetched up hard on her anchor chain 600 feet to windward of *Cheers*.

It was 4:40. The bosun heaved the lead, letting it bump along the bottom when we dropped into a passing through, and repeating the maneuver amidships and astern. The captain had chosen his spot with hair-splitting accuracy. There was 20 feet of water at the bow, shoaling to just 15 feet at the stern. *Dong Won* had only two feet of water beneath her keel when she lay in a trough.

The wind blew 15 knots from the east. The height was five feet, swelling to eight feet before breaking in a frothy barrier between the two vessels. But for the late hour, conditions could not have been better to attempt an exit through the surf.

Still, *Cheers*' chances of survival looked poor. I could envision the mighty hawser coming under strain. *Cheers* would pivot on her keel until she pointed seaward. Then, resting on her keel and starboard bilge, she would be dragged through the foam. She could survive that, just as she had the night we struck the reef. But when she got enough water under her keel to give her buoyancy, she would rise high on each oncoming crest, then be thrown with the full force of her 15 tons against the coral bottom as each wave dropped beneath her. Her 5½-ton internal lead ballast, I feared, would batter the mast upward, splintering the cabin sole, springing bulkheads, popping the deck and crushing the hull like an eggshell.

But it was our only chance. The captain was at that moment

risking his own vessel to save mine. Two hours of daylight remained and darkness would be our deadline.

The 28-foot fishing boat I'd engaged came along our port side. We needed radio communication with Don while setting up the job and hoped to talk with him through the 28-footer's VHF radio. But Pedro had only a single sideband radio and it was broken.

We returned to the wheelhouse and Jack asked the captain to turn on his loudhailer. *Cheers* was dead downwind and it might just carry the 600 feet to her. But the loudhailer, too, was broken.

We would have to float a long messenger line downwind to Don to enable him to pick up the hawser, and so I penned this note to him along with a diagram:

Don:

Pull in messenger until you get to nylon hawser. Pass hawser entirely around Cheers *like a girdle: lead it from stem, aft through propeller aperture and back to stem with a bowline. Fashion a bridle so load is even and hawser cannot slip. End of hawser is shackled to a long wire rope. Make sure it leads fair and clears bowsprit.*

Stow all deck gear below or lash it securely on deck. Lash tiller firmly between port and starboard stanchions. Kick up steering vane rudder. Dog all hatches and ports. Get everyone off boat. If you choose to stay aboard please wear life jacket and harness.

Get plywood, drill, screws and bedding compound ready for patch.

No way to communicate with you by radio. Air horn in locker beneath chart table. We are anchored and cannot pull port or starboard, only ahead. Use these signals to direct us:

One long blast—slow ahead
Two long blasts—fast ahead
Four short blasts—stop

Please check bilges as soon as you're afloat. Cross your fingers.

I hurried down the ladder to the afterdeck. It was 5 o'clock. I slipped the note in a plastic bag, then sealed the bag in a jar, wrapped the jar in more plastic and sealed the whole thing with duct tape. The bosun tied a bright orange life ring to the bitter end of the messenger line, secured the message-bearing jar to the life ring, waved the ring high over his head and tossed it into the sea.

We watched intently as the orange ring drifted downwind, tumbled through the breakers and stopped 10 yards south of *Cheers*. We waited and watched for someone to retrieve it. Unbelievably, no one seemed to see it. We waved our arms high overhead and pointed to the buoy. Finally a figure slipped over *Cheers'* rail, waded to the ring and dragged it aboard.

Five minutes passed, but no one pulled in the messenger. Had they read the note? Ten minutes. It was 5:15. Only 75 minutes of daylight remained.

With slow, exaggerated gestures I acted out a pantomime on the fantail, urging them hand-over-hand to pull in the messenger. Nothing happened.

I hurried up to the bridge and trained the binoculars on *Cheers*. Don stood in the cockpit waving the orange buoy, which he then threw over the side.

What went wrong. Didn't he know time was running out?

"He attached something to the ring," said Jack, looking through the binoculars. "It's probably a note. We better pull it in."

While the bosun retrieved the long messenger I hurried to the afterdeck to get the note. On a piece of lined paper was scrawled a crude sketch and these words: "No go. Too dangerous."

We turned the paper sideways and upside down but could not make any sense of the diagram. It showed two vessels with a ripple of water in between. But which was which? What did it mean?

It was 5:30. An hour of daylight remained. I turned Don's message over and scribbled on the reverse side:

> "Must try. Pull in messenger. Secure hawser. Signal when ready. Hang on."

The bosun stuffed my reply in the jar, taped it to the buoy and threw it into the sea. The orange ring again drifted down to *Cheers* and a wader retrieved it. I watched through the binoculars as three bodies scurried about the deck securing things, then someone pulled in the messenger line, passed the hawser around the mast and back to itself in a loose bight. It was not the towing bridle I had wanted, but time was short and Don evidently thought it adequate.

Two bodies jumped off the boat and swam to Pablo's anchored skiff. Only Don remained aboard *Cheers*. Wearing a yellow foul weather jacket, he stood on the cabin top and signalled "all ready." It was 6 o'clock.

Captain Kim signalled the crew on the afterdeck to winch in on the cable drum. When they'd taken all the slack out of the wire towing cable, he ordered them to clear the afterdeck. The captain looked at me. I nodded. There was no turning back.

Thirty seconds later the engine responded with a powerful growl. The cable strained tight as a piano string. I clenched the bridge railing with white knuckles and held my breath. The engine revved louder and louder. *Dong Won*'s stern swayed and squatted under the strain. Susan stood behind me, her fingers digging into my shoulders. At the last moment I turned away. I could not watch.

"Here she comes. She's moving, Betsy, she's *moving!* Oh God! No!"

"Shit," muttered Jack.

I spun around to see what had gone wrong. Susan covered my head with her shoulder. I broke free and saw *Cheers* teeter upright, hesitate, then topple over with a crushing jar and a tremendous splash hard on her port side. The captain let up on the throttle, but *Cheers* burried her port rail and came to rest with her mast nearly horizontal.

"I thought she'd pivot and come free," I muttered, my face buried in my hands. I was crushed, my spirit was broken. I believed her port side was stove in. Waves now broke over her cabin trunk, sending spray flying high into the air.

With binoculars I searched for Don, fearing he'd been hurt. A moment later he stood in the cockpit and motioned us to try again. Captain Kim looked to me for direction and then quickly spoke to Jack, who translated for me.

"The captain fears she will roll if we pull again. He thinks we may rip off the deck."

I studied *Cheers* and wished for wisdom. I was over my head, facing a decision beyond my experience. Finally, I told the captain through Jack, "If we stop now, she is lost. Please, will you try again?"

The captain walked to a quiet corner of the bridge and kneeled with his head in his hands. Finally he rose and spoke to me through Jack. "We will try again, but you must promise not to hold me responsible. I believe your boat will be destroyed."

I had been studying *Cheers*'s position carefully. "If we can reanchor a hundred yards to the south we will have a better angle of pull. Then she cannot bury her rail. I take full responsibility for my boat, Captain, and regardless of the outcome I am grateful to you for your help."

The captain nodded. It was 6:15. The sun would set in 15 minutes, then we would have another 15 minutes of twilight before darkness dropped its curtain.

At the captain's command, the crew on the afterdeck slacked off the wire towing cable and bent on a half-inch-diameter rope tail to give the ship the necessary slack to raise it and reset its anchor 100 yards south.

At 6:30 the sun slipped into the sea, and with nerve-tingling clatter the anchor again was lowered. We drifted astern in neutral while the foredeck crew paid out anchor chain. Suddenly the bosun gave a frantic shriek. Coral heads reared around us in the fading light. A deck hand snubbed the anchor chain, but the anchor did not bite. We continued to slip toward the breakers. The captain threw the telegraph control ahead and we all held our breath, waiting for the crunch. Half a minute later the forward gear engaged.

Suddenly another cry of panic rang up from the afterdeck. The towing line had fouled in the propeller. With no maneuverability, we continued to slip toward the breakers, dragging our anchor.

The captain buried the throttle. The engine droned, the entire superstructure shuddered, and with a belch of black smoke, *Dong Won* surged ahead. The mate stood on the afterdeck holding the severed tail of the line that had fouled in the propeller. We had lost the entire wire cable, 600 feet of it, our only tie to *Cheers*.

The captain's shirt was soaked in perspiration. He powered due east, away from the reef, for 10 minutes without looking back. Then he turned the wheel over to his mate, spoke briefly to Jack, then called the owner in Venezuela.

We sat in silence, numbed by the narrow escape. Jack listened attentively to the Spanish portion of the captain's call, then shook his head in disbelief. "He's asking the owner's permission to try again in the morning at first light."

Even I had been ready to admit defeat.

No understanding of Spanish was necessary to comprehend the owner's rage as he bellowed angrily at the captain and ordered him to proceed immediately to Bonaire.

The captain pointed out that he had passengers aboard he had promised to deliver to Aves de Sotavento and that he had lost his 100-fathom wire cable and must retrieve it in daylight.

The captain also pointed out that a crew member was dangerously stranded aboard the boat on the reef. Since a human life was at stake, he felt responsible to proceed around to the island, launch a boat into the lagoon and rescue the stranded man.

The owner's patience was exhausted. He ordered the captain to enter in his log that the distressed vessel was damaged beyond hope. He was to drop off the passengers and return immediately to Bonaire, or lose his contract and face deportment back to Korea.

There was no more discussion. The captain emerged from the radio shack a beaten man. I shook his hand warmly with both of mine and tried to convey in the few words of Spanish I'd learned how deeply grateful I was for his efforts.

Now, in total darkness, the captain set a southerly course for Pablo's island, where he would leave us. The next day we would salvage what gear we could from *Cheers*. My spirits were at their lowest ebb since we'd struck the reef four days before. My despair knew no bounds. I stared, mesmerized, at the inky surface of the sea and thought how like an evil tar pit it was, an oily black mire covering the bones of countless sailors, their ships, their broken dreams.

Images of the horrors of this past month blotted from memory all the joy *Cheers* had ever brought us. I accepted then that my sailing days were over. I was utterly and completely defeated. Slumped in a darkened corner of the bridge, I slipped into a lifeless sleep.

CHAPTER FIFTEEN

SUNDAY, AUGUST 2

———————————— Strong fingers gripped my shoulders and shook me like a rag doll. I tried to focus on the face before me, still in the world of lunacy between mindless sleep and wakefulness. My sister's face was inches from my own.

"Snap out of it, Betsy. We're here. You were out of your head, Betsy. You really gave me a fright."

"I was dreaming."

"Your eyes were open. What's this curse you kept talking about? Some sort of curse on *Cheers?* You kept saying, 'It's jinxed.' "

"I don't know, Susan. I think the strain is getting to me. Where are we?"

"We're off the point of Pablo's island. Better decide now whether you're going to stay on Aves or return to Bonaire."

"Where's Don Brown?"

"Unless Pablo got him off, he's still aboard *Cheers.*"

The flashing strobe atop *Dong Won's* bridge illuminated a well-defined circle in the lagoon. Anchored on the periphery of the circle, in the same spot she had chosen three days earlier, was the gray hull of the Guardia Nacional gun boat. Her presence made Captain Kim uneasy and more than once he trained his binoculars on the darkened ship.

Suddenly lights appeared in the windows of the igloo two

hundred yards away. We heard the whine of an outboard motor and moments later Pablo and Rafael were alongside *Dong Won* in their blue skiff.

"You spoiled all our work," said Pablo in a trembling voice. "We moved your boat to a shallow pool where she was safe from the waves." He held his cut and swollen palms under the light. "We cleared the coral with our bare hands for you."

"I'm sorry, Pablo. I didn't know."

"You should have talked with Don and waited until morning to tow your boat."

"We have this ship only for today. We had to try before dark. Where is Don?"

"He is aboard your boat. We could not get to him through the surf in the darkness."

"How was *Cheers* riding when you left?"

"Very bad. She is sideways to the waves. They pick her up and throw her against the coral. But your boat is stronger than the coral. She crushes the coral to sand."

"Is she holed?"

"Before you came there were only scratches on the hull. Now, I don't know. She hit the coral very hard when she fell over. Maybe now she is holed. You will try again to pull her off in the morning?"

"No, the captain is ordered to return to Bonaire tonight."

"At first light we will get Don. Then we will try to pull your boat back over to her right side and patch her if her hull is broken."

"Good. I'm going back to Bonaire tonight. I'll try to hire another boat and return as soon as I can. Susan, try to monitor VHF and single sideband tomorrow at nine, noon and six. I'll get word to you as soon as I can."

A bright searchlight flashed from the Guardia boat and came to rest on the *Dong Won*. "They've seen your ship," said Pablo, "Go now, before the captain gives you trouble."

Susan climbed over the *Dong Won*'s high bulwarks. Pablo and Rafael reached up, lowered her into their skiff, and hastily pushed off for shore.

Captain Kim snuffed out both the strobe and his running lights and idled slowly westward. When the searchlight from the Venezuelan gunboat was only a white spark on the eastern horizon, he revved the engine and bore away for Bonaire.

Again I nodded off on the wing of the bridge. Sometime later

Captain Kim awakened me with a tap and led me into the state-room, where he had made up a bed for me on the floor. There, beneath a *Penthouse* poster, I laid down my head in deep restorative sleep.

We reached the mouth of Kralendijk Harbor just before sunup.

Moments after we stepped ashore at the cement pier, Pedro's 28-foot fishing boat tied up. Its cockpit was in disarray and the two crew were bleary-eyed from exhaustion. At Jack's request I peeled off four hundred-dollar bills from the wad in my Ziploc bag and left them dickering over the spoils.

It was Sunday, August 2, *Cheers'* fifth day on the reef. Though Kralendijk Trading Company was closed, I had a hunch José Marchena would put in an appearance, and I wanted to be waiting out front if and when he unlocked the door.

With two hours to kill, I roamed the sleepy village until I found a waterfront café. Over a cup of coffee I withdrew an inch-thick stack of napkins from the table-top dispenser and began to map out a new salvage plan.

I'd lived through one hair-raising attempt to bring *Cheers* out through the breakers. There was no telling what the weather might brew up for our next attempt. And little likelihood our next salvage captain would persevere with the dogged resolve of Captain Kim. Thinking about Don, I vowed with deep remorse never again to risk someone's safety to save my boat.

Over coffee I thought of Don's words when morning dawned our first day on the reef. Maybe, just maybe, we could tunnel through the reef and bring *Cheers* into deep water inside the lagoon. According to Pablo, they already had muscled her some distance using only her own ground tackle. Why then, given time, a good work boat, a crew of men and the right equipment, couldn't we multiply that effort a hundredfold?

Cheers lay in three feet of water. The path to deep water inside the lagoon was obstructed by gardens of live coral—heavy boulders of brain coral, brittle forests of branchy staghorn coral, dense fields of antler-shaped elkhorn coral and menacing patches of leathery, orange-brown fire coral. Another obstacle was the shallow lagoon bottom itself, composed of dead coral thinly covered with sand. Though we might be able to clear a channel through thickets of living coral, nothing short of dynamite would dislodge the bedrock plain of dead coral, which limited any cleared channel to between two and five feet depth for a distance of 400 feet, where the water deepened to a consistent five to six feet. There *Cheers* would float if we could reduce her six-foot draft by emptying the boat, heeling her over and/or building some sort of buoyant raft beneath her.

First, I made a list of heavy gear we could easily unload ashore to lighten the boat, reduce draft and make her easier to pull:

Empty water tanks (85 gallons) .	680 pounds
Empty diesel tank (60 gallons) .	480 pounds
Books	400 pounds
Three anchors, 200 feet chain .	600 pounds
Canned goods	800 pounds
Misc. gear: life raft, outboard motor, typewriter, hardware, sewing machine, batteries, stove, tools, sails, spare parts . .	1,000 pounds
	3,960 pounds

In the course of a morning we could shuttle approximately 4,000 pounds of gear ashore by small boat, reducing *Cheers'* displacement to 26,000 pounds, giving us three inches less draft.

As for increasing buoyancy, I calculated that if a gallon of water weighs about eight pounds, a 55-gallon oil drum weighs 440 pounds filled. That same drum empty would provide 440 pounds of buoyancy when submerged. *Cheers* could easily accommodate five such drums on each side. That would give us roughly 4,000 pounds of buoyancy, further reducing her displacement to 22,000 pounds. The total reduction of weight might reduce her draft from five feet, 10 inches to five feet, four inches.

Eventually, lightening a boat reaches a point of diminishing returns. Each additional inch of freeboard calls for reducing proportionately greater amounts of weight.

An assisting vessel drawing six feet could enter the lagoon and approach to within 600 feet of *Cheers*. Assuming that any vessel we hired would have enough power to drag *Cheers* over the reef, she also could pluck out the massive boulders of brain coral in *Cheers'* path.

I opened my plastic bag and beneath the skirt of the tablecloth counted the money I'd withdrawn from *Cheers'* safe; $1,200 U.S. remained. That should be plenty to cover my expenses for awhile. José had offered to give me a line of credit for other expenditures until I could wire for more money from the States.

That left just one problem: finding a powerful shallow-draft boat with an owner who was willing to try. If anyone could find that special combination, it was José Marchena.

He was standing at the picture window, peering through binoculars out to sea when I slipped unnoticed into his office. His spontaneous cry of elation upon seeing me gave way to blasphemous oaths in three languages when I told him the *Dong Won* mission had failed.

Sunday was no obstacle for the seven-day-a-week magician whose alphabetical card file contained home telephone numbers for shipping tycoons and owner/operators of commercial vessels throughout the Dutch islands and Venezuelan mainland. By 10 o'clock he had worked his way through the M's and, cursing in the face of adversity, plowed through the rest before noon. Their excuses were varied; their logic was sound: the reef was too treacherous, a fiberglass yacht too fragile, the Guardia Nacional too diabolical and routine business too brisk.

I'd missed my 9 a.m. radio transmission to Aves, so at 11:45 I hurried to the pier where two American tugs were berthed and spoke with the captain of *Marianne McAllister*. The captain, a slow-moving, slow-talking Texan, led me to the wheelhouse and turned his radio equipment over to me. I broadcast on Channel 16 VHF, but heard no reply. Oddly, the tug did not have Channel 2182 on single sideband, nor any of *Cheers'* 14 other frequencies.

" 'At's too bad, Ma'am," drawled the captain. "You c'mon back an' try again jes as often's you like, hear? Jes let herself aboard."

At noon, José drove me to the Hotel Rochaline, where I rented a small room at the end of an alley off the kitchen. It swarmed with roaches and was a bit of a dump, but it perfectly suited my pocketbook and my mood. José promised to find me there if he lined up a boat.

I could no longer postpone that call to Jim. It was eight days since we'd sailed from Bequia; my call was four days overdue. I gave the operator his parents' number in New Jersey. Surprisingly, it was Jim who answered the phone.

"Betsy, are you all right? God, I've been worried. Where are you?"

"I'm in Bonaire. I'm fine. But are *you* all right?"

"I'm recuperating at home. I see Dr. Rumundo twice a week. What happened?"

My voice began to tremble. "We've had an accident. No one is hurt, but *Cheers* is. . . . she's on a reef. Aves de Sotavento, it's called, a Venezuelan atoll thirty-eight miles east of Bonaire. But we're going to get her off, Jim. I'm sure of that . . ."

Jim's strong voice and quiet acceptance gave me strength. I quietly explained how *Cheers* had come to grief. Without second-guessing, he accepted the news and tried to reassure me. "I know you'll do everything you can to save the boat," he said. "I love you. No matter what happens, we can start over."

You'd think I'd just creased the fender on our car, so calm, optimistic and reassuring was his voice. He'd made the dreaded call an encouraging vote of confidence, something the three of us sorely needed. I promised to call as soon as I had more news and we rang off.

I wandered outside and took a seat at an umbrella-shaded table in the hotel's pebbled courtyard, where two magnificent green Colombian parrots shouted insults at one another in English, and goaded female passersby with shrill wolf whistles from their hidden perches.

I liked Bonaire. Inland it was cactus country, but the waterfront was trade-wind swept—comfortably langorous without the inevitable cloud cover and oppressive rainfall of the more mountainous islands to the northeast. I was dazzled by Bonaire's striking Dutch architecture and pulsating Latin American music, by its intriguing mixture of races, which produces exotic, fanciful women and industrious yet playfully-childlike men. Bonaire, I thought, might be just the place to start over: to rebuild our boat, and if we lost the boat, to rebuild our lives.

At 6 p.m. I tried again without success to make contact with Aves on *Marianne McAllister's* radio.

I forgot once again about dinner and passed the night in my room, scribbling on squares of bathroom tissue designs for elaborate ways to move *Cheers* with A-frames, greased skids, rollers, wedges, slings, jacks and prybars.

MONDAY, AUGUST 3

Early in the morning I found José at his desk with promising news written on his face. He'd turned up a Curaçao man, who owned a tugboat company and who ran a few line boats—powerful maneuverable work horses, smaller than a tug, that carry the great hawsers from tugs to ships. Maduro, as José called him, was experienced in salvage work and believed his best line boat, *Donald*, which drew just seven feet, could pull *Cheers* into the lagoon. He was willing to try, for a price of $100 per hour, including commuting time, on one condition: that José obtain necessary permission from Venezuelan authorities to work their waters. At that price, even a smooth salvage operation that went without a hitch would wipe out my entire savings. Without hesitation I agreed.

But how to get a work permit for *Donald?* For $1,000 I could fly to Caracas, as José had said, and a week later I might have the permit. Or we could visit the Venezuelan Consul in Bonaire, who could issue the permit that day. But José had misgivings about working through the consul, for reasons known only to him.

José rolled a sheet of paper into his manual typewriter and with rapid, two-finger chicken pecking, hammered out an authorization form, in Spanish.

"This is not entirely legal," he grinned. "In fact it is a worthless piece of paper. But unless we can produce signed authorization from a Venezuelan official, no one is going to risk losing their boat to the Guardia. You said there are two men living on Aves? Two government officials? Do you think one will sign this?" asked José.

"Pablo would do anything he can to help. But how do we get it to him?"

"You hire Pedro and his boat. If he leaves in the next hour— say by nine a.m.—he can be in Aves by four p.m., get Pablo's signature and deliver the form to us by midnight. No, that's too slow. *Phantom* can make the trip in one hour, so we can have it by six o'clock tonight. As soon as we get the paper *Donald* will get under way immediately. She can reach Bonaire by midnight tonight. What do you say?"

"Sounds good."

José phoned Curaçao and told Maduro we expected to have work papers later that night. Meanwhile, Maduro said fly over Aves, locate *Cheers* on the reef and assess from the air the best path to deep water.

José sent his office boy to the pier to find Pedro, and while we waited, I typed this letter to my crew on Aves:

Monday, August 3, 8:30 a.m.

Don and Susan:

I tried without luck yesterday to reach you on VHF from Bonaire tug Marianne McAllister.

We have lined up a line boat (small tug), Donald *to bring* Cheers *out via lagoon, but water depth poses greatest obstacle. Owner of* Donald *leaving Curacao this moment by air to assess situation. He cannot land on Aves. He will not get underway to rescue without written permission from Venezuelan government. For this purpose José has prepared permission form for Pablo or Rafael to sign. SOMEONE MUST SIGN FORM AND RETURN IT TO US IN BONAIRE BEFORE DONALD WILL EMBARK. If Fernando is willing, have him return authorization to us via* Phantom. *If not, send it back with 28-footer. If form is returned without delay, we can arrive Aves to begin work by sunup tomorrow.*

If Cheers *cannot be brought out via lagoon, we will have to try again through breakers.* Donald's *owner is experienced in salvage work. I expect him to be reluctant to risk his boat in the lagoon, so it might be wise to sound a channel through the lagoon, clear of coral heads, and if time permits, to buoy an exit channel.*

I phoned Jim at home yesterday and told him the news. He took it very well and was greatly relieved to hear we all were safe. He required no further surgery and is recuperating at home, where he must remain for at least another month. I told him to inform Dad and Don's partner Skip Fick, but no others. His phone is ringing day and night with calls from well-wishers

*following the stabbing, so for many reasons it's best we keep
this under wraps.*

*Please convey my thanks to Pablo, Rafael, Pepe and Fer-
nando for their courageous assistance. I hope we did not spoil
all your hard work with* Dong Won *and that we did not seri-
ously damage* Cheers.

*Given the difficulty of establishing radio communication, I
can only suggest you monitor VHF 16 beginning tomorrow
morning at seven and every hour on the hour. When not aboard*
Cheers, *use the portable VHF. You might have better luck by
climbing up wind generator platform behind igloo. Even if you
cannot transmit, I will talk to you briefly every hour and tell
you what's up. We will not attempt another rescue without
first talking with you.*

*Please be careful and take no unnecessary risks. Return
signed authorization as soon as possible.*

Betsy

At 8:45 a.m. José's messenger returned with Pedro, owner of 28-
footer, and with Lino, the mechanic who had worked on *Phantom's* outboard. At 9 a.m. the 28-footer was speeding for Aves
while I hurried to the *Marianne McAllister* to make my morning
broadcast. Again there was no reply, but I transmitted a brief
message in case *Cheers'* crew could receive but not transmit.

Back at my hotel room, I made an exhaustive list of gear we
could round up that afternoon to aid the rescue. At 2 p.m. I
checked out of my hotel room and visited José to find out which
route Maduro had chosen, based on his morning flight observation, to pull *Cheers* off the reef.

José sat slumped at his desk nervously chomping a wad of gum.
His face was ashen and he didn't even feign a smile.

"Better sit down," he began. "I have not seen your boat. I know
only what you have told me. I also know Maduro has much experience in these things. Tugs and salvage are his business. He flew
over your boat this morning. He says she is too far on the reef.
She cannot be saved. He says your boat is high and dry. She is two
hundred meters from deep water, and would be crushed by the
coral if he tries to take her out through the surf."

"We can pull from the lagoon. A small tug can get to within 700
feet of *Cheers* and we can clear a trench through the coral."

"Maduro says there is much heavy coral inside the lagoon. He cannot work from such a great distance. And how are you going to clear that much coral? The Venezuelans will not let you dynamite their reef."

"I don't know, José. We could clear the coral by hand. How do you think they built the Panama Canal? With a crew of Chinamen and picks. We can do the same."

"You think too much with your heart my friend. I know you love this boat, but why throw good money after bad? I can try to find a buyer for the boat as she sits, on the reef. Make me a list of everything that is left and I will sell the equipment for you."

"I don't want cash. I want my boat. I agreed to pay Maduro's price, a hundred dollars an hour. Win or lose, he gets paid, so why won't he try?"

"Because he believes it is impossible."

"Then we have to find another boat."

"That is easy to say. There are no boats left."

"Then I'll just have to fly to Venezuela and start over there."

"Let us wait until *Phantom* returns this evening with the permission form. Then early tomorrow morning I will call every company again."

At 7 p.m. I was waiting on the dock for *Phantom* to arrive. José and Jack van de Eem arrived soon after in separate cars. When by 9 o'clock *Phantom* still had not arrived, our anxiety gave way to concern that something had happened to the boat en route to Bonaire. At 10 p.m. Jack and I drove south eight miles along a lonely, flat stretch of highway to Lacrepunt where we watched for *Phantom* until midnight.

I thought of Fernando and Pepe, so eager to help but so innocent to the ways of the sea. I worried that their ailing engine had died and they were somewhere between Aves and Bonaire, drifting in the darkness, with no chart and an unknown current. At 1 a.m. Jack dropped me at my hotel room.

TUESDAY, AUGUST 4

Today was *Cheers'* seventh day on the reef. By first light neither *Phantom* nor the 28-footer had returned. At 7 o'clock, Jack and I met in José's office. Something obviously had gone wrong. I didn't want to impulsively launch another government search and rescue mission—not yet—not when there were private planes available for hire, so José phoned the local flying club at Bonaire airport and I chartered a four-seat single-prop plane to search for *Phantom*. The pilot explained that he could not land on Aves without official permission from Venezuela, but he agreed to let me drop a written message out the door of the plane for my crew to retrieve. Hastily I penned this letter in José's office.

August 4, 7:15 a.m.

Don and Susan:

We're concerned because neither Phantom *nor the 28-footer returned to Bonaire with the signed permission form.*

The line boat Donald *fell through, but José is trying to line up a shoal-draft, self-propelled barge with a powerful winch to pull* Cheers *into the lagoon. Max speed four knots. Time Curaçao—Bonaire—Aves about 25 hours. Failing that, there's nothing more we can do in ABC islands and I will fly to Caracas, then Puerto Cabello to start over there. Our priority remains lagoon exit. Try to flop* Cheers *back to starboard side, out of wave action.*

Still important that Pablo sign permission form, which we can modify for another rescue attempt. Please get it to us without delay.

I folded the note and stuffed it in one of José's empty coffee tins.

Jack offered to come on the flight, and at 8 o'clock we were airborne. The plane climbed swiftly to 1,000 feet and set off on a course due east for Aves. Three pairs of eyes scanned the sea for signs of *Phantom*, but we might as well have been looking for a freak wave as a speedboat with white decks and a white Bimini top in a sea of whitecaps.

We flew the rhumb line course to Aves, made a wide circle over *Cheers*, low enough to determine that *Phantom* was not assisting near the reef, then we swooped in low over the island.

Three sailboats were anchored just inside the lagoon. "That's odd," I remarked. "*Cheers* was the first yacht to stop here in three months. Now suddenly there are three others."

"Vultures," said Jack, matter-of-factly.

The Guardia Nacional boat was still anchored off the settlement. Pablo's 28-footer, which had carried our message, was tied to the wood pier in front of Pablo's igloo, but *Phantom* was nowhere to be seen.

Four figures ran out of the igloo upon hearing our plane pass low overhead. I looked intently for Don, to be sure he was all right. Just as the pilot pulled the nose up I saw him, his face now bearded. He waved, and though it's doubtful he knew I was in the plane, I was greatly relieved he appeared uninjured.

The enormous Venezuelan flag snapping from the tall pole outside the igloo gave me an idea. I scribbled a postscript to my note:

> *Plane has VHF. Tune in 16 on portable VHF set. If we cannot make radio contact, lower flag to signal we should search for* Phantom. *Leave flag flying if* Phantom *is all right or has returned to Venezuela.*
>
> —Betsy

I stuffed the note in the coffee can, dropped in some stones the pilot picked up before take-off to ensure the can would not be sucked into the plane's propeller, sealed the lid with tape and placed the can inside a red plastic bag. The pilot dipped the starboard wing, dropped the nose and began a long clockwise descent.

When directly over the grass landing strip, Jack opened the passenger window and threw the "letter bomb" smartly toward the ground. The red object struck the grass field and bounced a few feet short of the red lagoon. Rafael sprinted to the field, retrieved the can and brought it to Don.

While giving them a chance to digest the message, the pilot stood by on Channel 16 and flew east to make a series of low observation passes over *Cheers*.

Viewing *Cheers'* position from the sky I could understand Maduro's skepticism. The shallow water in which she lay was absolutely invisible from the air, giving the false impression that *Cheers* lay stranded on a completely dry reef. She lay on her port side, perpendicular to the line of breakers, her deck and cabin posing a near-vertical obstruction to the waves.

Jack, seated next to the pilot, produced a 35 mm camera and began taking pictures.

"What are you doing?" I asked from the back seat.

"A reporter gave it to me at the airport. He wants some photos for tomorrow's paper."

"No photos. And no story for tomorrow's paper. We'll have every scavenger in these islands coming here to see what they can pilfer."

"Looks like she's holed," said Jack, changing the subject.

The pilot dropped into a lazy clockwise arc. As we descended I could clearly see a large charcoal-gray area at the turn of the bilge on the exposed starboard side.

"I think it's just bare fiberglass showing where the gel coat has abraded through," I countered.

The pilot made another low pass. The damaged area was about three feet long and extended a foot above and a foot below the waterline, about amidships, where *Cheers* took much of the punishment our first four days on the reef. Though I didn't doubt that the hull by now could be holed, this dark gray area was the color of bare fiberglass, not void.

The pilot was unable to raise the crew on the VHF radio, so there was no way to verify the condition of the hull. We flew over the tiny settlement once again to check the flag. It had not been lowered. In unison, three figures on the ground beneath us pointed due south, which we interpreted as meaning that *Phantom* had returned to Venezuela.

Chartering a plane to drop a letter bomb was an extravagant way to achieve one-way communication, but well worth the expense to find out that Don had survived his night-long ordeal on the reef, that there was no reason to search for *Phantom*, that *Cheers* was holding up and that the Guardia ship was still lurking.

José was waiting at the airport when we touched down. He bore more bad news. In the course of our hour-long flight, final hope for a salvage vessel had collapsed when the owner of the self-propelled barge, apprehensive of the open-sea voyage to Aves, withdrew his offer in favor of harbor work in Curaçao.

It seemed we'd reached the end of the road.

I thought of the U.S. Coast Guard, but we were hundreds of miles beyond the range of their nearest foothold in the Caribbean. But the next day, on the off chance some U.S. Coast Guard boats were in the vicinity, I telephoned the U.S. Embassy in Caracas, and spoke with Roy Apple, an embassy official. The closest Coast Guard vessels were now on a training mission in Brazil. "But there's someone here who might help you," he said.

Next I spoke with the U.S. Naval Attaché, who said he might be able to arrange for a Venezuelan Navy vessel to tow *Cheers* off the reef.

"I'll speak with Carlos Luengo. He's chief of staff here and Venezuelan fleet commander. Their Navy has come to the aid of yachts in the past, so let me see what I can do."

I explained the risk of bringing *Cheers* out through the breakers and asked if the navy had a powerful shoal-draft vessel that might work inside the lagoon.

"I very much doubt it, Miss Hitz. But if I can get you a vessel to pull you out the way you came on, through the breakers, are you willing?"

"Only as a last resort," I said. "Let us continue to work on a lagoon exit and if that fails, I'd be grateful for any assistance the Venezuelan Navy can give."

"Let me talk with Commander Luengo, check the specs on his fleet and get back to you when I have something."

At 10 Tuesday morning, Jack and I again convened in José's office to discuss our options. A lagoon exit was the only viable solution, and since we'd exhausted all possibility of hiring a shoal-draft tow boat, our only resort was to assemble heavy equipment, a crew of men and somehow get to Aves to begin clearing coral and inching the boat over the reef using her own ground tackle.

Jack, Lino and Pedro would work on Aves along with Don, Susan and myself and whomever we could enlist in Aves. Pablo would transport the crew and equipment to Aves in his 28-footer. Though his boat could not offer much pulling power as a tow boat on the reef, it would remain on the scene to tow *Cheers* back to Bonaire if we could free her.

Pedro had twice made quick turn-around trips to Aves without official permission. This time he would need to stay and work until *Cheers* was free or until we gave up. But to do so without a work permit for his boat and visas for the crew could mean big trouble. Mindful of the vendetta seething between the neighboring islands, we dared not risk a confrontation with the Guardia. We now had no choice but to seek written authorization from the Venezuelan consul in Bonaire. At 10:30 José telephoned the consulate and spoke in Spanish with Federico Martinez-Isturiz. He refused to issue a work permit to a boat of the Netherlands Antilles to work in Venezuelan waters. José explained that he could find no Venezuelan boat to take the job, and that if we did not move swiftly, *Cheers* would be lost. Consul Martinez suggested several tug and salvage companies along the Venezuelan mainland. José replied that he had tried them all but they had declined the job. Consul Martinez suggested he keep trying and hung up.

"Ay, ay, ay," sighed José. "What we going to do now?"

"I've seen a vessel, berthed at the town pier, flying a Venezuelan flag," I recalled.

"The fruit boat?" exclaimed José. "You would go to sea in Obdulio's old fruit boat?"

It was an awkward-looking roughly-built, wood-planked cargo vessel of about 40 feet.

"He makes the round trip from Venezuela to Bonaire, doesn't he?" I asked. "So the boat's capable of open-sea passages. It's certainly got the load-carrying ability we need to get the crew, gear and barrels to Aves."

At 10:45, while José went to the dock to speak to the owner of the fruit boat, Jack and I set out to round up gear. By noon, we had amassed an impressive pile of equipment: 10 55-gallon steel drums; 20 gate valves; three sledge hammers; three crow bars; three six-foot pry bars; three cold chisels; a 6½-ton-capacity portable mechanical winch; four sheets plywood; five gallons axle grease; six pairs heavy leather work gloves; four eight-foot galvanized pipes; 100 fathoms half-inch polypropylene line; a 20-ton hydraulic jack; 30 feet clear plastic hose.

When we returned to the office at noon, seated opposite José's desk was a Venezuelan man of middle age, dressed in a faded denim work shirt and baggy khaki trousers flecked with red bottom paint. He sat humbly stooped, fidgeting with a tattered straw hat in his lap. José introduced the man simply as Obdulio. He stood and I shook the enormous hand of a working man.

José explained that Obdulio was willing to transport crew and gear to Aves, and to bring us back after the work is finished. The permit would be issued to his boat, but it would remain at anchor. "He will not bring his boat into the lagoon or assist you in any way. He will bring back only your crew and gear. He will not tow your boat back to Bonaire. He will hold the work permit and he will stay until the job is finished, but no longer than two weeks."

We discussed various forms of payment and settled on a flat rate of $100 per day, which suited Obdulio admirably. After transporting us to Aves, he was free each day to fish, swim or loll about, so long as he was there with the permit.

We shook hands and agreed to reconvene shortly at the Venezuelan Consulate to get the necessary paperwork.

At the Venezuelan consulate, José, Jack and I were shown inside the plush, air-conditioned chambers of Consul Martinez. To my surprise, Obdulio had been admitted beforehand. A jovial man approaching 50, Consul Martinez greeted us warmly, then listened carefully as José explained in English our plan.

"I see," he said when José had finished. "You have been through a great ordeal, Señorita, and I pledge to do everything in my power to help you. Now, tell me, what do you intend to pay Señor Rodriguez for his services?"

"We agreed on a price of a hundred dollars U.S. a day," I said.

"One hundred dollars a day? You must be joking! You will pardon me, but that is laughable. One hundred dollars a day? That is an insult. You would take advantage of Mr. Rodriguez because he is a poor, uneducated man?"

"We are asking Obdulio—Mr. Rodriguez—to transport four people and gear from Bonaire to Aves de Sotavento—eighty kilometers," I pointed out. "We are not asking him to work or to use his boat, only to transport us."

"Ah, but the permit. Surely that is worth something."

"A Venezuelan boat needs no permit to work Venezuelan waters," challenged José.

"On the contrary, he must have a permit issued by my office. I say your offer is an insult to my countryman."

"He agreed to the price," said José angrily. "And I'll wager it is more than he has made in his best day selling fruit."

"I cannot sanction an agreement that takes advantage of an

ignorant man." Consul Martinez rose. "Good day, Miss Hitz, Mr. Marchena, Mr. van der Eem," he smiled.

"Just a minute," I said, feeling the blood rise in my face. "My boat is on that reef and has been for seven days. I care about one thing and that is getting her off before she breaks up. I made a deal with this man to take me to Aves so I can save my boat. I have never earned one hundred dollars a day and I don't think Obdulio has."

"Madam, your offer is an insult. If you would care to return tomorrow morning we can discuss this again."

"My boat will not wait. My crew—my sister—is stranded on that island. I have arranged transportation to Aves. Now are you going to prevent me from rejoining my boat and my crew?"

"If you would care to return later this afternoon, say in one hour, we can discuss the matter further," said Martinez, showing us to the door. Obdulio remained seated in the consul's office.

We climbed in José's car. "Do you see now why I did not go to the honorable consul in the beginning?" asked José.

"He's not going to give us a work permit without a payoff, is he?"

"That's right."

"What was that you said in his office about Obdulio not needing a work permit for the job?"

"That's right. He is the licensed Venezuelan operator of a licensed Venezuelan work boat. He does not need a special work permit."

"Then why are we bothering to go to the consul?"

"If he leaves you at the island and the Bonaire men are found working on Venezuelan soil without a work permit, they can be arrested and your boat impounded. That is why he must stay there with the permit."

"José, what are we going to do now?"

"We could get drunk."

"Filthy drunk!"

"Let me out," pleaded Jack in the back seat.

We deposited him at the nearest corner and drove to the bar at Hotel Rochaline, where we took two stools and asked the bartender to set up four beers.

"We should hear what he has to say," advised José.

"You go. I don't have the stomach for it."

We drank the beers, then José ordered another round.

"I guess I misjudged you," José said thoughtfully.

"What do you mean?"

"I thought you would do anything to save your boat."

"I would. But a person's got to draw the line somewhere. You know, José, I can't remember a time I didn't dream of one day sailing around the world on my own boat. That boat was bought with Jim's and my hard-earned money. Hell, together we didn't earn a hundred dollars a day. But we owned every nut and bolt on *Cheers* and never left behind an unpaid debt."

"Bartender, another round."

"I don't expect charity, but I don't like being fleeced either. I'll pay more than a fair wage, but I don't like being blackmailed by some slimy consul who figures he's entitled to a piece of the action. What good's the dream, José, if it's built on fraud, on extortion."

"Then why don't you go home to this man of yours and be with him? Put this behind you. This is no place for a woman, and frankly I do not think you have a prayer of saving your boat. If you persist until a storm comes or until thieves clean out your boat, you'll be worse off than you are now. I can sell. . . ."

"No." I looked at my watch. "It's already three o'clock. We better get to the consulate."

José grinned.

We scaled the consulate steps two at a time and were ushered into Consul Martinez's chambers without delay. Braced for the worst, I was determined to listen without opening my mouth. Consul Martinez rose from his seat and sandwiched my hand compassionately between both of his.

"Let me assure you, Madame, that I have only your best interest at heart," he gushed. "Please, be seated."

I took a chair beside simple Obdulio.

The consul paused and cleared his throat. "Upon talking with Señor Rodriguez, it became obvious that he did not understand your offer. With my help he has arrived at an arrangement which I trust will suit you both and will protect both parties."

Consul Martinez's attractive secretary laid a typed contract on the desk. The consul passed one copy of the contract to me and another copy to José. I found my name and *Cheers'* name and some eye-popping figures, but I could not read the contract because it was written in Spanish. José translated aloud:

> "I, Obdulio Rodriguez, with residency in Bonaire, agree to transport from Bonaire to Isla Aves and back to Bonaire Elizabeth R. Hitz, American, owner of the North American sailboat *Cheers*, and the following citizens of the Netherlands Antilles: Jacob van der Eem, Johan Soleano, Lino Craane.
>
> Also I agree to remain in Las Aves during the rescue of the sailboat *Cheers*. The sum for my services will be $3,000 U.S., to be paid as follows: $2,000 upon signing of this agreement and $1,000 to be paid upon departure for Las Aves."

"You are asking three thousand dollars to transport my crew and gear 38 nautical miles?" I asked in disbelief.

"Señor Rodriguez is providing more than transportation. He will hold the official permit, without which no vessel can work Venezuelan waters. It is not my rule; it is the law of my country."

The room fell silent, then José spoke: "Let us talk this over. I will telephone you later."

Consul Martinez again clasped my hand solicitously. I felt dirty and I wanted to take a bath. We returned to José's office.

"How much of this $3,000 do you think Martinez will keep for himself?" asked José.

"None," I said flatly.

"You are more naive than I thought, my dear."

"None because I won't sign it."

"It is a lot of money. But what if I can talk him down to two thousand?"

"I won't deal with that man. He's a crook and Obdulio's a crook if he's giving him a kickback. Two thousand now and the rest when we leave the dock—what kind of fool do they take me for?"

"A desperate fool. They are right, eh? Listen, I will tell Martinez two thousand is our top price. You can pay half in advance and the other half on your return to Bonaire."

"José, you don't understand. I don't want to do business with men I don't trust. No good will come of it. Suppose we have to return to Bonaire for more materials? Obdulio's going to milk me for every cent he can get. I don't see much hope of getting the boat off in ten days, when the permit and visas expire. What will he charge me for the next permit?"

"I cannot argue with that. But Betsy, I tell you this sincerely, I know no other way."

"No, I'm sorry, José. Let me go back to the hotel and think this through. I'll call you later."

It was 4 o'clock when I turned the key to my hotel room and found a letter that had been slipped under the door.

Dear Betsy:

I did not know you and Susan were aboard Dong Won. *When you arrived we were very close to moving* Cheers *into a five-foot pool, though we were moving very slowly, perhaps four inches an hour with three anchors going to three different winches and a block and tackle. My thought on going ahead into the pool was that either way it was a step in the right direction. She would ride better there and even if we decided to pull her through the breakers, it would be easier to turn her around in the pool.*

The boat has survived incredibly well. This morning after you flew over we flipped the boat back onto her starboard side. She fell into the pool without damage.

Phantom *returned to Venezuela, but Fernando left us his Zodiac and outboard as a work skiff. Pablo is not authorized to give any foreign vessel permission to work Venezuelan waters. He has tried since yesterday to contact his superiors by radio, but they cannot help. He feels very badly.*

I feel strongly the safest exit is through the lagoon. The biggest obstacle is clearing a path through the coral. Carolina, a Venezuelan fishing boat, arrived yesterday, and I contracted with them to bring Cheers *into the lagoon for $2,000, which I intended to pay myself. But after a day's work they gave up and returned to the mainland. We were able to keep their best hand, a fisherman named Oriol. We cleared a channel for about 70 feet, but had to stop when we ran into lots of fire coral and some heavy brain coral, though I was amazed at how fast the latter can be removed.*

What we need now is a strong work boat, more men and most

important, heavy equipment with which to clear coral: picks, shovels, gloves, crowbars, plywood, lead pipes, stone chisels, sledgehammers, hydraulic jacks, the biggest portable winch you can find, a come-along, one or two hooking-type anchors, lots of food, bread, rum, and dynamite if you can get it.

We need to talk by radio. The portable VHF set doesn't receive or transmit, and anyway it seems Bonaire is beyond VHF range. We will monitor VHF 16 and SSB 2182 and 2638 at 9 a.m., noon and 6 p.m.

Your boat will come out all right, Bets. Bring help as soon as you can.

> Don
> Aves de Sotavento
> August 4

His letter was reassuring but posed a mystery of how it had reached me. I walked to the hotel's front desk and asked the receptionist if she'd seen anyone slip it under my door. She pointed to a couple seated at the bar.

I introduced myself to Henk Befort and Maryke Schravesande, a Dutch couple who'd sailed their ketch *Gunn* all the way from the Netherlands. *Gunn*, their husky wood double-ender, was one of the three boats I'd seen anchored in the Aves lagoon that morning. Henk and Maryke had stopped at the remote island when they came upon the wreck and stayed for two days to help my crew, and offered to deliver the letter to me when they left Aves that morning.

I explained to them that I'd rounded up the crew and equipment but had run afoul of the Venezuelan Consul. I asked if I could hire them to transport us to Aves to join the crew, but they explained apologetically they had pressing business in Curaçao. From their reactions I sensed they thought my boat a hopeless cause.

José showed no surprise when I returned to his office late in the afternoon and asked, "Is it too late to make a deal with the consul?"

A moment later he had Martinez on the phone and was talking in rapid Spanish. He covered the receiver and whispered to me: "Two thousand dollars and you can leave Bonaire at nine o'clock tonight. You'll be in Aves by sunup tomorrow to start work."

I nodded.

José concluded his call, hung up the receiver and glanced at his watch. "It's five-ten. You go buy food before the market closes while I get the new contract."

I whisked through the aisles, clearing out shelves and filling first one cart, then another and another. Next, I checked out of my hotel room. Then, defying my conscience and better judgement, I put my signature at the bottom of the new contract. The tired old boat, fruit flies and all, wasn't worth much more than the $2,000 I'd agreed to pay to charter her.

By 9 p.m. the boat was fully loaded. Ten barrels and all the gear was lashed on deck or wedged into corners where it wouldn't roll in a seaway. But where was Obdulio?

When he didn't turn up by 9:45, Jack and I drove to his house while Lino waited on the boat. Jack went inside and returned a few minutes later.

"There's been a misunderstanding," he said. "Obdulio says he thought we were leaving at midnight. He wants to get a few hours' sleep and won't get underway now."

Shortly before midnight, Jack and Lino returned. Again we waited, but Obdulio did not appear. At 12:30 Jack and I drove back to his home.

Jack leaned impatiently on his car horn and a teenage son stumbled outside. There was not enough diesel fuel aboard the boat to make the trip, the youth explained, so we would have to wait until morning. The eight-hour delay would cost us a full working day since we would not reach Aves until 4 the next afternoon. Jack ordered the boy to awaken his father. A few minutes later Obdulio appeared in the doorway, wearing baggy pants and suspenders. Lightning-fast Spanish broke the still night air but didn't change Obdulio's line of defense.

Seven hours to wait. I was leery of hanging around the dock or the fruit boat alone, so I returned to the hotel and dozed off on the lobby sofa.

When Obdulio did not appear Wednesday morning, I can't say I was surprised. Jack and I drove a third time to his house and found Obdulio sitting in a patio chair in his front yard, surrounded by screaming children.

"Bad back," said Obdulio. "Slipped a disk. The trip is off."

WEDNESDAY, AUGUST 5

It was *Cheers'* eighth day on the reef. When Jack and I opened the door to José's office at 9 o'clock, he let out a pained moan and shook his head. "Why aren't you both in Aves? No, let me guess: Obdulio withdrew from the contract."

"That's right."

"So, there was not enough money for the consul."

In the next instant José was on the phone with Consul Martinez trying to convince him to issue a permit to Pedro's 28-footer. He refused, saying we must find another Venezuelan boat.

"There is no other Venezuelan boat," insisted José.

"Keep looking," suggested the consul.

José had an idea. He led me to his car and we sped to Bonaire Marina where half a dozen yachts were berthed. I followed him down the dock to the largest boat, a stout steel motorsailer of about 48 feet. A tattered blue and yellow Swedish ensign drooped unceremoniously from the backstay, and there was no sign of crew aboard the boat.

José rapped on the hull with his knuckles. Several minutes later a bleary-eyed Swede of about 40 trudged on deck pulling on his shorts. His naked back bore the wrinkled impressions of rumpled bedsheets.

"José Marchena, what trouble have you brought me now?" asked the Swede, struggling with his fly.

"Stellan, I bring you the opportunity to do something purpose-ful with your wasted life."

Without waiting for an invitation, José leapt aboard and pulled me over the rail behind him. I introduced myself. With practiced expertise, José presented our case to Stellan, who listened distantly without speaking while he rolled a cigarette, lit it, then rolled an-other, watching the blue-gray smoke curl upwards in the sun-bathed wheelhouse.

"What do you say, my friend?" José concluded, "Will you help this woman save her boat?"

"I can get her boat off," Stellan said arrogantly. "But I'm not going to mess with the Guardia unless all my papers are in order. You get me a visa, work permit or whatever the hell they require and I'll get that boat off. For a price, of course."

"Before we talk about the price," said José, "let me see what Consul Martinez has to say."

After 30 minutes of head-butting persuasion, José convinced the consul there was no Venezuelan boat available for the job. Sanctioning a Swedish boat for the work seemed to him an infinitely more palatable solution to the problem than authorizing a Bonaire boat.

We raced back to the marina, alerted Stellan to get the boat fueled and ready and set a departure time for 9 o'clock that evening. Just then, José's office boy, William, appeared with a message.

"Betsy, you had a call from someone at the embassy in Caracas," said William. "It sounds important. Here, he left his number."

I left the men to finish transferring gear to Stellan's boat, and at José's office I called the embassy and spoke with Roy Apple.

"I thought you'd want to hear that the Venezuelan Navy sent an eighty-footer to Aves de Sotavento last night to tow your boat off."

A week ago, I could not have asked for better news. But now the prospect of a navy ship arriving in my absence to pull *Cheers* out through the breakers was grim news, indeed. Those on Aves would assume I dispatched the naval vessel and that it was my wish to again assault the breakers. The naval attaché, in his eagerness to help, had put my query into action and though I was grateful for the interest he'd shown, I could not conceal my dismay.

"Is there any way we can call off the mission?" I asked sheepishly.

"The ship should have reached Aves by sunup," he explained. "My guess is they've already pulled your boat off that reef."

There was no sense in my continuing to mount a rescue attempt if my boat already had been pulled off the reef. I had to talk to my crew on Aves.

José telephoned the airport. There were three planes, but no pilots available. Next he phoned Bonaire Petroleum Corporation (BOPEC), which maintained a twin-prop corporate plane. "It's available now, said José, "Two hundred dollars an hour."

"Ask the pilot if he'll let me drop a message canister?"

"He says that's okay."

Not knowing whether it was already too late to forestall the navy ship, I hastily penned this note:

August 5, 3:00 p.m.

Don and Susan,

*After many failures, I've found a steel motorsailer to transport
myself, crew of three and gear to Aves. We depart Bonaire at 9
p.m. tonight. Will arrive Aves by sunup tomorrow morning to
bring* Cheers *through lagoon. We are bringing all the gear you
requested plus a six-ton mechanical winch and as many 55-
gallon drums as deck space allows.*

I stopped there, deciding to complete the letter after assessing
the situation from the air.

At 3:30 we were airborne and 10 minutes later dropped down for
a close look at *Cheers.* There was no navy ship in sight. On the
first pass, I could see *Cheers* had been flopped back to her starboard side and was heading into the lagoon. Two figures on the
bowsprit and two more in the water were apparently clearing coral.
Two parallel walls of dislodged coral rubble delineated the man-
made channel through which *Cheers* had moved a distance of two
boat lengths. I was thrilled at the progress they had made. But
where was the navy ship?

The plane peeled off toward the tiny island. Anchored just inside the lagoon were two yachts, but no navy ship. I could only
assume the naval vessel still was en route from Puerto Cabello, so
I penned this conclusion to my letter:

*Through misunderstanding, Venezuelan navy dispatched
from Puerto Cabello last night an 80-foot ship to rescue*
Cheers. *Expect ship any time. Under no circumstances exit
through breakers. Try to persuade captain to anchor and stand
by. We're coming.*

Betsy

I sealed this letter bomb like the last one, in a tin, with stones
for ballast and a plastic bag for buoyancy. The pilot swooped in
low over *Cheers'* mast. I threw the letter bomb out the passenger
window. The pilot flew in a tight arc until we saw someone retrieve
the red plastic bag from the lagoon. Then we returned to Bonaire.

José was not waiting when I returned. Instead, I was met by

William who explained that José was at that moment delivering the work permit to Stellan at the marina. The boat was loaded and the crew was standing by to depart Bonaire as planned.

The paper chase was over. In just five hours we'd be underway. The next morning I would be reunited with my crew and we could devote full energy to the job at hand. Based on the progress I'd just seen from the air and the heavy equipment and manpower we would deliver, this effort promised to succeed.

José's car was parked out front at Kralendijk Trading Company. I reeled into his office to thank my ally and to say good-bye. Beneath the avalanche of a week's neglected paperwork, I found a broken man, his face buried in his hands.

"I send him to hell," he muttered. "I send him . . ."

"Who, José?"

"Stellan." His voice was a flat monotone. "I knew better. I must have been out of my mind to rely on that no-good Swede."

"Will you tell me what happened?"

"I go to his boat with his visa, the permit for the boat and there is Stellan, on his knees. He has most finished a bottle of Scotch and he tells me to go buy him another bottle. I send him to hell."

"We'll just have to go sober him up. I can get his boat to Aves if I have to."

"No good. He'll go two, maybe three days like this. It's no good, no good."

It was 5 o'clock Wednesday afternoon. The workday at the shipping company had come to a halt. Typewriters were covered, the switchboard was dead. Dust has settled in the empty parking lot.

José and I sat alone in the silence of his office for a very long time, tracing in our minds one deadend after another.

Finally I struck on an idea: I would buy a boat—any boat—in Bonaire and transport myself, the gear and whatever crew I could muster to Aves. I had to find a boat in decent running condition and an owner who was willing to sell. Now. Cash on the table.

Our planning was interrupted by a gentle knock. A small, unassuming man of 50 stood in the open doorway wearing sandals, a sports shirt and Bermuda-length kahaki shorts.

José bounded to his feet and embraced the man he called Julio Soza Rodriguez, formerly a Venezuelan ambassador to the United States, and the most revered resident of Bonaire. He'd stopped in to pay his friend José a social call, but soon was embroiled in our plight. His handshake was genuine and he spoke in carefully-measured English. "Can you not find a boat to hire?"

"Pedro Soleano has made the Aves run twice already without a permit," explained José. "He has one of those 28-footers in the fishing cooperative and has agreed to take the job, but he won't risk it again without a work permit. Martinez, the consul, refuses to issue the papers to a Bonaire boat."

"You tell your man Pedro he will have his permit. Round up your crew, young lady, load up that boat and leave the consul to me. You'll have your permit tonight and by tomorrow morning you can be working with your friends to save your boat."

The man inspired confidence. He made it all sound so simple. I couldn't help but have faith in what he said.

By 9 that night Pedro's 28-footer was fueled, loaded with 10 drums, all our equipment and food stores and the crew was standing by. José left his home, stopped briefly at the consulate and at 9:30 delivered to us visas for the crew and a work permit for Pablo's boat. José planted a kiss on my cheek, and promised a champagne welcome when I brought *Cheers* to Bonaire.

His confidence was infectious. I tumbled into bed at the hotel for a quick, five-hour sleep a thoroughly happy woman. I didn't yet have my boat, but at last I had a fighting chance to save her.

CHAPTER SIXTEEN

THURSDAY, AUGUST 6

—————————————————— The heavily-laden fishing boat bucked into the oncoming seas carrying a queasy crew and an unlikely cargo. Her large, shallow fish hold beneath the cockpit was stacked with picks and pry bars, sledges and slings, galvanized pipe, jacks and winches. Above the closed hold were laid four sheets of marine plywood, then 10 shiny new 55-gallon drums stacked end-up and lashed, affording little room for her crew.

Young Pedro, the slightly-built, dusky brown, pigtailed captain, sat atop one gyrating barrel steering toward the rising sun. He whistled a haunting tune and thumbed the frayed visor of his Red Sox cap. The spray-drenched windshield gave him only an occasional, distorted glimpse of the horizon, so he steered a careful compass course, poking his head out occasionally between waves to search for low-lying Aves.

Pedro spoke only his native Papiamento and could neither read nor write, but was nonetheless a fine seat-of-the-pants navigator who took nothing for granted. He knew the current that swept this stretch of sea was diabolical. A navigator who failed to spot the low film of land when it first became visible three miles distant would, at our speed of seven knots, find himself on the reef inside of 30 minutes.

So Pedro tuned his senses to signs of land. Soon, the ground-swell flattened in the lee of the unseen island. By 9 o'clock we threaded the wide, deep-water entrance into the lagoon and backed stern-to the wood dock in front of Pablo's fiberglass igloo.

After many days of aborted attempts to return to the island, our arrival caused wild excitement. Don and Susan had lost a bit of weight in the week I'd been away, but they appeared trim and fit, their skin roasted a crackling brown from the sun. Susan was her optimistic, energetic self, but Don seemed distant and withdrawn. No doubt the tension and frustration was getting to him. While I had been in Bonaire chasing down one deadend after another, Don had endured a night-long ordeal stranded, alone, on the stricken vessel in breaking surf, then had singlemindedly labored many days on end to budge the yacht inch by inch across the reef.

"*Cheers* is holding up well," Don reported. "But I might as well tell you, the hull has a three-foot crack on the starboard side at the turn of the bilge where she pounded against brain coral for three days. With the two manual pumps we can keep up with it during the day. Each morning we find the bilges full. There's another leak in the forward bilge just abaft the mast step where water appears to be seeping in through the keel. If you've got some underwater epoxy I'll try to patch the leaks.

"I tried to start the engine the other day. It turned right over, ran for a few minutes, then something shorted out and caused an electrical fire. It went out by itself. The wiring's pretty well melted. The fuel pump's shot and so is the alternator. I can't be sure what caused the fire. There's a trace of diesel in the bilge water, so maybe there's saltwater in the fuel tank. I'm hoping it was just a short in the fuel pump."

After eight days on the reef, I was thankful the damage was no worse. Having dispensed with the bad news, we set about using the remaining daylight hours to best advantage with a strong and willing crew which now numbered nine.

No one had as yet been appointed to supervise the rescue task. It remained to be seen who would be best suited to coordinate the effort, joining together the multilingual factions.

Don Brown, who spoke only English, naturally spearheaded the Aves crew which had worked on the reef the past week. He had good, workable ideas and a thorough understanding of *Cheers* and her gear. But perhaps because of the language problem, Don found it easier to carry out each task himself, however menial. His soft-spoken manner wore well but was ineffectual in commanding rough-and-tumble laborers who responded best to direct orders.

Pablo Silva, our 41-year-old Venezuelan host, was an eager, cheerful and tireless worker who exhibited immense strength for his squat build. He was a strong swimmer and was wonderfully adept at clearing coral. After putting in long days on the reef, he would pull his three wire fish pots, cull out the junk fish and moray eels, then would prepare a sumptuous and nourishing evening meal for the entire crew. Lobster, turtle, barracuda and grouper were our favorites, always generously laced with fresh garlic. Castaways could hardly have asked for a better ally than Pablo, whose sole interest was to save the boat, eschewing pay, while enjoying the camaraderie of the crew. His fluency in both Spanish and English was immeasurably valuable in breaking down the language barrier that at times divided the labor force.

Each evening after supper, he would serenade with his ukelele and lead us in foot-stomping dances to unwind from the toil on the reef.

Rafael Useche, Pablo's 24-year-old colleague who spoke only Spanish, was a kind-hearted Venezuelan who loved to clown. He had endured two miserable days of coral clearing before declaring himself infirmed to the igloo to look after the housekeeping chores. His coral cuts became quickly inflamed and without antibiotics the open sores on his legs and feet grew dangerously infected.

Plump Rafael had a pronounced distaste for physical toil, but he cheered us on in our effort and was always willing to run the launch out to the reef and to ferry crew and materials.

A relative newcomer to the Aves company was 41-year-old powerhouse **Oriol Marval** the star of the short-lived *Carolina* salvage effort. Susan and Don had lured him away from the Venezuelan fishing boat after a day of watching him singlehandedly clear a field of elkhorn coral. Pronouncing Oriol's given name gave us fits. It came out either as the chocolate sandwich cookie, the Baltimore baseball team or butter's polyunsaturated substitute. We settled on "The Incredible Hulk."

I enjoy the sight of a well-developed set of biceps as much as any woman. But overdeveloped bodybuilders always seemed to me rather foppish and vain. But Oriol had the physique of a body builder without ever having seen a barbell. From the age of 13 he'd known only honest hard work. His years of fishing had given him the strength of Atlas, the coordination of a ballerina and the thick hide of a water buffalo. The father of 13, Oriol was an uncomplicated man, quiet and kind, given at times to shy retreat whenever conversation turned to his superhuman strength. For $50 a day he worked like a team of mules and if I did not tap him on the shoulder each afternoon to signal the end of the workday, I believe he would have toiled on into the night.

Oriol was a coral-clearing machine who could not be convinced to wear gloves or shoes. Each night when we treated the day's coral wounds, his always were the worst. Oriol's favorite job, because he was the only man capable, was resetting anchors, which we did many times daily. Changing the angle of pull by only a few degrees often necessitated moving an anchor a hundred feet through dense coral forests. Oriol would coil the 35-foot length of ⅜-inch chain rode upon one shoulder, sling the 45-pound plow anchor over the other shoulder, and climb, barefoot across whole fields of razor-sharp antlerlike coral while someone on the foredeck payed out the line. But for the Herculean efforts of this indefatigable man we might still be on Aves, digging.

Vying with Oriol and Rafael for my medal of honor was 41-year-old Frenchman **Jean-Jacques Roscian** who, with his lovely Bahamian girlfriend **Leslie Claridge,** sailed into Aves on August 2 on their brilliant red former Admiral's Cup racing sloop *Red Rooster*. The pair stumbled upon our castaways when *Cheers* had laid on the reef just five days, and immediately invited Don and Susan to share their quarters on the spacious sloop. Awed by the sight of the stranded vessel and the monumental task that lay ahead, the couple soon threw in with the effort and gave us five good days.

Jean-Jacques, a seasoned sailor, scuba diver, skilled mechanic and experienced fiberglass man, was an inexhaustible source of information whose expertise neatly dovetailed Don's. They worked well as a team, fixing broken winches, troubleshooting engine problems, calculating the surest path to deep water and jury-rigging a constant stream of broken gear.

Nassau was home to Leslie Claridge, whose face and figure

could drive a crew to mutiny. Beneath the voluptuous exterior hid the mischievous heart of an incurable tomboy who spent her childhood exploring the reefs and wrecks of the Bahamas with her brothers. Born to English parents, she was reared in Nassau, educated in Switzerland and, like Jacques, was fluent in English, French and Spanish. Leslie occasionally cleared coral with the men, but the moment she sensed she was in the way, she would climb out of the water, leaving that job to the muscle men, of which there was no shortage. Aboard *Cheers*, she helped prepare mid-day meals and busied herself clearing pulverized glass from lockers, cleaning the bilges and winching in anchor rodes with Susan and me.

Two days after my return to Aves, *Red Rooster* sailed for Bonaire. Leslie's lips were blistered and disfigured from the sun, and Jean-Jacques's festering coral cuts, which covered every limb of his wiry body, finally drove him out of the water.

My sister, **Susan Hitz,** rounded out the Aves troupe. A month before, I could not have guessed how she would react to being shipwrecked on a remote island. Though at first I worried this was one hell of a way to spend her precious two-week annual leave from the Washington graphics studio where she was an account executive, she revelled in the excitement of a great adventure no poolside piña colada holiday could match.

Susan gave me stamina when my own reserves flagged. She would make the morning coffee before we awoke at 6 each morning, herd us into the boat, work beside the men clearing coral, treat their coral wounds in the evening, help prepare the supper and wash up all the dinner dishes. The self-appointed watchdog of *Cheers'* gear, she spent many hours keeping damage to a minimum.

Susan matched wits with the innovative crew and became skilled at anticipating their needs and tactfully producing the right tool for the job. She tended anchor rodes as needed and if she couldn't get a fair lead over the rail or around the cabin trunk, she would pad the area with chafing gear.

Susan's coral wounds, by no means the most severe, were certainly the most novel. Her thighs and calves bore the perfect imprintation of brain coral where she had brushed the slimy, somewhat toxic polyps. A blue-eyed blonde with an Ivory soap complexion, her skin erupted in itchy red lesions in an allergic reaction that lasted many weeks. On the day she was scheduled to return to work, *Cheers'* 13th day on the reef, she was still beside me, clearing coral.

Pedro Soleano, of Bonaire, the pigtailed owner and skipper of the unnamed 28-footer, had joined the venture for the good daily wage he earned between fishing seasons. An irrepressible angler, Pedro would troll a lure just beyond the wake of his boat each morning and evening as we traversed the lagoon. Invariably he would land one or two thrashing, silvery barracuda, which he would pull in hand-over-hand, beat on the head with an abbreviated baseball bat and clean there and then. A four or five-footer would become steaks; smaller fish became fillets that he would toss immediately into a perpetual pan of grease and fry over his portable kerosene stove to a delicate, golden crispness.

So abiding was Pedro's affinity for fishing that when I would notice his prolonged absence from the coral-clearing brigade, I could generally bet on finding him napping in the cockpit of his boat, his slim legs slung over the transom with a monofilament fishing line laced between his toes.

Happy-go-lucky Bonairian **Lino Craane** was the brains behind the salvage effort. A 35-year-old unemployed jack-of-all-trades, Lino was the only one of us experienced in salvage work. Lino spoke only Papiamento and could not even write his name. But he had a keen mind, a rudimentary grasp of physics and the good sense to follow his instincts. Lino's ideas were presented by Jack as his own, which fooled no one.

It was Lino who had fixed *Phantom*'s outboard engine, Lina who had flopped *Cheers* safely back to her starboard side, and Lino who masterminded the logistics of attaching the drums to *Cheers* for added flotation. He tackled the project as a personal challenge to outwit nature and dupe the reef. He'd already succeeded in bringing one yacht off Aves that same year and was becoming something of a local legend in the lucrative game of salvage.

Strong as a bull, with arms the size of most men's thighs, Lino thrived on hard work. Standing waist-deep in water, Lino would throw his entire weight into pumping and wailing the 6½-ton winch, thrashing the water, straining to hear my cheer from the bowsprit: She's moving!" He would pump on the winch until his arms cramped in pain, then throw me a thumbs-up before sinking, exhausted, into water up to his neck.

Burly, blonde **Jack van der Eem,** last but certainly not least of the Bonaire contingent, was a third-generation Netherlands Antillian of pure Dutch descent. He was the spearhead of the Bonaire work force. University-educated in Holland, Jack was an intelligent, ambitious and shrewd businessman. At 35, he held one of Bonaire's few salaried positions as head of the government-subsidized fishing co-op.

Jack's motives, from the beginning, were a mystery to me. Altruism? Friendship? Adventure? Profit? His participation, in the beginning, was voluntary. From the first day he appeared in José Marchena's office he maintained close daily contact with me, exhibiting, I thought, genuine interest in the success of the project. He communicated well with the Bonaire crew and was instrumental in obtaining salvage gear, some of which was borrowed.

Jack had a quick, calculating mind and was actually a cunning genius. He epitomized the manual laborer who has made the grade to management. In the beginning, he worked in the water as hard as any man and thereby gained the confidence and respect of the entire crew. He was a kind and benevolent leader. But Jack also had a mean streak that surfaced as biting sarcasm delivered with a mischievous smile.

Jack alone spoke English, Spanish and Papiamento, the trilingual key to controlling the labor force. And thus he came to command the entire crew.

✳   ✳   ✳

When I first saw *Cheers* upon my return to Aves, I marveled at the progress the crew had made in my absence. They had cleared a channel 100 feet through the reef and had pulled the 15-ton vessel three-quarters of that distance using only her own ground tackle and winches. Unless the weather worsened, we could bring *Cheers* into the lagoon in less than two weeks.

As the channel was cleared through dense coral thickets choking the vessel's path to the lagoon, the broken, dislodged coral was tossed to either side, forming retaining walls rising two feet above the water's surface. The mounded coral had turned a deadly black in the sun, and in the still early morning hours the stench of decomposing coral hung heavy in our nostrils.

A change had come to the reef in the days I'd been away. Where great waves once had crashed upon the unbroken nine-mile expanse of reef and dissipated into frothy wash, blue water now sought *Cheers'* path into the lagoon. The longer the channel grew, the faster became the current's velocity until, by week's end, the current reached a turbulent four knots when the wind blew strong from the east, making it all but impossible to work in the water. As we could neither wade nor swim against such current, we used the taut anchor rodes to pull ourselves upcurrent from the work boat to *Cheers,* and to brace ourselves while clearing coral. The current flooding from the sea was an exciting symbol of our progress, and when its velocity thwarted the coral clearing, as it would those afternoons when the wind blew fresh, it became a welcome kick in the stern as we strained at the winches.

Evenings back at the igloo I thought plenty about our intrusion upon the reef and the consequences to the lagoon habitat. But the seabed itself exists in a state of perpetual upheaval, battered by a roiling, turbulent ocean. As we were later to see, one summer storm opened random arteries of its own through the reef into the lagoon. If our task seemed at times insurmountable, our determination to succeed was unwavering. At the risk of offending environmentalists I confess that conversation on most evenings centered not on the fragile reef habitat, but on how we might get our hands on some dynamite.

CHAPTER SEVENTEEN

──────────────────────────── Our first order of business upon returning to the reef to begin the long trek to the lagoon was to thoroughly assess the damage to *Cheers'* hull. We all were relieved to find only the one long crack at the turn of the bilge and some severe abrasion. Our next order of business was to begin relieving *Cheers* of all removable gear and securing the 10 empty drums to her sides to give her added flotation.

I was surprised, since Jack van der Eem had been in all along on the planning, when he opposed vehemently stripping *Cheers* of what we estimated was 3,000 pounds of removable, unnecessary gear and cargo. Even though losing that much weight was the equivalent of seven and a half barrels' worth of flotation, he argued strenuously it would make no difference in our ability to move the boat over the reef. Jack refused to participate in the operation with what he now termed "my crew". Even without them, Rafael, Pablo and I had the boat cleared in a matter of hours. The rest of the work force set to clearing coral around *Cheers* to make room for the 55-gallon barrels.

Securing the drums beneath the turn of the bilge posed a dilemma that stymied all but Lino, who had thought it through beforehand. The problem, of course, was how to sink an airtight drum with 400 pounds of buoyancy.

Lino's solution was to open the two spigots he had welded to two small lids in the top of each barrel. The barrels filled with seawater and sank. One by one, we lashed them on their sides, end to end, all around the boat, five to each side. In order to fit the drums under the starboard bilge, which lay on the coral, two anchors were run out to port and wedged securely in the coral. As we winched in on the two rodes, *Cheers* gradually righted herself enough to fit the barrels to the starboard side. Numerous lashings were passed under the keel and others were led fore and aft to secure the barrels.

Jean-Jacques was able to borrow from *Hispañola*, the black French ketch anchored in the lagoon, two diving tanks of compressed air. With the assistance of *Hispañola's* French captain, Joel Congal, Jean-Jacques and Lino set about displacing the seawater inside the drums with air. They simply connected an air hose from the dive bottle to the open spigot in the top of the barrel's end. When the valve was opened on the dive bottle, air entered the barrel, forcing the water out through the open spigot in the bottom of the barrel.

The 10th drum was filled just as the sun, hanging low in the western sky, signaled the end to our first workday.

I clambered across *Cheers'* slanting deck and gave a few last pulls on the bilge pump. Though the keel was still firmly aground and the starboard rail lay just awash, a change had come to the vessel. While only that morning *Cheers* lay dead and motionless as a cement barge, the deck beneath my feet now rolled with a slow, intoxicated motion.

I slept well that night knowing that the drums which encircled her like a collar would take the brunt of the night's punishment on the reef. She was moving and would be ready to make some progress through the channel when we returned next morning.

*   *   *

Our first day with full crew on the reef was a day of hard-won successes marred by a streak of gear failures, a test of patience and ingenuity.

Arriving at the reef shortly after sunup, we found that the five drums lashed along *Cheers'* starboard side had been severely battered by coral during the night. Three were dented; one was crushed and full of water and a fifth was holed and slowly filling. Overnight *Cheers* had lost 800 pounds of buoyancy.

Half the crew set to work to winch *Cheers* through the channel while the other half cleared coral ahead of the boat to widen and extend the channel.

Clearing what we estimated was 20,000 cubic feet of coral was not the impossible chore it first seemed. We were fortunate to be working in warm, gin-clear water. Only a snorkle and facemask were required. We discovered the task demanded agility more than brute strength. Except for Oriol, whose hands *were* his gloves, we wore heavy leather work gloves and found that a flipper on one foot and a shoe on the other was the best combination for maneuverability.

Easiest to clear was the brittle staghorn coral, whose branches snapped with a turn of the wrist. We cleared great patches of the stuff the way you would clear a field of deciduous shrubs in autumn.

Removing the sturdier elkhorn coral called for heavy tools and a bit of cunning. They grew from the sandy bottom to the water's surface like a great graveyard of moose antlers. With six-foot pry bars, sledge hammers and picks, we waged war on the dense, antlerlike fronds, swinging, bashing and prying the limbs until the bare stumps could be uprooted and cast onto the refuse piles.

Orange-brown fire coral was a curious obstruction. It resembles some of the antlerlike corals—until you touch it. It is soft and leathery and its toxic polyps inflict a painful sting, followed by a rash which lasts for days. So we handled it like you would the sea nettles its sting resembles—well clothed and with great respect.

Dislodging the massive boulders of brain coral called for the strength of our brawniest men and a trial-and-error approach. Working in the weightless underwater world with heavy tools took some getting used to for all of us. Many times I picked up a pick or sledge hammer and, with feet splayed, raised it in a slow backswing, only to lose control in a backwards somersault.

Pry bars and galvanized pipes proved best suited for dislodging brain coral, whose bases were far smaller and more vulnerable than their rotund masses. Typically, three or four men would pry from one side of the base until the boulder broke free, then together they would roll it out of the channel. It was amazing to see what enormous boulders they could move underwater, with only a fraction of the normal gravity to inhibit them. Brain coral too massive to dislodge or roll required tedious fracturing with cold chisels and sledge hammers to break it into manageable chunks. Only two boulders, both the size of compact cars, proved impenetrable barriers the men could not budge. And so we built a dog leg around them and continued to extend the channel toward the aquamarine deep water which grew closer, more alluring with each day.

*   *   *

Late Friday morning it was time to see how far we could move *Cheers*, adding the new portable winch to our pulling power.

Oriol set the two 45-pound plow anchors deep in coral to give just the right directional pull. One rode led to the powerful 40-to-1 anchor windlass on the bow and the other to the 47-to-1 sheet winch in the cockpit. The lead from the 6½-ton mechanical winch from Bonaire was chained to a massive coral head on the fringe of the channel 20 feet ahead of *Cheers*.

First we took all the slack out of the lines, and at Don's signal, three teams threw their weight to the winches. We hunkered down and cranked, throwing arms, backs and legs to the winches.

"That's it!"

The lines squeezed tightrope taut.

"Don't stop!"

We cranked, straining breathlessly. *Cheers* shuddered. She rumbled and she creaked, but she did not move.

"More heel," muttered Don. "We've got to reduce her draft."

"We've got fifteen knots of wind on the port quarter," I added. "Let's set the flying jib."

Again we strained at the winches. *Cheers* shuddered. She pivoted five degrees to port, and then she shouldered down and began to move. Without speaking, without stopping, we winched and cranked in unison, driven by the sound of coral crushing to powder beneath her keel. Pulling together with all the strength we could muster, we cranked for five minutes, then rested for five, and so on throughout the morning. For the first time, *Cheers*'s hourly progress was measured not in inches but in feet.

Then gear began to break under load. First was the starboard cockpit winch that Susan and I cranked. We moved the rode to the port cockpit winch and resumed cranking.

Next the anchor windlass gave out. Don and Jean-Jacques hurriedly unbolted it from deck and found two of the gears crushed.

With no possibility of repair without spare parts, the windlass became just another hunk of useless weight. Don moved the anchor rode to the main halyard winch and resumed cranking, while Oriol tailed from the end of the bowsprit.

Next to go was the 6½-ton portable winch. With a snap, the quarter-inch-diameter steel pin in the ratchet mechanism sheared under load. In the time-consuming hunt for a suitable substitute part, I narrowly avoided losing to eager scavengers the gooseneck clevis pin by offering up the kick-up pin to the outboard motor. That part lasted only ten minutes before shearing off just as the last one had. Next I dismantled the sea rail on the Shipmate stove. But by the time it was in place it was 5 o'clock and time to make our way through the lagoon before the coral heads were hidden by the sun's low rays.

We measured *Cheers'* forward progress that day at a record 24 feet. If we continued at that rate, I calculated that in 13 days we would reach water five feet deep with far fewer coral heads to thwart our progress.

Still, we had to do better. Time was the enemy. Not only were we working to get to safety before the first tropical storms arrived, but also to get off the reef before our work permit expired, eight days hence.

SATURDAY, AUGUST 8

During *Cheers'* 11th day on the reef, we made our best progress yet. Pedro agreed, over Jack's objections, to add his boat's 80-horsepower engine to our pulling power.

We cut crew weight aboard *Cheers* by stationing Susan and myself at the two winches. Oriol teamed up with Lino to operate the 6½-ton winch in the water, pushing and pulling the long handle like a seesaw.

At the signal from Don, we fell to. With a throaty rumble, the 28-footer fetched up taut on the hawser. Pedro nudged the throttle ahead. The stern squatted and swayed under load.

"Here she comes!" cried Don. "Keep cranking! By God, she's moving. Pedro, more throttle!"

Cheers fairly lunged ahead. Once she overcame inertia it was not difficult to keep her moving. We worked like demons, stopping only to reset anchors, move the portable winch and reanchor Pedro's boat. By 10 o'clock that morning we had dragged *Cheers* 40 feet. Aquamarine water marking the five-foot depth lay 250 feet ahead.

Then, suddenly, Jack summoned the Bonaire crew to the 28-footer, announced over the idling engine that work was done for the day and offered to transport the rest of us back to the settlement.

"It's ten in the morning, Jack," I objected. "Why are you stopping now?"

"You cannot pull the boat any further," he insisted. "The channel is not dug."

"So let's get to work clearing coral."

"You can do anything you want. We're going back." Then he spoke in Spanish and Pablo and Oriol climbed into the 28-footer.

"You better come now," Pablo advised. "unless you want to spend the night here. Rafael hauled the launch this morning to fix that leak, so he cannot come for you."

Pedro raised the anchor. Susan, Don and I climbed reluctantly aboard the 28-footer and returned to the settlement.

I took Jack aside. "What's up?" I challenged.

"I've decided that from now on we'll work at night. I've been studying the current. There is no tide, but in the late afternoon, when the breeze blows hardest, the water comes up six inches. That will be the best time to pull."

"We've got more than two hundred feet of channel to clear before this is going to get easier. We can't clear coral at night, in the dark."

"Your people can clear the coral. I'm going back to Bonaire for more drums."

"We don't need more drums. We're pulling the boat fifteen feet an hour, now that Pedro is pulling with the twenty-eight-footer."

"He will not pull anymore. It is too much strain for the boat."

"Is that what you've told him?" I bridled. "He was willing enough this morning."

"I am merely looking out for the welfare of my men. We will go to Bonaire tonight for ten more drums."

"You're taking Pedro off the job?"

"And Lino."

"Three men to get ten barrels? You may be running the crew, Jack, but I'm paying these men to work on Aves, not to run errands."

"You put your boat on this reef. I didn't. You need my crew of men. If I walk off this job, Pedro, Lino and the boat go, too. Now if you'd like to do it alone, go right ahead. We can take our gear and leave right now."

There was no more discussion. I tried to see his point of view, and it only added to the growing realization that Jack wished to prolong the salvage effort. I wondered what scheme had taken seed on the fertile floor of his mind. He was a man of few words, whose mind I could not read. Why was he taking so much time from his job to save my boat? Why, the day I chartered the plane, did he take those press photos of *Cheers* on the reef? Why did he try to dissuade me from removing cargo to lighten *Cheers?* Why did he deny us the pulling power of the 28-footer? And why did he suspend our visible progress on the reef for a time-consuming mission for more barrels?

Jack alone held the trilingual key to commanding the labor force. His control over Pedro and Lino was absolute. And though he was unsuccessful in drawing Oriol into his fold, Jack's influence, I realized, was sufficient to deal the salvage effort a crippling blow at will.

Why would a man sabotage the very mission he led? It didn't add up. Many were the times I'd dismissed the thought from my mind. Now I suspected that this man, who had quickly become the indispensible leader of the crew, was driven by the unthinkable ultimate motive: to gain possession of the boat for himself.

For more than a week I'd been unable to pin him down on a wage agreement for himself and his men. I felt a surprise was in store, one I could not leave to chance now that Jack had become the indispensible link in communication.

When the 28-footer left the dock Saturday night for Bonaire, I was aboard.

CHAPTER EIGHTEEN

———————————————— That night, as the 28-footer surged westward before a brisk northeast wind and following sea, I decided to let the pieces fall where they would. If it was the power play I suspected, calculated to deal the salvage effort a crushing blow, I would deal with it when Jack played his hand.

At 8 o'clock Sunday morning I put in an overseas call to Jim in New Jersey from Bonaire. It was wonderfully reassuring to hear his voice and to learn that he was feeling stronger. Though he tried to sound assured, I knew his days were consumed with worry about me and anxiety over the salvage. I tried to encourage him with news of our progress and shared with him my misgivings about Jack.

"Smells bad to me," he said. "I know something about salvage and about salvagers. First on the scene are usually the vultures— amateur salvagers who scavenge a living off the misfortunes of others. They'll promise to save your boat, then they'll string you along till the money runs out or until your spirit's broken. Then the pickings are theirs. It doesn't matter to them what shape the boat's in. The equipment alone's worth plenty and if they can get the hull off, so much the better. Has Jack asked you how much the boat's worth?"

244

"Yes, but I was evasive. I didn't answer him."

"Has he asked you how much you're prepared to spend to save the boat?"

"I told him, 'Whatever it takes.' "

"But he has no idea how much money you have?"

"I'm afraid so. He was in José's office when I transferred seven thousand to an account in Bonaire."

"You can count on one thing: Your total bill for the job will be that or more."

"That's why I came to Bonaire to pin Jack down on a firm price."

"You must get a wage agreement before you go any further. If you don't, and you get the boat off the reef, he can demand any price he wants and if you don't pay, he can put a lien on the boat and force a sale."

"I hadn't thought of that."

"If Jack should ask you anything more about how much money you have, how much you're willing to spend, what the boat's worth, what the gear's worth, be evasive. Tell him you've talked to me. We've agreed that if your best effort to refloat the boat fails you're going to burn her to the water."

"He won't believe that!"

"I want you to tell him that. Now what would happen if you told him his services were no longer needed?"

"I'd lose the other two crew, the boat and some of the gear we borrowed. Let me pin him down on a price. Next time I call I hope I'll have good news for you. I'm not giving up until we get her off."

Sunday was a lost day. The stores were closed; we could get no barrels; and Jack was unavailable to meet with me.

Monday, August 10

Early in the morning José Marchena knocked on my hotel room door.

"Jack said he wants fifteen dollars per man hour, and he needs one more man in the crew. And he wants two hundred a day for the boat."

I did some quick calculating. "That comes to eight hundred a day. I can't afford that. I'll be broke by the end of the week."

"He knows that. I told him he is crazy to demand so much. He says if you don't want to pay it, the men don't want to work."

"Can you get in touch with the crew, José? I'm tired of talking through Jack. I know only what he wants me to know; he tells the crew what he wants them to know. It's time I spoke with them myself and I'd like you to translate for me, José."

At 10 Monday morning Jack, Pedro, Lino and I sat face-to-face around a round table in José's office. I spoke to the crew as a whole and José translated.

"I appreciate your efforts thus far and I am confident that if we continue we will succeed. But I cannot afford to pay you the amount Jack has asked. Anyone who has joined this project thinking he is going to get rich from my misfortune is here for the wrong reason.

"I offer each of you one hundred dollars a day, plus one hundred dollars a day for the boat. I am offering you a good day's wage for an honest day's work. I will not pay you to run errands to Bonaire.

"Let me assure you of one thing: As long as my boat is on that reef I am going to work to get her off. And if I decide she cannot be saved I am going to take off my personal belongings and burn her to the water. When I leave Aves the next time, I am leaving nothing behind. Regardless of the outcome, you will be paid for each day you work on Aves.

"What do you say?"

All eyes fell on Jack, who gave them no lead. After a moment of silence, Lino nodded. Then Pedro nodded.

"What about you, Jack?" asked José.

"I cannot ask more than my men," said Jack benevolently. "If they want to work for a hundred dollars a day, then I will, too. You must pay for the boat to be at Aves, but you cannot use her to pull your boat."

"Why not," I asked, "if Pedro's willing?"

"You could break the clutch plate or damage the propeller."

"The propeller is protected by a strut. I will buy a clutch plate to take as a spare."

José translated and Pedro agreed.

"Who will be in charge of running this crew?" I asked.

"I will," said Jack.

"Then I will continue to talk directly with you and I ask that you consult me on major decisions. When can we get underway for Aves?"

"Tonight. Three a.m."

I agreed to add a fourth man to the crew, and José Marchena convinced the consul to issue a visa for Ron Domacassé, a cheerful multilingual Bonairian whose sportfishing excursion business was suffering during the slow tourist season. Pedro repaired his broken steering cable and we loaded 10 more barrels and more provisions aboard the 28-footer.

TUESDAY, AUGUST 11

At 9 o'clock, we slipped into the cut at Aves, wholly unprepared for yet another strange twist of fate. There, anchored off the rickety pier, was the gray hull of a Guardia Nacional gun boat.

"Sheet," muttered Pedro. It was his first word of English.

Don took our lines. His face was softened with a smile of renewed optimism that had replaced the look of dispiriting frustration he had worn the previous week. Pablo ambled down the dock with a springy gait to welcome us inside the igloo to meet El Capitán.

Instead of the dour, toothless old crank that had commanded the previous gun boat, I shook hands with a robust, ruggedly handsome and enthusiastic young captain.

"Capitán Jorge Alberto Martinez-Rodriguez," he smiled, giving me a vice grip handshake.

"The Capitán requested permission to come as soon as he learned about your boat," beamed Pablo. "I showed him your boat today. He says he can get her off. Is true! He has saved fourteen boats before this. Already he is like a legend in the Guardia."

The young captain beamed with pride, still pumping my hand. "Cheers, numero quince!" he declared.

We lost no time in getting out to the reef. In my absence the crew had cleared another 80 feet of channel. We off-loaded the additional drums we'd brought, filled them with seawater and lashed them five to each side in a second tier beneath the original drums. *Cheers* rose a full two inches on her lines.

Captain Martinez maneuvered the 60-foot gunboat into position inside the lagoon and anchored 600 feet southwest of *Cheers*. Since neither vessel had a hawser long enough to connect the two boats, we bent one of *Cheers'* 300-foot ⅝-inch nylon anchor rodes to the gunboat's 300-foot one-inch nylon deck line and secured the bitter end to the heavy nylon bridle that girdled *Cheers*.

Captain Martinez was not a thinker but a doer, a natural leader whose mere presence commanded attention. He brought to the effort a decisiveness that was sorely needed. If he said "Jump," we asked only, "how high?" He could maneuver his ungainly vessel through coral-infested shoal water with the finesse of a launch driver.

The one man who did not share our enthusiasm for the impetuous Captain Martinez was Jack, who became moody, argumentative, unapproachable, and finally withdrawn. His power to control had been usurped.

I stood on *Cheers'* bowsprit and checked the bridle. Jack stood below me, waist-deep in water.

"Don't try this," he urged. "I'm warning you, you'll destroy your boat if you try to pull with that ship."

I waved my hand high overhead, signaling the gunboat to pull. I heard the rumble of the gunboat's engine and watched the long rope fetch up taut. The steel drums creaked, *Cheers'* bow dipped gently and slowly she began to move. The hawser stretched to a fraction of its former thickness, the three strands began to unlay with a dangerous recoiling whiplash, the hawser parted. *Cheers* settled back down in the grip of the coral.

Three times more the gunboat fetched up taut on the towline, but each time, the line stretched, distended and parted under load with a dangerous whiplash. Unless we could come up with a stronger hawser, there was nothing the gunboat could do to help us. Frustrated, the captain returned his vessel late that afternoon to the deep-water anchorage off the settlement, leaving our original crew and the 28-footer to make best use of the remaining two hours of daylight by clearing coral.

While filling the barrels with air, we discovered quite by accident that the compressor made a marvelous device for blowing sand out of the channel. By sweeping the air hose from side to side as far as it would reach, we effectively added a precious one to two inches to the channel depth. While snorkeling with the air hose, I heard a rumble, looked up and saw the 28-footer weigh anchor and power away toward the setting sun.

Without a word, without looking back, the Bonaire crew had called it a day and left Don, Oriol and myself stranded on the reef in the fleeting light.

"We can inflate the Zodiac," I suggested.

"I barely made it out here in that thing," said Don. "It's leaking badly and the fuel tank's about empty."

"Where are the oars?" I asked.

"There aren't any. It's getting dark. Let's not waste time. Betsy, grab a screwdriver from *Cheers*. We can take the floorboards apart and paddle with those if we have to. Better bring a couple of buckets, too. Hurry!"

I grabbed the gear, locked *Cheers'* cabin and climbed down into the Zodiac. The metal gas tank was floating in the calf-deep water inside the boat. Don picked up a face mask and slipped over the side for a look. The sun set behind clouds in the west.

"The center seam's split from bow to stern. She'll sink this far, but no more."

He climbed aboard and pulled the starter cord. The engine sprung to life. Slowly, to conserve fuel, we made for the island, invisible now three miles across the black lagoon.

After an hour we could make out lights in the windows of Pablo's igloo. Then the engine droned to a slow, thirsty halt. Gripped by the current, we watched as the lights on land slipped eastward. We were being sucked out the pass to open sea. Again and again Don pulled the cord, but the engine wouldn't start. I shook the gas tank; a trickle remained. I raised the tank high over my head and squeezed the siphon ball. Again Don pulled the cord. The engine coughed to life and we limped the remaining mile to the pier.

Jack and his Bonaire crew were frying fish in the cockpit of the 28-footer when we tied up beside them.

"Why did you leave us there?" I asked him. "Why did you call off work without telling us?"

"It was getting dark. You know we always leave by six o'clock." We exchanged few words after that.

WEDNESDAY, AUGUST 12

On *Cheers'* fifteenth day on the reef, the entire crew was on the job soon after sunup. Captain Martinez put to sea early in an attempt to retrieve the 600-foot wire cable left behind by the *Dong Won* when the messenger line had parted. Pablo volunteered to search for the cable. It was a perilous job to dive in the breaking surf trying to extricate the tangled cable from a labyrinth of coral, but one Pablo insisted on doing himself.

At noon, Captain Martinez gave three blasts of the horn and a blood-curdling war cry to say they had retrieved the cable. At 2 o'clock the gun boat entered the cut and anchored 600 feet southwest of *Cheers*, ready to pull.

My stomach knotted with anticipation as the captain approached *Cheers* in his launch. He peeled off his shirt, then slipped over the side and swam the length of the channel. He gave me the thumbs-up and passed me the end of the wire cable.

"I'm warning you," urged Jack. "Don't try it. You'll damage your boat. Slow and sure is the way to go," he insisted. "Call off this madman and his ship."

Don connected the cable to the nylon bridle. "Jack, get your weight off the boat, please."

"I'm warning you, you're going to destroy this boat. The ship cannot control the direction of pull from such a distance. You'll careen into that wall of coral and . . ."

"Betsy," said Don, "give us a signal from the bow. Use the flag on the man overboard pole to direct us. Use straight up for ahead, and wave it back and forth for stop. I'll be on the Guardia boat watching with binoculars."

Don sped in the Guardia launch to the anchored ship and climbed aboard. Susan lashed *Cheers'* tiller amidships, then put her weight to leeward by swaying outboard on the starboard shrouds.

I stood on the bowsprit and raised the flagpole to go ahead. The ship nosed ahead. The cable fetched up taut under strain. *Cheers* pivoted ever so slightly and pointed her bowsprit straight down the channel. More throttle. She rumbled and creaked and slowly began to move. Five feet, 10 feet, 20 feet, crushing the thrumming barrels like beer cans as she moved. Thirty feet, 40 feet. Then she rode up on a ridge, listed heavily to starboard and stopped dead, her starboard deck awash. More throttle. She wouldn't budge. I waved the flag to stop.

Don sped over in the launch. "It's too shallow here," he said. "We'll have to try to deepen it with shovels and straighten out that bend. And we better work fast." He studied the eastern sky. "A tropical storm's coming. The mate just heard it on the radio. It hit Margarita with fifty knots this morning and is headed this way at fifteen knots. It should reach us around midnight."

"We better sat all the anchors and stow the sails below," I said.

"We'll ride it out right here," said Don.

"Aboard *Cheers?*"

"You bet. It might be just what we need. Don't you see, the only tide range we've got is wind-driven current flooding from the sea. If we get fifty knots out of the east, the seas are going to come right over the reef. We could get a foot or two of tide pushing us through the channel."

"*Cheers* will be battered to bits!"

"Relax, Bets. The barrels will take the beating beneath the waterline and we can set anchors to maintain position or to pull."

"I don't know, Don. It sounds pretty risky. This thing could develop into a hurricane. I want to stay aboard, but the rest of you. . . ."

"Let's clear as much coral as we can before dark and get rid of this dog leg."

The Bonaire crew opted for a quiet night ashore. I couldn't blame them; it seemed like insanity to me. But with five other ready volunteers eager to ride out the storm aboard *Cheers*, I couldn't very well argue.

Captain Martinez was the ringleader of the ludicrous plan. He set a second storm anchor from his ship, left his mate in charge of anchor watches and fell in body and soul with my crew. Wearing only tattered cut-off shorts, a snorkel and face mask, he grabbed a pry bar, tumbled over the side and decimated coral until darkness fell and the dog leg was gone from the channel.

Oriol and Pablo also cleared coral until dark, then they stayed aboard *Cheers* throughout the night to tend lines and carry out the anchors. Don intended to sail out the storm, hard aground, with as much sail as *Cheers* could carry. Susan was there, as I was, to watch the bizarre night unfold, to look after *Cheers*, and to call off this lunacy if it got out of hand.

At 6:15 the sun in colorless oblivion slipped into the sea. Two days from full, the moon cast long shadows as we settled into the cockpit to wait. Soon after sunset the wind began to build in the east, from 15 to 20 knots, with higher gusts.

The night was magnificent, the air clear and cool, sparked with expectancy. So bright was the moon, it cast a perfect shadow of *Cheers'* keel upon the channel, and we watched by moonlight as scores of tiny fish darted in and out of the submerged coral rubble.

Three anchors were set to guide us down the channel, and as the wind built from 20 to 25 knots, *Cheers* began to rock and sway. We winched in on the anchor rodes, taking every inch of slack we could get. The reef astern knocked the stuffing out of the waves as they rose, curled, broke and cascaded past us. Divested of its destructive force, the great volume of water sought our channel as the surest path into the lagoon and surged past us with the force of a river.

Gradually, thick black clouds began to gather in the east. Don raised the full mainsail, eased the sheet and vanged it to starboard. *Cheers* heeled, we strained at the winches, and she inched down the channel to the ear-splitting din of crushing steel. In half an hour we had dragged ourselves a full boat length and had come up short on the anchors.

Pablo and Oriol were over the side simultaneously, vying for the honor of walking out the anchors.

My protests only added to their bravado. They handled the swift current by drifting down hand-over-hand, along the rodes. When they reached the anchors Susan and Don slowly paid out each rode as the men walked their respective anchors to their new sets. Then, hand-over hand, they returned to the boat, shivering, bleeding from coral cuts, but proud as warriors.

The night now was filled with the noise of booming surf and shrieking wind. A curtain of thick clouds veiled the moon and all was black around us. Don sheeted in the mainsail for more heel.

"This is insanity," I muttered, "sailing, hard aground, in thirty-five knots of wind. You're all crazy."

Susan took me below and tried to put me to bed. The noise below, of steel drums crushing between coral and fiberglass, was torturous. I began to cry, a whimper at first. Then, for the first time since the long ordeal began, I sobbed uncontrollably. I could not understand what all the people were doing on my boat or why we were sailing hard aground. I'd lost my grip.

"Sleep," Susan insisted. "You're just exhausted. Lie down and get some sleep."

I lay down in the dark cabin and soon I did not even hear the din of the drums crushing against the coral or the shriek of the wind in the rigging.

MIDNIGHT THURSDAY, AUGUST 13

I awoke in a horrible, sweaty fright, marched on deck and ordered all the pirates off my boat. Whether dreaming or hallucinating, I was up and down the companionway many times during the night ordering the pirates over the rail. My crew had the good sense to ignore me and to send Susan down to sit on my chest when I got in the way.

In the morning, I went on deck to find enormous waves bashing the reef, a bedraggled crew, an empty bottle of Amaretto and a soul-satisfying scene. We had "sailed" not less than 100 feet during the night. The beautiful aquamarine line of deep water lay just another 100 feet ahead. Captain Martinez was approaching in the gun boat to reanchor and set up the tow. For the first time since we'd struck the reef 15 days before, I knew that *Cheers* would float free, that she would be mine to sail again.

Jack was on the reef just after sunup, trying again to persuade me to choose the slow and certain path of letting his crew winch the boat, inch by inch, to deep water. I just looked at that line of blue deep water and ignored him.

The captain anchored his ship southwest of *Cheers*, and at 8 o'clock carried the cable to me on *Cheers'* bow. I secured it to the nylon bridle. I stood on the bowsprit, Susan in the cockpit, and Don on the afterdeck of the gun boat.

I raised the flag. Go! Don motioned to the captain, and as natural as kids on a slide, *Cheers* bumped and skidded, twisted and slid 100 feet straight through the canal and bounded free in five feet of water.

I knelt and kissed the gently-rolling deck beneath my feet. Then, giddy with excitement of a child, I embraced my sister, as much to hug her as myself.

CHAPTER NINETEEN

———————————————— The 28-footer approached *Cheers*, throwing a big wake and, before I could fend off, bashed into her port side.

"Careful!" I shouted to Jack in the cockpit.

"Look at your boat," he sneered. "You think one more scratch makes a difference?"

With knife in hand, Jack slipped over the transom and cut the lashings on the 20 drums secured to *Cheers'* underbody.

"Those are my dock lines you're cutting!"

Singly and in rafts of two and three, the dented drums popped to the surface and drifted with the wind and current toward the pass and out to sea.

"You can't just set those adrift," I protested. "They're a hazard to navigation. They could sink a small boat."

"Then you chase them. We're getting underway for Bonaire. The job is over. Your boat is floating."

"I hired the 28-footer to escort us to Bonaire or to tow us if we need it."

"We will do that, but the men want to get back. Only Pedro is getting paid for steaming time, and we don't want to waste another day here."

"This boat has laid on that reef for fifteen days. She's not ready for sea and I don't intend to take her out to deep water now and risk sinking her. Her engine is broken and there are at least two cracks in the hull where she's taking on water. Most of her gear is ashore in the shed and we've got to reeve new halyards if we're going to try to sail. It's one-thirty now; there's no way we can leave before tomorrow with the boat in this condition."

"Then you tell that to my men. You hired us for the job. You had no right to bring in the Guardia Nacional."

"So that's what's eating you. The job didn't drag on long enough to suit you. You'll get paid for every day you worked here. Now excuse me. I have work to do."

Pedro passed me a line and while the 28-footer towed us the three miles to the settlement, Susan steered *Cheers* and Don and I combed the inside of the hull for damage. The leak through the crack in the starboard side had slowed to a drip. Don had patched the forward bilge leak with underwater epoxy, and though it didn't arrest the leak, it slowed it to a weep. We checked the bilges frequently, and to our amazement, pumped only six strokes that hour.

We anchored *Cheers* in 15 feet of water off the landing and rowed to the dock. I looked long at *Cheers*, bobbing at anchor, still light on her lines.

"Poor boat," sighed Susan. "She looks like someone picked her up and ran her through a cheese grater."

"She's never looked more beautiful to me," I said. And it was true.

Our Venezuelan friends who had labored so hard to see this moment greeted us with the gruff and sentimental abrazo of the South American latino. One by one, they pulled us onto the dock. A tear slipped down Oriol's strong, smiling face and hung in the cleft of his chin. The dynamic Captain Martinez picked me up off my feet, whirled me around, then thrust in my hand an open green drinking coconut he'd brought on the ship from Venezuela. Then he walked toward the beach, now strewn with broken coral rubble from last night's blow, and with bare, cupped hands, planted a sprouting coconut to commemorate the occasion by giving Aves its first palm tree.

On my last trip to Bonaire, Pablo had asked me to bring him

back a case of beer which he had sequestered in the outdoor cooler. Now, to toast our victory, he graciously passed cold Amstels to all the crew.

"The relief ship comes for Rafael and me tomorrow," said Pablo. "Now we can go back to Venezuela with happiness in our hearts." With a boyish grin, he reached behind his back and presented me with the steel rotator from my Walker log, the distance-measuring device we had been towing and lost the night we struck the reef.

"I found it when I dove for the *Dong Won*'s cable."

"Amazing!"

The Bonaire faction remained aloof on the 28-footer, tied to the dock. So I gathered up some cold beers and walked down the dock to invite them to join us. A little political fence-mending was badly needed. With sullen faces, they rejected the beer and my thanks and looked to Jack for expression.

"They want to get underway for Bonaire. No more delays, hear?" he said firmly.

I deeply lamented whatever divisive factors had so splintered the crew. With my tail between my legs, I walked up the dock and broached to Don the subject of departure. That proved to be a mistake, for Captain Martinez picked up enough of my conversation to launch him into a seething rage. He stormed down the dock, and shaking his fist threateningly, vowed to confiscate the 28-footer then and there if they forced us to leave in the next 24 hours. He would release us when he was good and ready. Meanwhile we had beers to drink and a cause to celebrate.

The salvage of *Cheers* had been plagued with enough ill will as it was. So Don and I decided to make peace by compromising. Against our better judgement, we agreed to get underway at 4 the next morning. On a Friday.

Susan occupied the good captain on shore while I hoisted Don up the mast to reeve new halyards and check the rigging. With help from the Bonaire crew, we retrieved *Cheers*' gear from the storage shed and divided it between our boat and the 28-footer. While Don inspected the hull underwater, I examined all the through-hull fittings inside the boat.

All in all, *Cheers* had weathered the stranding magnificently, and we would even have enough battery power to use running lights.

Pablo cooled the captain's fire by explaining that we were eager to return to Bonaire to begin repairs. Reluctantly he agreed to let us sail at 4 a.m.

"If you are going to Bonaire," he added, "you must look up my uncle, the Honorable Frederico Martinez-Isturiz, who is the Venezuelan consul there. He will be most interested to hear your amazing story and to learn what his nephew has done."

"I know your uncle," I said numbly. "He gave us our visas. I shall be pleased to tell him it was his nephew who saved my boat."

For the first time in five long weeks, I slept that night in my own bunk aboard *Cheers*. At 4 o'clock, the 28-footer was alongside.

Friday, August 14

"I don't think we will need a tow until we get to the marina," I said. "But stick close by. We'll give you five blasts on the horn if we run into trouble."

"If we see your lights disappear we'll know you sunk," quipped Jack sarcastically, and off they sped for Bonaire.

"Hey!" called Don, "You've got our life raft!"

It was too late. The fishing boat disappeared into the night.

Nothing was going to spoil this sail for us. Susan, Don and I were determined to bring *Cheers* safely into port, under her own steam with the same crew, still friends, who had begun the trip 19 days before.

We hoisted the full main, raised the anchor hand-over-hand, then ghosted slowly out the wide pass. So as to minimize strain on the hull and rig, we raised no more canvas, and broad-reached eastward at an easy five knots.

The moon was nearly full overhead, and from time to time we could glimpse the white stern light of the 28-footer a mile or so ahead on the horizon.

By dawn, the 28-footer was nowhere in sight. But we weren't troubled because our bilges were nearly dry and our sails full and drawing. Only by handling the tiller, guiding the boat and feeling her respond to our touch did our hard-won victory seem at last a reality.

When we reached Bonaire Marina at 11 o'clock that morning, the 28-footer was drifting outside the bottleneck entrance, waiting to tow us inside. We furled the sails, passed Pedro a line and cast it off a minute later to steer ourselves into a slip. The 28-footer's crew dumped our belongings on the nearest finger pier and left.

The dock was choked with curious on-lookers. José Marchena was the first aboard, with customs and immigration following close on his heels. The courteous three-man team cleared us in quickly.

Then I hurried to the nearest phone to call Jim.

"I didn't think you could do it," he confessed. "I thought *Cheers* was finished."

"She's held up amazingly well," I reported. "But we're looking at a long haulout. There's a 100-ton lift right here at the marina and I'll get on the waiting list. I'll call you again with a list of materials to bring down from the States. We can do all our own work, if you're up to it."

"You bet I am. I've got to see the doctor again next week, but I've made a reservation to fly down in ten days."

Leslie and Jean-Jacques of *Red Rooster,* who had helped us on the reef, were there to help us empty the boat, salvage what gear we could and assess damage to the hull. Marina manager Nico Block designated a 100-foot-long finger pier for us to sift through our gear, and by late that afternoon the pier was piled high with camera equipment, electric sanders, a power drill, a jig saw, binoculars, books, a radio direction finder, short wave radio, boxes of new fuel filters, a case of engine oil, sleeves of sandpaper, boxes of spare parts, and sentimental, mutilated photographs. We stripped the bunks and sent six bags of clothing to the Chinese laundry. We heaped the dock with canned goods, rusted tools, a punctured inflatable dinghy, drowned outboard motor, tangles of rusted anchor chain, coils of chafed running rigging, rusted propane tanks, moldy charts and sodden books.

The amassed gear must have looked like the garage sale of the century. A South African pilot from a nearby boat asked me how much I wanted for the life raft!

Don arranged a flight back to St. Croix for Sunday, two days hence, and until his departure, worked tirelessly at numerous mechanical chores that were beyond me. He tinkered many hours in the engine room, but concluded that the engine was in need of a major overhaul. He got the Shipmate stove working, and so we were able to make coffee to keep the vigil going. He plunged all the corroded tools in a 10-gallon jug of diesel fuel to retard rust and gave the boat a thorough washdown.

Lying two weeks in the caustic spray of the wave-swept reef, *Cheers* exhibited extensive corrosion all the way to the masthead. Aluminum was pitted, stainless steel was streaked with rust, moving parts of deck fittings were seized fast. The Seagull outboard, which had been clamped to the stern pulpit, was a moulten mass of immovable mixed metal. Its fuel tank and muffler were rusted through. All the galvanizing had worn off the four 35-foot lengths of anchor chain. The stock of one of the two 45-pound plow-type anchors was bent in a 90-degree arc from the sideways load we'd put on it trying to winch the boat. The steering vane was seized immovable. The varnished brightwork was an expanse of yellow flaking fish scales with innumerable deep lacerations from mis-aimed crowbars. Masthead sheaves were crushed from the sideways pull of halyards used to heel the boat, and only one of four halyards was still in one piece. Five nylon dock lines, two jib sheets, two 300-foot nylon anchor rodes and an 80-foot deck line were destroyed. Four winches were broken but repairable.

Once the boat was emptied, Susan hosed out the cabin and we surveyed the interior damage. Most bulkheads had torn away from the hull as it flexed on the reef, but all bulkheads remained in their proper positions, showing only cracked fiberglass tabbing. Bulkhead damage was concentrated amidships, at the boat's greatest beam, and was most extensive on the port side, where the vessel had fallen during the unsuccessful *Dong Won* rescue attempt.

Locker and passageway doors opened and closed as easily as ever. Remarkably, only two insignificant joints of interior woodwork facia had sprung; the hundreds of others still fit together with the same surgical precision as the day *Cheers* was built. The hull-deck joint, one of an Alajuela's notable strong points, remained absolutely watertight.

I was concerned we might have ruptured the two stainless steel water tanks, located beneath the cabin sole, or worse yet, ruptured the fiberglass fuel tank molded as an integral part of the keel. But since the forward bilge area continued to weep slowly and the engine was inoperative, there was no quick and easy way to test the integrity of the tanks. The extent of engine and electrical system damage would have to await Jim's appraisal, as there was no skilled marine mechanic on the island.

Damage to the hull was superficial above the waterline and could not accurately be assessed below the waterline until the boat was hauled. Until then, I could only glean clues from what I saw through a face mask. The bottom third of the two-inch-thick fiberglass rudder had carried away, exposing the quarter-inch-thick steel reinforcing plate, which was bent and mangled. The rudder was cracked at two out of three gudgeon attachment points and the massive bronze pintles and gudgeons had worked loose and had become misaligned. Though there was some play in the tiller, we were able to steer the boat as well as ever from Aves to Bonaire.

The three-foot-long crack in the starboard side of the hull at the turn of the bilge was invisible from the outside and appeared only as a subtle yet long fracture in the woven roving inside the hull. The starboard topsides were badly scarred, with bare roving exposed, and the port topsides showed only subtle hairline cracks in the thick white gel coat. The entire underbody was gouged from the coral, but most lacerations penetrated only the ultra-hard bottom paint or gel coat and did not expose bare fiberglass.

Abrasion to the bottom of the keel was severe, revealing chunks of fiberglass, but exposing no lead. The extent of water penetration into the keel could only be determined once the boat was hauled.

It was painful to strip the boat and see all our familiar belongings spread like refuse on the dock alongside our battered boat. I could only feel the greatest relief that we had good friends to help and a strong hull to build upon. It is testimony to the incredible strength and resiliance of a well-found fiberglass hull that we escaped with more than our lives. Had we chosen a lesser boat, our ill-fated passage would certainly have ended in tragedy.

Rebuilding *Cheers* ourselves was a financial necessity we never questioned. Whether something of the dream to cruise the world could be salvaged, only time would tell.

SUNDAY, AUGUST 16

Early in the day, Don boarded a plane for St. Croix, his boy-ishly-handsome face hidden beneath the uncharacteristic beard he'd grown on Aves. He had spirited the seemingly-impossible plan by which we tunneled through the reef and he had done every-thing in his ability to ready *Cheers* for the rebuild, absolving him-self, I could only hope, of the tremendous guilt which at times threatened to break his spirit. On parting, he reached in his pocket and thrust in my hand his personal check for $2,000. "Put this toward the rebuild," he insisted. Then he turned and walked to his plane.

I wanted to be gallant and tear up the check, but instead I returned to *Cheers* and put it in a drawer—just in case.

MONDAY, AUGUST 17

I struck out right after breakfast for Kralendijk Trading Com-pany to settle my account and pay the Bonaire crew. José Mar-chena caught me on the marina dock.

"Bad news, my friend," he said. "We go back to your boat and cry in our coffee."

"Now what?" I asked, putting on the pot.

"Jack's bill." He reached in his shirt pocket and handed me a folded sheet of yellow lined paper.

The hand-written bill was a triumph of creative writing. In-cluded was labor for every man while in Bonaire as well as on Aves, materials I'd billed through José's office, underwater flash-lights I'd never seen and a whopping $1,000 bonus for Jack beyond his per diem rate for services performed in Bonaire.

I outlined in writing details of our August 10 wage meeting, itemized each man's labor based on that agreement, and set out to pay each man exactly what I owed.

At 1 p.m. I met with Jack in José's office to iron out the $2,500 discrepancy. Heated words ensued. Jack wadded my accounting into a ball and tossed it into a waste basket.

"I hope you anchor that boat with chain," he said vengefully and walked to the door. "You owe what's on my bill. If you do not pay, there is no telling what my men will do."

Unable to sleep that night, I got up and bolted the hatches. But still sleep would not come. I found the revolver, loaded it and tucked it under my pillow. The same fear that stalked me those long nights on Bequia had returned.

Tuesday morning I was waiting outside Kralendijk Trading Company when José unlocked the door. He led me into his office and closed the door.

"José, you were at the meeting. You translated my offer to the crew and you watched as every man agreed to a wage of a hundred dollars a day for their work on Aves. I'm sorry to put you in the middle of this, but you have to tell Jack what you heard."

"I hate to argue about money. I know you are right, but how can you ask me to take sides? This is a very small island. Jack van der Eem may be a stubborn Dutchman, but his people are in these islands now three generations. You will sail away on your boat soon enough, but I must live here with these people."

"But I cannot pay what I do not owe. Is there some sort of court here?"

"You want to go to court against Jack? Present the word of an American tourist against that of a native Antillian—of four Antillians? You have no chance."

"Then you think I should pay what he demands?"

"I don't think even Jack expects you will pay that much. That is why he threatened you. He thinks he can scare you. I've told him it is too much. But Jack is not stupid. He can put a lien on your boat and you cannot take it away from this island until his bill is paid. In the end it will cost you more to fight him, believe me.

"Go back to your boat, Betsy. Clean up your mess and think it over. I will add up all the expenses we have billed through this office and we will see what you have left."

"Did my bank draft come through?"

"Yes you have seven thousand on deposit in our account."

"What will you charge for your services?"

"How I hate to talk money. How does seven hundred and fifty sound?"

"Fair enough."

"I will ask Jack to meet you here at two o'clock."

"I want to meet with the entire crew, all four men. I want to see them face to face."

"I will have them here at two o'clock," said José.

I returned to *Cheers* and tried to work, but the impending confrontation gnawed at my mind. Bonaire had ceased to be a friendly haven. Moreover, I couldn't bear the thought of Jim returning to face a strenuous rebuild of a boat he had no hand in wrecking, with sinister characters lurking in the shadows.

We had sailed the boat 38 nautical miles to Bonaire in her battered condition, and Susan and I could take her another 30-odd miles to Curaçao just as well. I would settle this claim and tell only customs officials my destination. Curaçao, capital of the ABC islands, had a choice of haulout facilities, and Spanish Water, with its myriad protected inland bays, offered an ideal hurricane hole.

Susan agreed it was time to get out of Bonaire. After dark we planned to load the whole mess back aboard *Cheers* in preparation for our covert departure. I composed a waiver for each of the men to sign when they were paid, acknowledging payment in full for their labor and relinquishing any later claim to my boat.

At 2 o'clock I began negotiating with the four men. Ron Domacasse, the crewmember Jack had insisted on hiring when we returned for more barrels, gratefully accepted his check for $400, signed the waiver and left the meeting. Pedro, skipper of the 28-footer agreed with my reckoning and left with a check for $1,900. Only Lino and Jack held out. Lino admitted he had agreed to work for $100 a day, but saw that Pedro's check was greater and objected because he felt he'd worked harder than Pedro.

For two full hours we debated the remaining $2,500 discrepancy in the total bill. Tempers flared, threats flew, fists pounded the table. Getting nowhere with arithmetic and logic, and with no end in sight, I called an end to the meeting. I crossed off Jack's bill the materials I already had billed through Kralendijk Trading Company and ordered José to write their checks.

"I am not paying you your wages; I am buying you off. You know it and I know it. I bought you. If I see either of you near my boat, or if you threaten me again, I am going right to the police."

With Don's $2,000 check and my $7,000 bank deposit, I had just enough to pay the entire $9,000 bill. With empty pockets I returned to *Cheers*, where Susan and I stowed gear well into the night in preparation for our sail to Curaçao.

Tuesday, August 18

The day dawned with a lusty breeze out of the northwest. Silently we hoisted working canvas, coiled our dock lines and slipped unnoticed around the breakwater. *Cheers* scudded past Klein Bonaire. We eased the sheets and pointed the bow west, flying free.

*   *   *

Four days after we dropped anchor in Spanish Water on the Dutch Island of Curaçao, Susan returned to her job in Washington. It was a sentimental parting, for we'd become close allies and I'd come to depend on her perseverance and optimism.

Two days later, the same plane brought Jim to Curaçao, his thin frame laboring under the weight of heavy boxes of power tools and materials he'd brought for the rebuild. His month-long convalescence had restored his lung, but he still was in fragile health. His pale blue eyes seemed lost in deep sockets, but still flashed with determination and that indomitable, toothy smile.

It was a joyous homecoming when, after piling the dinghy high with boxes, we rowed out to *Cheers*. Jim pulled on his old face mask and a moment later slipped over the side for a look at the damaged underbody. It was only then I realized how great his frustration must have been these long weeks, his head swimming with ideas, yet impotent to do more than wait for my phone call.

Since the epoxy patch had temporarily stemmed the inflow of water through the badly abraded keel, Jim turned his attention to the ailing engine room. For many days I saw little more of him than the soles of his shoes sticking out the engine room door as he lay belly-down over the engine coaxing loose salt-frozen parts, pumping saltwater out of the crankcase and rewiring the electrical system.

In his absence I had made the rounds of shipyards in Curaçao's commercial port, Williamsted. However, with storage rates of $35 a day, we simply couldn't afford to haul at one of the commercial yards, anticipating as we did a lengthy rebuild.

Finally I found the perfect spot right in Spanish Water, a hundred yards from where *Cheers* was anchored. I rowed ashore and struck a deal with Henk Bieldeman, the middle-aged Dutch manager of the Asiento Sail Club, a private waterfront club offering water sports to the predominantly Dutch employees of the colossal Shell oil refinery on Curaçao. I rowed back out to *Cheers* to tell Jim the news.

"We've joined the yacht club," I announced, pointing to the sprawling colonial landhaus high on the hill at the head of the dock.

"We've what?"

"I signed up today. We'll rebuild *Cheers* right on that gravel lot beyond the crane. We can do all our own work and can use the table tools in the covered shed. There's running water, 110 electricity, and a bathroom with a shower."

"What's it going to cost?"

"Ten guilders—six dollars a day. And we have privileges at the bar."

His face brightened. "Cold beer?"

"Cold Dutch beer! There are only two problems. Details, really. There's only five feet of water on the approach to the crane."

"And?"

"And the crane can only handle a one-ton vessel."

"Details? How are we going to haul our six-foot draft, thirteen-ton vessel there?"

"I found an Englishman, Ed Wilson, who'll bring us out with his thirty-ton mobile crane."

"What will that cost?"

"He said, 'It will fit your pocketbook.' I didn't tell him we're broke."

Jim eyed me skeptically.

"Come on, we better start lightering gear ashore. The crane will be there at seven tomorrow morning and we've got to drop three thousand pounds if we're going to get into the dock. I've rented space in a storage shed for all our things. Monday morning I'll buy some rat poison . . ."

"Rats?"

Load after dinghy load, we emptied *Cheers* throughout the night and stored our gear in a locked shed at the club. With flashlight and leadline we sounded a channel by dinghy that would bring *Cheers* to within 300 feet of the bulkhead where the crane would be waiting.

At sunrise the next morning we towed *Cheers* until she ran

aground in the soft mud. Then we swung the boom out to starboard, slung the dinghy from the boom's outboard end, which
heeled the boat and reduced her draft. Lines were run to bollards
ashore. Then we winched *Cheers* through the mud using the main
and jib halyard winches.

At 7 o'clock the yellow crane was waiting in position as we
breasted the cutter alongside the dock. Jim dove down and muscled the two nylon slings into position beneath the keel, which
required a bit of cunning since we still were firmly aground in the
sticky mud. After several dives he dragged himself out of the water,
winded and caked with mud to his armpits.

"Next time," he choked, "we wait for a full moon."

Jim picked up a saw and began laying out a cradle from a pile of
discarded lumber. By 9 o'clock *Cheers'* battered hull was cradled
on the hard, her mast and boom laying beside her on sawhorses.
Among the gouges and grass that marred her underbody was one
ominous reminder of how narrow had been our escape—the branchy
fronds of staghorn coral that had taken root on her propeller as
the reef began to boldly assert its claim. I picked up a chisel and,
with quiet satisfaction, chipped away the nest of brittle branches.

This vessel, so much more that just a boat, had been our looking
glass on a world that still held, for me at least, irresistible intrigue.
She demanded much, but had given far more in return. Now it
was time to pay our dues—to rebuild *Cheers* and rebuild our lives.

Part Four

The sun slipped toward the eroded phosphate hills of Spanish Water, casting a long, spiderlike shadow from the cradled yacht upon the gravel lot. Like clockwork a cloud of mosquitoes rose from the nearby mangrove swamp, penetrating *Cheers'* cabin where Richard and Robyn, Jim and I sat around the salon table in the fading light, swatting.

I struck a match. "Now I've done it again," I apologized, touching the flame to a mosquito coil. "I've talked the day away."

"How's the patient?" asked Richard. "Suturing done?"

"Neat as teeth on a zipper," said Jim, showing off Robyn's handiwork.

Richard cast a hesitant sideways glance at Jim's leg, then stared morosely into his empty glass. "I'll 'ave another spot of that rum, mate. Amazing, this boat of yours, fortnight on a coral atoll and she's still turning out ice blocks. Tell me—you've had no more trouble from Jack van der Eem?"

"He's in jail," I said brightly. "There was an article in last week's paper."

"It seems the Bonaire government wanted to learn why the fishing co-op he ran for the past two years has lost so much money while van der Eem's personal assets grew," explained Jim. "When detectives came to examine his books, they found the ledgers had been destroyed by a fire in his office the previous night."

"Jack seemed to me a man desperate for money," I added, "but I had no idea at the time how desperate. Perhaps by gaining possession of *Cheers*, he hoped to repay the money before it was discovered missing."

"And Calvin Hunte?" asked Robyn.

"There's been no trial," I said. "And still officials on St. Vincent have not replied to my letters. I can't get them on the phone and they don't return my calls. They seem to find it easier to forget."

"You're fortunate to have a strong boat to build upon," said Robyn. "When *Cheers* is launched and you've left the Caribbean, you'll learn to forget, too."

"Running away is not the answer," I insisted. "It seems I've been on the run for a very long time. Sometimes I feel . . ." I searched for the right word. ". . . dirty. Does that make sense? You consort with swine and before long you begin to smell of them."

Richard shook his head and faced me squarely. "Rolling in the muck is not the best way of getting clean."

"Richard!" scolded Robyn. "Where are your manners?"

"Beggin' your pardon," Richard winced. "So, you're doing all the repairs yourselves?" he asked on a lighter note.

"Have to," said Jim.

"How much longer do you figure it will take?" Richard asked.

"I don't know, Richard, we're still finding new damage," sighed Jim. "All our materials must come from the States. Flammables like resin, paint and thinner must come by ship, which takes six weeks. By the time we've paid freight charges and customs duty, the price for materials has effectively doubled. Rich, if I had the money, I'd ship her by freighter back to Florida where we can get everything we need. She might even make the trip on her own bottom, but it's not something I'd chance during hurricane season. No, we'll rebuild her here. Everyday we get a little closer."

"Then what?" asked Robyn. "Will you continue cruising or go back to the States?"

Jim gave me a pensive glance. "That we don't know ourselves."

The weeks that followed were a different kind of voyage as our hopes soared and plummeted.

Our days were long and physically demanding. We would rise at sunup, climb into heavy overalls, then grind and glass under the relentless tropical sun. Arms and legs grew lean and tough to match the job. Muscles burgeoned. Sore hands grew rough and calloused. Like routines worked out at sea so long ago, we fell into work as a team. Conversation became unnecessary.

When the sun set and there no longer was light enough to see, we would strip off the heavy clothing, shower off the itchy fiberglass particles and salve our irritating skin, then fall lifelessly into our bunks to wait for sleep that would not come.

Our nights were haunted by images of the horror of that not-so-distant night in Bequia. Each nightfall would drop a curtain of uncertainty. The slightest disturbance—the rustle of wind in the mangroves, the creak of the wooden dock nearby, the eerie howl of a dog on the far shore—would trigger the same familiar, painful drama to play again in the stage of our darkened stateroom, the patter of feet over my head, Jim's angry, accusing cry, the glint of steel, the tearing of flesh. Again each night the same scenario until I could hear only the percussion of my own heartbeat pounding in my chest, resounding in my ears.

In point of fact, we were safe enough. Each night before retiring, Jim would haul up our makeshift ladder and lay it on deck. Portholes were sealed, hatches were dogged. New cannisters of mace lay at our pillows, posed and ready.

The weeks and the months dragged on. For Jim, our unfinished boat hung like an albatross about his neck. For not until *Cheers* was back in the water, ready for sea, could we leave the Caribbean and the horrible images of that night back in Bequia.

"Fleeing is not the answer," I insisted. "It's the knowledge that Hunte is a free man that's really eating at us. We've got to finish the hull work. Get *Cheers* to the point where we can leave her and return to St. Vincent for the trial, however long it takes. Once Hunte is convicted, the nightmare will end. You'll see."

"There'll be no trial," Jim scoffed. "It's a cover up, a deliberate whitewash."

"Don't attribute to malice what can be explained by simple stupidity," I countered.

"You're naive."

When the scheduled trial date of October 6 came and went with no word from officials on Bequia or St. Vincent, no reply to my letters and phone calls, my determination was broken. We were up to our eyeballs in expenses and placing more unanswered overseas calls to elusive bureaucrats was like beating a dead horse. I gave it up. Closed my file. Conceded the whitewash. Never again would I mention Hunte's name. He was Bequia's problem. A thing of the past. And we were busy building our future.

We threw ourselves body and soul into our work, laboring now under spotlights into the nights. Exterior fiberglassing was finished. Interior bulkheads were retabbed. The ruptured diesel tank was reglassed. The topsides were faired, primed and ready for paint. The massive outboard rudder was repaired, hoisted by block and tackle and fitted in place.

Cheers no longer drew gasps and grimaces from passersby. "New boat?" they'd query, eyes following her sweet sheerline.

We lived for launch day.

Then, in late October, a letter arrived from a man in Bequia I'd never met. Bats fluttered in the pit of my stomach as I slipped open the envelope and read the letter aloud to Jim:

Bequia, St. Vincent
September 27, 1981

Mrs. Betsy Hitz
YACHT "CHEERS"
Asiento Yacht Club
Spanish Water
CURACAO, NETHERLAND ANTILLES

Dear Mrs. Hitz-

I am the owner of Friendship Bay hotel for the past twelve years. I was away at my home in Montreal when the sad happening occurred at Friendship Bay. I was very much distressed when I heard of the happening and even more so when I learned that Hunte was out on Bail.

He needs to be put away for a long time. He has a long record of thievery and assault charges and we are all very anxious that you appear together with your husband for the trial. I have examined the record at the post office and the trial written down is to take place on the 3rd of December.

No matter how long the trial takes, I wish to offer you accomodations together with meals at my hotel for as long as you must be here—and longer—to see that we really have a nice friendly Island. All of the people are distressed over what happened to you and your husband here in the Bay.

Sincerely,
Niels Peter Thomsen

*   *   *

We sat in silence at the foot of the ladder. Carefully I folded the letter and replaced it in the envelope.

"So there *is* going to be a trial, Jim."

"Sure. December third. You wrote Jackson that we were leaving the Caribbean in November. If we're not there to testify, there'll be no trial. Jackson told you that himself. He's banking on our not appearing."

"We have to be there to testify," I said simply.

"Haven't you had enough? We've no money left." His voice was bitter, accusing.

"Look at us." He dusted his filthy overalls. "We're not kids anymore. We're two ragtag cruisers with a broken-down boat. This boat has eaten our savings." He pointed to the storage shed. "The rats are eating our sails. And we're eating cold food out of rusted tin cans. You want to jet off to Bequia, then St. Vincent, for more punishment?"

"I don't *want* to, Jim. We *have* to. Do you want it on your conscience that Hunte gets off scot-free because we won't return to testify? Police Commissioner Jackson has assured me his government will pay our airfare."

The next morning, October 28, I wrote to Jackson asking for confirmation of the December 3 trial date and requesting that airplane tickets be sent as promised. Next I wrote to Thomsen, the Bequia hotelier, and accepted his kind offer of lodging during the preliminary trial, pending confirmation from St. Vincent.

As October gave way to November we labored to complete repairs so *Cheers* would be ready to launch when we returned from the trial. As each day was X'd off the calendar we looked toward the approaching trial date with a mixture of anxiety, hope and dread. Thomsen's letter had unleashed the sleeping demons. Only Hunte's conviction, it seemed, would banish them forever.

As the trial date loomed, it seemed that no matter when I awoke during the night I would find Jim in the same posture, lying flat on his back, wide awake, unblinking eyes riveted on the overhead.

"I saw him for one hour of one night nearly five months ago," he said softly, his gaze fixed on the ceiling. "What if I can't identify him?"

Two weeks passed. Daily I thumbed through the morning mail at the yacht club. But there was no confirmation from St. Vincent or Bequia. And no plane tickets.

By the middle of November *Cheers* was coming together and we looked with a sense of deep satisfaction and pride at the progress we'd made in the nine weeks since she was hauled. The final coat of white gloss paint hid once and for all the scars of her ordeal. In another month she would be ready to launch and we would have to decide what to do with our future. Our longed-for circumnavigation, seven years in the making, hung in the balance. Whether we continued west across the Pacific as planned, or limped north to the security of home would have to be Jim's decision. He was leaning, I feared, decidedly toward the familiar waters of home.

The middle of November also marked the end of hurricane season in the Caribbean, the time for westbound yachts to be on their way. The long summer hibernation was over. The migration had begun. Daily Spanish Water played host to new arrivals and daily we watched their departures from our vantagepoint atop the deck of our cradled boat. We ached to be among them.

Though nine weeks into the rebuild, we could not look with certainty toward a launch date. Antifouling paint and materials to finish the job were on some ship somewhere in the Atlantic Ocean, in transit to Curaçao. Even after launching it would be weeks, maybe months, before we could repair all the broken gear to put *Cheers* in shape for sea again.

It was a sad parting when, on November 18, we said farewell to Richard and Robyn Roderick as they began their homeward leg to Sydney, Australia to complete their circumnavigation. We met *Walu* at the yacht club's fuel dock that morning and handled lines as they tended to last-minute chores. The tanks were filled, sail covers removed and steering vane set in place. Jim tossed the docklines to Robyn on the bow.

"Whatever you do," she said, "wherever you go, keep in touch."

We embraced them both, then gave *Walu* a shove. The blue ketch turned and threaded her way toward the channel.

Jim cupped his hands and shouted. "Put the Fosters beer on ice, Richard. We won't be long behind you."

I turned to Jim. "You mean it?"

"Why not? It's what you've wanted, isn't it, Bets?"

"We can make it this season, Jim. I know we can. The trial's only two weeks away. If officials in St. Vincent persist with their silence, my conscience is clear. We've spent long enough beating a dead horse."

On November 26, with only one week to go until the supposed trial, I received a second letter from Thomsen.

Bequia, St. Vincent
November 16, 1981

Dear Mrs. Hitz:

The police advise me that the trial is still set for the third of December. I will be leaving for my home in Montreal on Saturday, but will be returning on about the fifth or sixth of December for the rest of the season. When you come to Bequia simply see my Chef Carroll Barker and he will know how to take care of you both.

Hunte has been back and forth to the Tobago Keys. I am of the opinion that they are gambling on your not showing up and then the case can be dismissed. I hope you will be able to make the trial, and I can assure you that many people here will be grateful to you. You should probably arrange to come a day or two earlier so as to be sure to be on hand.

The Inspector Rodriguiz is a nice chap and has your interests at heart.

Sincerely,
Captain Thomsen, USCG(ret)

If the trial was on for December 3, I was determined to be there with Jim. If Police Commissioner Jackson would not send tickets as promised, we would fly there at our own expense and take the matter up with him in person. I made plane reservations to fly to St. Vincent December 1. With an overnight stopover in Trinidad to change planes, we would arrive in St. Vincent December 2 and catch a ferry to Bequia that same afternoon. We would attend the preliminary hearing in Bequia on December 3 and then the trial in St. Vincent immediately afterward.

But still I had only the word of Thomsen, a Bequia resident I'd never met, as indication there would be a trial when we arrived. It would be foolhardy to make the long trip without official confirmation that a trial would indeed take place.

Monday morning, one day before our departure, I checked the mail at the yacht club. Nothing. I caught a taxi to town, where I telephoned Police Commissioner Jackson. Jackson's stern voice came on the line.

"I have turned the whole affair over to Monica Joseph . . . I did not reply to your letters because I told you you would hear from us when a trial date was set. That has not changed. No, the trial cannot be on December 3. There is no trial on December 3 scheduled here or in Bequia. We will contact you."

He hung up, leaving me stuttering at the end of a dead line.

Furious, I thumbed through the pages of the dog-eared notebook I'd kept during those days we tracked down Calvin Hunte. Scrawled on the back cover I found the number of Monica Joseph the prosecuting attorney. I had to learn if Jackson was telling the truth.

The overseas operator connected me with the Ministry of Legal Affairs in St. Vincent. Monica Joseph picked up the line.

"Police Commissioner Jackson said he turned the case over to me? Let me just see what is pending. No, I have no file on the case. No, the trial cannot possibly be heard on December 3. It is not even on the docket. The next open trial date is sometime in February next year. You'll hear from us. No, I'm afraid there is nothing I can do to expedite your case. These trial dates are set far in advance. As I said, you will hear from us."

I paid for those phone calls and washed my hands once and for all of the Bequia affair. There was no trial December 3 and clearly there was to be no trial. I cancelled our plane reservations and returned to *Cheers*.

Jim was sanding the bottom of the hull when I returned. He listened with a kind of numbed battle-weary indifference. Then, without comment, he turned the sander back on and resumed fairing the botoom.

Bitterly, we resigned ourselves to the inevitable and never spoke again of Bequia, Calvin Hunte or the trial. We ordered charts for Panama, the Galapagos and French Polynesia. Evenings we spoke excitedly of trolling rigs, the iguanas we hoped to find in the Galapagos, and landfall in the Marquesas. The old wounds at last were healing. We longed to be at sea again, back in control.

On Thursday, December 3, I received a package notice in the morning mail. "I'll be back by lunchtime," I called to Jim and caught a taxi to town.

At the main post office in Willemsted I waited my turn in the long queue, then presented my slip to the clerk behind the window. "I have a package, I believe."

He shuffled through his stack of postal slips. "No," he corrected, "it's a registered letter. Sign here."

He handed me the letter. I stared at the postmark. It had been mailed from Bequia on November 10, twenty-three days earlier. The return address, Police Inspector Ralph Rodriguez. I tore open the envelope and began reading:

> Police Inspector R. Rodriguez
> Port Elizabeth, Bequia
> St. Vincent Grenadines
> 10 November, 1981

Dear Miss Hitz,

Your letter was received and I did not reply before because I was trying to arrange an earlier trial date than the 3 December date set by the magistrate for your case. To save expense and inconvenience I tried to arrange the preliminary hearing in Bequia for October, to be followed by the trial in St. Vincent. But the October agenda was full and my efforts were in vain.

The date for the pre preliminary hearing in Bequia still holds good for 3 December, 1981 at 9 a.m. in the Bequia Court Room. The trial in St. Vincent will follow.

As for Calvin Hunte, I'm sure he will be present at the trial. He is still in Bequia and goes to the southern Grenadines to fish occasionally. I am confident that once Jim and yourself can say for sure that Hunte is the person who committed the acts without any doubt then he would be nailed to the cross.

Bequia, at present, is very quiet and the citizens are eagerly awaiting the trial of Calvin Hunte, as they see people like him a serious threat to the tourist industry here in Bequia.

How's Jim feeling now and how are the repairs to your boat progressing? I hope you will soon be sailing again.

My regards to Jim and yourself. See you at the trial on December 3rd. Please come.

> Ralph Rodriguez

I pored again over the tight, neat handwriting: "Trial 3 December, 9 a.m. . . . . Please come."

I looked at my watch: 10 a.m., December 3.

I hurried out of the post office and ran next door to the communications building where I placed a call to Inspector Rodriguez at the Bequia police station.

"Sorry," said the voice, "Inspector's at the court house. Big trial today. I don't know when he'll be back."

In desperation I rang Son Mitchell, the parliamentarian and owner of the Frangipani Hotel in Bequia. Son would know what was going on there.

The connection was poor. I cupped my hands and enunciated into the receiver, but could not make my questions fully understood.

"Betsy!" he exclaimed. "Why weren't you here? What's that? Where are you? I can't understand you. You're coming in broken. Listen to me. Your case was called by the magistrate this morning. I just came from the court house. You were not here. The case was dismissed."

*   *   *

Scapegoat. The word stuck in my mind as I walked up the drive to the yacht club, drained of emotion. *They found their scapegoat.*

I found Jim seated up on a weathered plank, his slim legs dangling from scaffolding he'd erected at the boat's port quarter. His figure looked dwarfed beside the great hulk of boat. He'd shed the heavy denim coveralls and wore only a pair of clean khaki shorts. His brows were knitted in concentration and his cheek was smudged with blue paint.

I stood morosely at the foot of the scaffolding. "It's over," I said flatly.

He peered down at me. "Aw, I wanted to surprise you." He leaned back and pointed with pride at the crisp blue letters, CHEERS, DEER ISLE, MAINE. "Well, what do you think?"

"A beautiful job, Jim." I studied the boat. "*Cheers* looks better than the day she was built."

"Stronger, too. We're ready to launch come next full moon," he beamed. "You know what that means? We'll be back in the water by Christmas!"

The lines of worry were gone from his face, replaced by the satisfied grin of a job well done.

"What's over?" he asked. "Hey, what took you so long in town? What was in the package?"

I crumpled Rodriguez's letter and stuffed it in my pocket, then rubbed the smudge of wet paint from Jim's cheek. "It's not important."

I picked up the paint brush and began stencilling the starboard side: C-H-E-E-R-S.

EPILOGUE

—————————————————— We left our home in the United States in the fall of 1980 to see something of the world from our own small boat. There were naturally those who asked why. Why leave all you've worked for? Why risk everything? The same questions have been asked on many shores since man first hollowed out a log in the shape of a canoe and climbed inside.

To us, on the eve of departure, the answers seemed obvious. To taste adventure; to be in control of our own destiny, free of social obligations; to find our own way across oceans using the sun and stars to guide us; to feel again and again the thrill of landfall after a long passage. Though we never considered ourselves escapists, the sailing life undeniably offered the only possible return to another age. We were curious to learn how other people adapted to life on our same planet.

"Sure there are risks," we explained, "but there are calculated risks. Many ordinary people just like us have made great voyages."

Within the year, one unguarded moment invited an act of violence for which we were ill prepared. Two weeks later, in a desperate bid to escape, an error in navigation brought disaster on a hidden reef. Our ordered, self-made world toppled like a house of cards. We found ourselves on the beach, broken cruisers with a broken boat.

But there's no better therapy than hard work and reflection. In Curaçao, during the seven months it took to rebuild our boat, there was time and need for both.

We had reached quite unexpectedly that feeling of remoteness, of high adventure we had yearned for. Nobody ever mentions that life's greatest adventures are hell to live through. Only long after their passing are they savored. Over nature, by its indifference, there can be no triumph, but merely a series of successful or unsuccessful confrontations. What it is that compels long-distance voyagers to confront so great a force as the sea I'm still not certain, but very little that is truly worthwhile in life can be accomplished without taking any risks at all.

We failed, perhaps. But more importantly, we picked up the pieces and again took the plunge.

Embarking from Curaçao in March, 1982, we found it harder to answer the skeptics who asked why. Why continue? Our former idealism was tarnished, our innocence lost. So we spoke, instead, of a typical, uneventful day aboard *Cheers*, the give-and-take of a couple at sea.

We sailed from Curaçao that spring with renewed confidence in our vessel, a greater awareness of our own shortcomings, and a faith in each other that has not been misplaced. We'd learned just how precious is life.

The fleet-footed cutter proved her strength on a four-and-a-half-day, 750-mile shakedown cruise to Panama. There, without bitterness, we left the Caribbean in our wake, slipped between the two great continents and struck out across the vast Pacific.

In the cold waters of the Galapagos we swam among the marine iguanas and sunned ourselves on volcanic cliffs. Pushed by brisk tradewinds, with only sea birds for company, we crossed 3,000 miles of empty ocean and 19 days later raised the fabled peaks of Fatu Hiva. In the Marquesas we stalked wild boars in the highlands and carried cargo of lumber and Marquesan passengers between islands. In the palm-fringed atolls of the Tuamotus, we dove for black pearls, feasted on baked dog, and tried in vain to help a shipwrecked sailor reclaim his yacht from the reef at Rangiroa. In the Societies we weathered the full fury of our first tropical cyclone. Living those months among the gentle Polynesians, we learned not to start at each bump in the night, not to shudder at the thunder of surf breaking on the reef.

And in Tahiti, the vibrant heart of French Polynesia, we welcomed cruising friends aboard *Cheers* to celebrate our marriage. I doubt Jim understood the oaths he uttered in French that day. It didn't matter. He'd lived them all the days we were together.

With the same strong boat, Jim by my side, the wanderlust continues.